Ian McPhedran is the award-winning bestselling author of five books. Until 2016, he was the National Defence writer for News Limited and during his extensive career as a journalist he covered conflicts in Myanmar, Somalia, Cambodia, Papua New Guinea, Indonesia, East Timor, Afghanistan and Iraq. In 1993, he won a United Nations Association Peace Media Award and in 1999 the Walkley Award for Best News Report for his exposé of the Navy's Collins-class submarine fiasco. McPhedran lives in Balmain with his wife Verona Burgess.

Also by Ian McPhedran

Afghanistan Australia's War
Too Bold to Die
Air Force
Soldiers Without Borders
The Amazing SAS

THE SMACK TRACK

Inside the Navy's war: chasing down drug smugglers, pirates and terrorists

IAN McPHEDRAN

HarperCollins*Publishers*

HarperCollins*Publishers*

First published in Australia in 2017
by HarperCollins*Publishers* Australia Pty Limited
ABN 36 009 913 517
harpercollins.com.au

Copyright © Ian McPhedran and Verona Burgess 2017

The right of Ian McPhedran and Verona Burgess to be identified as the authors of this work has been asserted by them in accordance with the *Copyright Amendment (Moral Rights) Act 2000*.

This work is copyright. Apart from any use as permitted under the *Copyright Act 1968*, no part may be reproduced, copied, scanned, stored in a retrieval system, recorded, or transmitted, in any form or by any means, without the prior written permission of the publisher.

HarperCollins*Publishers*
Level 13, 201 Elizabeth Street, Sydney NSW 2000, Australia
Unit D1, 63 Apollo Drive, Rosedale, Auckland 0632, New Zealand
A 53, Sector 57, Noida, UP, India
1 London Bridge Street, London SE1 9GF, United Kingdom
2 Bloor Street East, 20th floor, Toronto, Ontario M4W 1A8, Canada
195 Broadway, New York NY 10007, USA

National Library of Australia Cataloguing-in-Publication data:

McPhedran, Ian, author.
The smack track / Ian McPhedran.
ISBN: 978 1 4607 5292 0 (paperback)
ISBN: 978 1 4607 0755 5 (ebook)
Australia. Royal Australian Navy
Sea-power–Australia–21st century.
Drug traffic–Persian Gulf–Prevention
Drug traffic–Horn of Africa–Prevention
Pirates–Persian Gulf
Pirates–Horn of Africa
Illegal arms transfers–Persian Gulf.
Arms control–Australia
Arms control–Horn of Africa
Naval strategy–Australia–21st century.

Cover design by Philip Campbell Design
Cover photo courtesy of the Australian Government Department of Defence
Typeset in Bembo Std by Kirby Jones

*To the men and women of the
Royal Australian Navy and their families*

Contents

Glossary	ix
Preface	1
Prologue	3

The mission

1. Leaving Dar es Salaam	9
2. Cauldron of conflict	23
3. At the captain's table	35
4. A close call	49
5. Boardos	62

Piracy

6. Skulls and crossbones	73
7. Under the not-so-Jolly Roger	86

Hash highway to smack track

8. Seizing hash and saving lives	97
9. Not just coffee	106
10. The River Phoenix	114
11. Eye on the prize	126

Making it work

12. Tonnes of guns	143
13. Dunnies, drains and dinners	156
14. Beating the blues	171
15. Birdies	184

The smack track

16. Truckies of the ocean	199
17. Jackpot	211
18. More smack on the track	227

The end game

19. Catch and release	243
20. Chasing the Golden Crescent	258
21. Bringing them home	274

Acknowledgements	287
Appendix: RAN Middle East deployments 1990–2017	289

Glossary

2IC	second in command
AB	Able Seaman
ABOT	Al Basrah Oil Terminal
ADFA	Australian Defence Force Academy
AFP	Australian Federal Police
AIC	air intercept controller
ANZAC	Australian and New Zealand Army Corps
Birdies	aviation department
Buffer	Chief Boatswain ('bosun')
CAG	Central Arabian Gulf
CAOC	Combined Air Operations Centre
CDF	Chief of the Defence Force
Chippy	shipwright
CIWS	Close-in weapons system (pronounced 'Sea Whiz')
CMF	Combined Maritime Forces
CN	Chief of the Royal Australian Navy
CO	Commanding Officer

CPO	Chief Petty Officer
CTF	Combined Task Force
DC	damage control
DEA	(US) Drug Enforcement Agency
DSM	Distinguished Service Medal
EBC	Enhanced Boarding Capability
EOD	explosive ordnance disposal
FFG	guided missile frigate
FGS	Federal German Ship
FNS	French Navy Ship
Greenies	electrical or 'green steam' department
Head	toilet or bathroom
HMAS	Her Majesty's Australian Ship
HMS	Her Majesty's Ship
HQJOC	Headquarters Joint Operations Command
HUET	helicopter underwater escape training
IRGCN	Islamic Revolutionary Guard Corps Navy
IRTC	Internationally Recognised Transit Corridor
ISIS	Islamic state of Iraq and Syria
JTF	Joint Task Force
KAAOT	Khor Al Amaya Oil Terminal
Killick	navy slang for a Leading Seaman
LHD	landing helicopter dock
LS	Leading Seaman
Mess	place to eat, live and relax
MEAO	Middle East Area of Operations
MER	Middle East Region
MFU	major fleet unit
MOAS	Mine and obstacle avoidance sonar
MV	Motor Vessel
NAG	Northern Arabian Gulf

NATO	North Atlantic Treaty Organisation
NCIS	(US) Naval Criminal Investigative Service
NVD	night vision device
OpsO	Operations Officer
OPV	offshore patrol vessel
PAG	Pirate Action Group
Pipes	public address system
PO	Petty Officer
PT	physical training
PTSD	Post-traumatic stress disorder
Pusser	Maritime Logistics (supply) Officer
PWO	Principal Warfare Officer
Rack	bed or bunk
RAAF	Royal Australian Air Force
RAN	Royal Australian Navy
RAS	replenishment at sea
RAST	recover, assist, secure and traverse
RHIB	rigid hull inflatable boat
ROE	rules of engagement
RPG	rocket-propelled grenade
SAG	Southern Arabian Gulf
SASR	Special Air Service Regiment
Scab lifter	medical assistant
Scribes	writers or clerks
Sky pilot	chaplain
SOLAS	safety of life at sea
SOPs	standard operating procedures
SPO	Systems Project Office
SQT	system qualifying trial
Stick	members of a boarding party
Stokers	engineers

Storbys	stores department
Swain	Chief Coxswain
SWO	Ship's Warrant Officer
Tiff	artificer or skilled navy mechanic
TS	training ship
TTPs	tactics techniques and procedures
UN	United Nations
UNCLOS	United Nations Convention on the Law of the Sea
USS	United States Ship
VERTREP	Vertical replenishment
Wardroom	the officers' mess
WEEO	Weapons Electrical Engineering Officer
XO	Executive Officer

Preface

Landing in a helicopter on the rolling and pitching deck of a warship at sea for the first time can be a white-knuckle experience, even for veteran flyers.

Sitting in a rigid hull inflatable boat alongside a navy boarding party as it bounces across the open ocean is a different type of wild ride, but when these two things happen on consecutive days they have a major impact.

So it was in 2007 when I joined the Anzac Class frigate HMAS *Toowoomba* on patrol in the Arabian Gulf for a brief visit and a taste of an Australian navy deployment in the Middle East.

As the RHIB sped across the oily waters of the Gulf, a dot appeared on the horizon. Soon that dot grew into a 300,000-tonne supertanker, and before I knew it I was following the agile young sailors several storeys high, up the ship's ladder and onto her vast deck. The boarding team, under the command of an officer who looked twenty years old, went about the business of searching the vessel and quizzing the Indian captain and his crew with a professionalism that belied their years.

The navy's three-decade-long Middle East story has been largely overlooked because of the higher profile and more immediate media access offered by the army and air force, but after a second visit aboard warships in the Gulf I knew that this terrific Australian story needed to be told.

Almost a decade later I was fortunate to join the guided missile frigate HMAS *Darwin* in Dar es Salaam harbour in May 2016 as she embarked on a two-week Indian Ocean patrol between Tanzania and the Seychelles. It was the ship's seventh and final Middle East deployment, and her prime targets were drugs and weapons smugglers on what Australian sailors have dubbed 'the smack track'.

The so-called war against terrorism has gone through many phases since it began on 11 September 2001, but one aspect has remained constant. That is the presence in and around the Gulf region of warships from the Royal Australian Navy, which has had vessels patrolling the waters of the Middle East, South Asia and East Africa almost constantly since 1990.

Over sixty-four rotations of twenty major fleet units, many thousands of Australian officers and sailors have forged their own stories in the calm seas of the Arabian Gulf or the wilder waters off the Horn of Africa and deep in the western Indian Ocean.

This book tells part of their story.

Ian McPhedran, Sydney 2017

Prologue

The young male and female sailors scramble down a rope ladder and into the bucking rigid hull inflatable boat that is tethered to the side of the Australian warship.

With the frigate steaming at fourteen knots in the open ocean, this is not a job for the faint hearted. In a dangerous sea-state four, with a buffeting wind and three-metre waves, the armed and fully kitted-out members of HMAS *Darwin*'s 'red' boarding team are dropping into a maelstrom.

It is 11.25 a.m. on Saturday, 21 May 2016, and we are in the Indian Ocean, several hundred kilometres to the east of Tanzania and north of Madagascar, hunting drug smugglers on the smack track. For one young woman, the conditions are just too severe and she is quickly replaced. Upper body strength is vital under these extremes.

Once the first group of boarders have made it safely into the RHIB it is set free and speeds away towards a suspect fishing dhow that is wallowing about a kilometre away under the watchful eye of the guided missile frigate.

Viewing the operation from the safety of *Darwin*'s deck it is clear that my wish to board a smuggling dhow is unlikely to be granted unless the sea calms down an awful lot. Sea-state four is at the upper limit for a water-based boarding by the Royal Australian Navy. As the RHIB approaches, the suspect dhow rolls through an alarming-looking forty degrees, and boarding officer Lieutenant James Hodgkinson deems it too risky to continue.

Climbing down into the RHIB from a moving 4000-tonne warship is one thing for these skilled and athletic sailors, but scrambling up a rope and onto a twenty-metre wooden dhow that is bucking about like an angry rodeo bull could be deadly. In addition, the team's radios have become waterlogged and communication with the ship is lost.

Just before noon they turn and speed back towards *Darwin*, but suddenly their radio crackles back to life and the skipper, Commander Phill Henry, orders the team to have another go.

The inflatable boat turns back to the dhow. This time its captain is instructed, via hand signals, to turn his vessel down sea to make conditions a little easier for boarding. Transferring sailors to the dhow is all about timing. In such a high sea-state the two vessels are almost level at the top of each swell. The boarders can therefore avoid using the rope ladder but must risk leaping directly from the RHIB onto the dhow.

Once safely on board, their first job is to herd the crew forward into the forecastle area and to secure the vessel while the RHIB returns to *Darwin* to collect the rest of the boarding party, along with the American NCIS agent Paul Lerza and his interpreter to interview the captain and crew. Time is of the essence.

It is soon clear that the skipper's story about why such a small coastal fishing boat is operating so far south of its home – on the Makran coast between Pakistan and Iran – and so far from land is ridiculous. The vessel is not flying a valid flag, her fishing nets have not even been deployed and the paperwork contains some major inconsistencies.

The authorities at headquarters in Bahrain authorise a search and the arduous task of checking every square centimetre of the vessel begins. Just before 5 p.m. a member of the dhow's crew secretly lets on that there are drugs on board, stashed beneath the 'snow' in the ice hold.

Rather than go directly to the spot, give the game away and potentially endanger the informant's life, the team continues to chip away at the edge of the ice before moving to the centre of the hold where they eventually find a suspect hatch hidden below the frozen sheet.

Able Seaman Eddie Tomsana, from Thursday Island in the Torres Strait, is used to living rough on small boats, but even he is shocked by the conditions on board the dhow.

As he and his shipmate Pete Irvine get down and dirty, urgently searching the rancid fish hold, their only company are rats nesting deep in the boat's bilge. Even the cockroaches swarming in the galley area up top don't venture down into this dark, filthy, frozen world.

The men use a crowbar to remove the hatch cover, and bingo – there is a stash of white bags underneath. Tomsana gets down on his belly and crawls into the stinking, rat-infested hiding place.

At first, he pulls out five, then another seven and finally dozens of bags containing an incredible 512 kilograms of heroin – a cache with an estimated street value of more than half a billion dollars that will no longer fund terrorist organisations and criminal syndicates.

THE MISSION

1

Leaving Dar es Salaam

The timber fishing dhows beached outside the bustling fish market frame a huge crowd of Africans undertaking their daily ritual of haggling over the catch. This colourful scene at the entrance to Dar es Salaam harbour plays out under the watchful eyes of Royal Australian Navy sailors who are manning fifty-calibre machine guns mounted high above the bridge of the guided missile frigate HMAS *Darwin*.

The warship's 228-strong company is embarking on a two-week patrol of the southern Indian Ocean in pursuit of a much more insidious catch – heroin and hashish grown and processed deep in the valleys of Afghanistan, and weapons bound for terrorist groups plying their evil trade somewhere on the troubled African continent. *Darwin* will be operating between Tanzania and the holiday paradise of the Seychelles islands, a smuggling hotspot.

A mere mention of the names Tanzania and the nearby island of Zanzibar conjures up images of darkest Africa and the slave trade.

Dar es Salaam, the capital of Tanzania, is a port city that sits about halfway down the east coast of the African continent. It has been a key Indian Ocean trading hub for centuries, and not just for the exotic spices carried on the ancient maritime routes by the favourable trade winds. During the 1800s, Zanzibar was the centre of the world's slave trade and more than 50,000 people were sold each year in its notorious market to buyers from America and the Middle East.

Large-scale human trafficking has long since given way to other destructive and highly lucrative trades in human misery. The waters off the east African coast are awash with fishing and cargo dhows attempting to land smuggled drugs – mainly hashish and heroin – or weapons. From this strategic staging post the guns are bound for trouble spots such as Somalia, Yemen and Sudan. The drugs will travel further afield – by air, using passengers as mules; by charter flights; or overland in trucks or cars, driving south through Mozambique and South Africa or northeast through Kenya and onwards to the wealthy criminal markets in Europe and beyond. In the post-9/11 era, the narcotics trade is one of the primary sources of funding for terrorist organisations.

The illicit drugs come from the 'Golden Crescent,' an opium-growing belt that stretches from Iran through Afghanistan and into northern Pakistan. Most of the opium is grown in Afghanistan, and heroin from the crescent supplies markets in Europe and the United States. The 'Golden Triangle' of Myanmar (Burma), Laos and Thailand feeds markets in Australia, the US and Asia.

Although engines have long since replaced sails, little has changed over the centuries for the men who work on board the fleet of timber dhows that are beached outside the busy fish market. Whatever meagre amount the smugglers get paid by drug barons to transport their lethal cargoes will far outstrip their poor income from fishing.

It is 8 a.m. and the crew of HMAS *Darwin* is on 'defence watch' and at high alert. The fighting ship moves away from her berth just forward of the German frigate FGS *Bayern* and slips slowly down the narrow harbour towards the Indian Ocean. Each gunner is in radio contact with the PWO – the Principal Warfare Officer – who relays warnings and commands from his armour-plated bunker. The PWO, Lieutenant Brett Schulz, and his staff monitor a suite of powerful electronic sensors inside the ship's locked and darkened operations room. These hi-tech tools of trade include radars, cameras and infrared equipment that scan the surroundings constantly. The most sensitive pieces of equipment are well hidden in a corner behind a heavy black curtain at the rear of the 'ops' room that is out of bounds to anyone without a security clearance.

Having joined the vessel two hours earlier, this landlubber author is greeted by the Commanding Officer (CO), Commander Phill Henry, who says, 'Welcome aboard. The WEEO [Weapons Electrical Engineering Officer Lieutenant Commander Jason O'Gorman] will be your escort for the first day or so and then you'll have the run of the ship.'

This is music to the ears of someone who is used to the strict media controls often imposed during Australian military embeds in covering the prolonged conflicts of the Middle East.

Crossing from the dock onto the ship is like venturing into another dimension where time and space become more finite and the norms of a life on land are left behind as the routine of the mariner takes over. Once the gangway is secured and the mooring lines stowed, the warship becomes a fully self-contained space. This new world is a mere 138 metres long and 13.8 metres wide. The trials and tribulations of the planet are distilled into this steel box and the lives of the 228 people who inhabit it.

As the warship glides past dozens of beached vessels and other boats crisscrossing the entrance to the harbour, every craft that passes by near the ship is regarded as a potential threat. No one wants a repeat of the USS *Cole* incident that took place in October 2000 when an explosives-laden terrorist skiff left seventeen sailors dead and the American destroyer badly damaged in the port of Aden in Yemen.

Nothing escapes the attention of the watchful security detail as I move close to them high up on the ship's gun direction platform. Even a local lad who floats by in what looks like an upturned car bonnet powered by nothing but a clear sheet of plastic mounted on a stick comes under close scrutiny.

Dar es Salaam is a rapidly changing city, and the harbourside central business district – dominated by new mini-skyscrapers – is being transformed by a gaggle of cranes that are erecting office and apartment towers to service an emerging middle class. It is clear that some of the glittering prosperity on display in the megacities that have sprouted from the desert sands of the oil-rich Gulf states has finally trickled down the east African coast, at least as far as the once-destitute Tanzanian capital. China's growing interest in Africa is also having an impact, along with the growing trade in oil, tourism, telecommunications and banking. Still, Tanzania's per capita income is just $1813 per annum or $34.80 per week. Its forty-five million population is divided between Christian (sixty-one per cent) and Muslim (thirty-five per cent).

Commander Henry has overall responsibility for the warship and is supported by a command team of seven officers for the deployment. In addition to O'Gorman and Schulz, they are the Executive Officer (XO), Lieutenant Commander Tina Brown; the Operations Officer, Lieutenant Commander Dale Axford; the Marine Engineering Officer, Lieutenant Commander Trevor

Henderson; the Supply Officer, Lieutenant Commander Chris Duke; the Navigator, Lieutenant Scott Benstead; and the Flight Commander, Lieutenant Commander Kye Hayman. Each will be on duty virtually around the clock during the fourteen-day patrol.

Brown is Henry's second in command and takes over when the captain requires a break. A professional and well-regarded officer, she is also the conduit between the crew and the CO and spends a lot of time meeting with the senior sailor on board, Ship's Warrant Officer Tim Brading. She also chairs many of the vessel's planning meetings.

Axford is a senior Principal Warfare Officer and most of his time is spent in the ops room planning and running the ship's program. That includes positioning *Darwin* where and when it is supposed to be and with all relevant permissions signed off. He also coordinates all of the ship's activities, brings the program together and juggles the demands of the various departments.

The bookish Schulz manages the fighting aspects of the ship from his glowing consoles, and that includes boarding operations. He is the link between the ship and the boarding officer and controls everything the boarding party requires from the ship.

Henderson keeps the ship operating and is responsible for all mechanical equipment, from the twin gas turbine engines to the soft serve ice cream machine in the galley. His knockabout personality makes the former sailor popular with all ranks.

O'Gorman is responsible for the ship's complex weapons and command and control systems, while Duke ensures that the warship has all that it needs to complete its mission, from fresh vegetables to toilet paper. Benstead plots the vessel's course and is responsible for its safe passage anywhere in the world. Hayman manages the 'birdies', who operate and maintain the ship's single Seahawk helicopter, designated 'Orko'.

The command team is supported by fourteen chief petty officers – the senior sailors who make the ship work.

I can feel a tension in the air as the crew snaps back into its sea patrol routines and the African coast slowly fades from view. It is 17 May 2016 and HMAS *Darwin* has remained in port for just thirty-six hours. Not only has a much-anticipated shore leave been cut short by a precious twenty-four hours, but the crew was also denied permission to spend a night ashore enjoying the luxury of a hotel room, a proper bathroom and eating at a restaurant table. Instead, they were ordered to be back on board by 9 p.m., in response to an Australian government travel warning about the dangers of the Tanzanian capital following attacks against Westerners and potential political unrest.

Little happens in the military outside of the chain of command. During operations, Henry answers to two direct bosses – the three-star commander of Headquarters Joint Operations Command at Bungendore near Canberra, and the two-star commander of Combined Task Force 633 at Al Minhad airbase near Dubai. All are guided by travel advice issued by the Department of Foreign Affairs and Trade in Canberra and by intelligence gathered from other sources. RAN ships deployed to the Middle East work for Joint Operations Command (JOC) from the moment they arrive or 'in chop' into the area of operations until they depart or 'out chop' when they leave the operational area and revert to navy command under the fleet commander. In May 2016, Dar es Salaam was simply deemed too risky for Australian sailors to stay ashore.

Tanzania has a troubled history and low-level terrorist attacks targeting Christians and tourists, especially in Zanzibar, have increased during the past two decades. In August 1998, hundreds died – including eleven in Tanzania – and thousands were injured when Al Qaeda terrorists simultaneously bombed the United States embassies in Dar es Salaam and in neighbouring Kenya. Parts of the country have also become havens for the Somali-based Al Qaeda affiliate group Al Shabaab. Tanzania has long suffered from grinding poverty and corruption. Many areas remain dirt poor despite the growing wealth on display in the capital and in tourist areas such as Stone Town in Zanzibar and the northern safari town of Arusha. Visitors to the capital are advised to exercise caution and to travel in groups after dark.

The ship sails safely into open waters after passing several merchant ships in the Dar channel, including a huge Korean car carrier, and the local pilot departs, proudly carrying a new HMAS *Darwin* baseball cap. *Darwin*'s two gas turbine engines are cranked up to propel the vessel eastwards into her 'patrol box' at twenty-six knots, burning almost a litre of fuel per second.

At 9 a.m. – precisely an hour after leaving the wharf – Commander Henry starts the day's drills by ordering 'action stations'. The ship's company has six minutes, and not a second more, to be prepared for war. Response times can be a little tardy immediately following a port visit, but on this day the crew performs well and the ship gets to 'action' in five minutes and twenty-three seconds. Next comes 'leaving ship stations' where the crew musters at their designated location to prepare to abandon ship. I am assigned to Warrant Officer Tim Brading at the centre of the flight deck, where some smiling sailors complain loudly about having to share rations with such a large civilian should they need to take to the lifeboats.

'How are we going to feed him?' they ask the Ship's Warrant Officer, whose nervous laugh says he really hopes it doesn't come to that.

HMAS *Darwin* is an Adelaide Class guided missile frigate built by the Todd Pacific Shipyards in Seattle, Washington, and commissioned into the RAN in July 1984. She is one of four American-built versions, with two more (HMA Ships *Melbourne* and *Newcastle*) built later at Williamstown dockyard in Melbourne.

It takes a newcomer some time to find his way around the ship even with the help of the 'Swaino', Naval Police Coxswain Denis McKenna. Judging where the bow and stern are can be tricky from inside the vessel's narrow passageways surrounded by noisy pipes and 228 other people. There are no portholes and the motion of the ship provides few cues as to which way is front and which way is back. Then there are the numerous steep ladders and tight hatches designed for young, slim and fit people such as most of *Darwin*'s crew, who must wait patiently for an older and less fit interloper to struggle up or down as he tries to find the wardroom, hangar or even the bridge without suffering a concussion or a fracture. It takes several days to unravel the mystery of which ladder, hatch and passageway leads to where.

At thirty-two years of age, HMAS *Darwin* is in very good order and a testament to her builders, the navy's engineers and maintainers and to a bold new support plan that closely bonds the ship and the civilian maintenance workers who look after her. The ship's two General Electric LM2500 gas turbine engines – a derivative of the four GE engines used to power some Boeing 747 jumbo jets – can push the sleek fighting vessel through the water at up to thirty knots, and she has a range of 8300 kilometres, steaming at twenty knots. The frigate can be underway from cold in just thirty minutes and can counter simultaneous threats from the air, surface and submarines.

At sea, the ship's power plant and machinery are in the capable hands of the marine engineers, Chief Petty Officers Andrew

'Goonga' Sims, Robert 'Turbo' Pearson and Ty 'Sparrow' Davis, who are led by Trevor Henderson. A quick tour of the main machinery space with Sims reveals two sparkling gas turbines and shiny gearboxes and pumps that are so clean you could eat your dinner off them.

The ship has a double hangar at the stern for two Seahawk helicopters, but for this operation she carries just one chopper from the navy's 816 Squadron based at HMAS *Albatross* at Nowra in New South Wales.

Two of the most vital pieces of equipment on board for operations in the Middle East and Indian Ocean regions are a pair of powerful rigid hull inflatable boats – known as RHIBs – mounted on each side of the ship. They are used for a variety of tasks, including the all-important boarding operations.

Based on the US Oliver Hazard Perry Class warship, the frigate was designed as an aircraft carrier escort or so-called 'missile catcher' for the United States Navy. The six multi-purpose ships acquired by the RAN have been the backbone of its fighting force for more than thirty-five years. Three remain in service – HMA Ships *Darwin*, *Melbourne* (III) and *Newcastle*, with *Darwin* due to be paid off in late 2017. *Newcastle* became the most capable frigate ever deployed by any navy when she set sail from Sydney for the Middle East in July 2017 following key upgrades that included the first ever deployment at sea of the Scan Eagle unmanned aerial vehicle and the new 'Romeo' model Seahawk helicopter.

At 10.30 a.m. we are clear of Tanzanian waters and steaming northeast under a 'reduced defence watch'. The ship is heading away from the African coast and towards her next patrol box to the north and west of the Seychelles as the crew settles into its routine. An introductory chat with Commander Henry fills in several blanks. These include what the patrol area will be and the fact that *Darwin* will be working closely with the French frigate FNS *Nivôse* and a French P-3 patrol aircraft flying out of Victoria in the Seychelles.

Phill Henry is an experienced New Zealand-born former sailor who came up through the ranks of first the Royal New Zealand Navy and then the Royal Australian Navy before taking command of HMAS *Darwin* in June 2015. After six months of intensive preparation, the ship set sail on 30 December 2016, first going to India for the International Fleet Review before moving into the Middle East Region (MER) to conduct the patrols. The ship was due to hand over to HMAS *Perth* on 24 June before making her way back to Australia.

'By the time we get home in mid-July it will have been in excess of sixty weeks operating, with nine weeks at home in Sydney,' Henry says. 'So the team is very much looking forward to getting home.'

After a pleasant dinner of spicy pasta and apricot crumble with the skipper in his cabin just below the bridge and forward of the ops room, and a chat about the job, family and rugby (he is a proud All Blacks supporter) it is time for the evening heads of department brief. This is an opportunity for each department head, from the Executive Officer and Chief Engineer to the Flight Commander and the Ship's Warrant Officer, to raise with the boss any issues affecting the ship and the well-being of those on board.

Most report that 'all's well' before the ship's chaplain, Richard Quadrio, raises the sensitive subject of morale, which he says has been negatively affected by the strict stopover conditions imposed during the shortened stay in Dar es Salaam. No one else at the briefing backs the chaplain's view about the impact of the truncated shore leave, including XO Tina Brown. Instead, she strongly supports the duty of care argument raised by the threat assessments and intelligence reports concerning the potential dangers after dark in downtown Dar.

'There is always give and take particularly on operations when the operation has to win out,' Brown says. 'They are tough calls and we have a responsibility to the government to make those calls.'

Phill Henry is well aware of the negative impact of the port visit on his crew and he has a plan in mind to make it up when the ship reaches the Seychelles.

Following the introductory guided tour by WEEO O'Gorman it is time for me to scramble back down to the chiefs' mess, which will be my home away from home for the next fortnight. After some brief introductions and a rundown on the facilities from 'Swaino' McKenna, it is time to transfer my worldly goods from a duffel bag into a small but perfectly formed metal locker and to settle in for the evening movie – *Sisters*, with Tina Fey and Amy Poehler.

It is amazing how quickly a non-sailor can learn to unpack, undress and dress one-handed in a passageway without bashing into a bulkhead as the ship pitches and rolls in the rising swell. Unlike in prison, where the newest inmate is apparently confined to the bottom bunk, the newbie on board a RAN vessel is traditionally assigned the top rack. In the chiefs' mess that means sleeping three high and two metres up, above two senior sailors in a compact six-rack cabin.

'I wish I could have taken a picture of your face when you saw that rack,' one of the chiefs says.

When you are ten years old, the top bunk is a prized berth and scrambling in and out of it is never a problem, ladder or no ladder. Here there is no ladder so hoisting my hundred-plus kilogram bulk two metres off the floor with only a narrow steel rack frame for a foothold is not so easy. The bed is called a 'rack' for a reason — there is less than fifty centimetres of headroom, a steel wall down one side and the abyss on the other. There is a roll bar to prevent serious injury or death in heavy seas, and the only privacy is provided by a curtain.

The roll of frigate and the constant hum of the ship's machinery soon lull me into a sound sleep, but waking up for the first time in the top rack presents a whole new set of challenges.

If defying gravity to get into bed isn't tricky enough, then working with gravity to reach the floor in one piece and without disturbing my shipmates is downright scary. Because it is not possible to sit upright, the best method is to lie flat on one side and swing out into space while seeking a foothold, without disturbing the chief who is fast asleep below. After twenty minutes of weighing up the pros and cons of the exit strategy, and with a screaming bladder, it is time for me to give it a go. Once the initial foothold is secure it is then a matter of finding the edge of the bottom rack or a stool strategically placed at the end of the cabin for the other foot before landing safely and happily onto the deck and finally racing for the bathroom, known as the 'head'.

After a couple of nights' practice the bedding-down routine advances from comical awkwardness to what feels almost like gymnastic grace as this portly landlubber scuttles in and out of his rack with ape-like agility.

The chiefs' mess is located amidships, one deck below the officers' mess or wardroom and adjacent to the ship's galley. Unlike the rest of the crew who queue up and are served their meals by galley staff or the chaplain, RAN officers enjoy table service from a team of stewards, all of whom have other jobs, including as boarding party members.

It is often said that the guided missile frigate must have been designed by an ex-chief because the chiefs' mess is in the best location on the ship with the finest amenities. Even with fourteen chiefs on board the recreation area is more spacious and user-friendly than any other mess, including the wardroom. The chiefs' facilities include a small combined galley area and dining room and a separate lounge area with a large flat-screen TV carrying numerous satellite channels. The head has two showers, two toilets, four sinks, a washing machine and a dryer. Internet is available via Wi-Fi, and a satellite phone enables direct contact with home and the outside world. This is a far cry from earlier days at sea when sailors could not talk with their loved ones for weeks or months on end and the only communication with home was via an unreliable snail mail service.

From the chiefs' mess it is one ladder up (maintaining three points of contact at all times) and through a circular hatch to the officers' wardroom, which is located aft and one deck below the CO's cabin and the ops room – the nerve centre of a warship. From the CO's cabin it is just a short climb up to the bridge.

Forward of the chiefs' mess is the ship's hospital and petty officers' mess, and a deck below are the male and female junior sailors' messes where up to sixty young sailors share a sleeping and recreation space not much bigger than an average suburban lounge room. Aft of the chiefs' mess is the junior sailors' café where all non-officers apart from chiefs and petty officers eat their meals. The senior sailors stand in line with everyone else to be served their meals, but they then retreat to their messes to eat in relative comfort. The chiefs' and petty officers' messes are strictly off-limits to all other ranks. Even the skipper has to knock and wait to be admitted by a mess member.

The junior sailors' café is the venue for combined crew briefings. Most games are played there, too, and can provide some robust entertainment and a welcome boost to morale, especially when a junior sailor is beating a senior officer at the traditional navy board game, Uckers. This take-no-prisoners game is like Ludo on steroids with two dice and some specific and aggressive rules and tactics, such as 'ucking' or knocking off an opponent's piece should you land on a square already occupied by their piece. The hints and tips section of the rules sheet provides some handy tips for ucking the offending piece with as much force as possible. There are degrees of ucking, and the most violent reaction should be reserved for ucking a double (two pieces) or when an opponent is lined up for a run home.

'It is a no-no to uck pieces overboard,' the rules state. 'Any sign of weakness or political correctness from any player should warrant a caution. Uckers is not a game for the weak, lily livered or soft hearted. It should be played with as much venom, underhandedness and spite as indeed is possible. The sensitive, introverted and touchy-feely type should avoid it at all costs.'

But for now, my first day living in HMAS *Darwin* as she steams across the vast ocean ends with ablutions at 9.30 p.m. Showering in a rocking frigate without crashing into the plumbing is another early test, with the water sloshing about thong-clad feet a constant reminder that we are indeed at sea in a steel box.

Following the clean-up it is time for bed, the ungainly scramble up to my designated top rack and a painful collision of skull with ceiling before settling in for a deep seven-hour sleep as the warship rolls on through the Indian Ocean swells, towards its perilous hunting grounds.

2

Cauldron of conflict

The Middle East is one of the most troubled and troublesome places on earth. Religious, political and territorial conflicts have raged for thousands of years, and Australia's military involvement dates back more than a century to 1914 when the first batch of soldiers from the Australian Imperial Force arrived in Egypt before taking on the Turks at Gallipoli.

In 1915, Brigadier General Harry Chauvel led the Australian Light Horse Brigade into Cairo and in 1917, as part of the ANZAC Mounted Division, it moved to Palestine – a cauldron of twentieth-century conflict – before heading north to Syria.

The Royal Australian Navy was represented in the World War I campaign by the submarine *AE2* and the navy's most decorated and possibly least known unit of the war – the RAN Bridging Train. This land-based engineering and logistics support team took part in two amphibious landings: at Gallipoli and at El Arish on the Sinai Peninsula. One of just fifteen fighting ships in the fledgling Australian navy, the *AE2* was the first Allied vessel to penetrate the heavily defended Dardanelles, running amok before being sunk a few days later. A further six navy destroyers served in the Mediterranean theatre of the Great War.

During World War II, Australians fought and died throughout North Africa and the Middle East, beginning in Bardia, Libya, in early 1941 and continuing through Tobruk, El Alamein, Syria and Lebanon. The navy had entered the fray in December 1939 when the 'scrap iron flotilla' – the derogatory name bestowed by Nazi propaganda minister Joseph Goebbels – of five ageing destroyers arrived in Malta. The ill-fated light cruiser HMAS *Sydney* joined them later, and eight Australian-built Bathurst Class corvettes were sent to Egypt in 1943 to support the invasion of Sicily.

So Australia's naval engagement in this ancient trouble spot dates back more than 102 years. And since early August 1990, when strategic and operational staff in Canberra began compiling a plan to participate in a possible multinational force after the Iraqi dictator Saddam Hussein invaded neighbouring Kuwait, the military's senior service has been almost continually focused on the Middle East Region, including the Horn of Africa and the western Indian Ocean. It is unlikely that any of the officers assembled in the 'head shed' that year would have imagined that their successors – many of them not yet born – would still be operating in the same waters nearly thirty years later.

Apart from some gaps between 1993 and 1996 and 1996 and 1999, the RAN has had at least one warship on patrol in the region since then. Twenty major fleet units and more than 3000 officers and sailors have patrolled countless square kilometres of ocean conducting diverse missions – from shelling land-based enemy targets during the Iraq War to counter-terrorism, counter-piracy and counter-narcotics boarding operations. They have secured Iraq's offshore oil terminals and even rescued shipwrecked fishermen. The deployment of the Anzac Class frigate HMAS *Arunta* in late 2016 marked the sixty-fourth rotation of an Australian navy ship in the region. She was followed by the upgraded frigate HMAS *Newcastle* in mid-2017.

Looking back on the 1990 planning, former Vice-Admiral Rob Walls told a Sea Power Centre conference in November 2003 that the RAN's operational philosophy for the United States-led multinational Maritime Intercept Force was, 'Give us a task and we will get on and make it happen.' That simple one-line mission statement has driven every one of Australia's sixty-four naval deployments since the world's first post–Cold War military coalition was formed in 1990.

Walls, who was a commodore and the director-general of naval policy and plans at the time, is a no-nonsense character from Colac in western Victoria who was ideally suited to being Australia's point man early in its first Middle East mission under the coalition, codenamed Operation Damask.

In typical Australian fashion, he marched into the office of the US commander, Admiral Hank Mauz, and proposed that the Australian rules of engagement should be the template for the entire combined force. With the Arab states, European Union, Britain and France all vying to promote their own, differing rules, Mauz was clearly impressed by the robust Australian template for war and by the man advocating them, and he was keen to have them tabled first at the planning conference in Bahrain.

After much debate, the Australian document was adopted as the baseline for the combined force under Operation Desert Shield and United Nations Security Council Resolutions 661 and 665 authorising the enforcement of an economic embargo against Iraq.

At first the Hawke government barred Australian ships from transiting the narrow Strait of Hormuz between Iran and the United Arab Emirates – one of the world's most dangerous sea lanes – and entering the Arabian Gulf (also called the Persian Gulf). They were ordered to remain at all times in the Gulf of Oman.

However, Walls used his close relationship with Mauz to ensure that the Australian Task Group – the guided missile frigates HMA Ships *Darwin* and *Adelaide* and the replenishment vessel HMAS *Success* – would operate where the action would be in the North Arabian Sea.

Former navy chief, retired Vice-Admiral Chris Ritchie, is an expert in anti-submarine warfare. He grew up in Melbourne's northern suburbs and joined the navy straight from school as a sixteen-year-old. The 1991 Gulf War and Operation Desert Storm were the culmination of his 'at sea' career as a seaman officer.

Ritchie's family spent their holidays at Queenscliff on the Bellarine Peninsula at the western entrance to Port Phillip Bay. The young lad who watched ships steam in and out of the bay and would one day command a fighting ship in a shooting war comes from a long line of seafarers. His great-grandfather was an able seaman in the Victorian colonial navy who fought in the Maori Wars in 1860 on board the steam sloop HMVS *Victoria* and was also on the ship when she went to the Gulf of Carpentaria in 1861 to search for the ill-fated Burke and Wills expedition.

'As a kid from about the age of seven or eight I intended to join the navy,' Ritchie says. In 1968, as a fresh-faced nineteen-year-old, he graduated as a seaman officer from the naval college at HMAS *Creswell* in Jervis Bay. Just five years later, in 1973, he was appointed commanding officer of the 300-tonne landing craft HMAS *Tarakan* and after more training and a stint in Canberra he became CO of the destroyer escort HMAS *Torrens*.

During the 1982 Falklands War, Ritchie went on exchange with the Royal Navy as an ancillary warfare teacher, and a number of his students went on to fight in the war.

'A lot of them came back and said, "Well, this was good and this was bad and this was right and that's rubbish, what they're teaching," and so I had a hint of what [war] would be like – but I didn't experience it until 1990,' Ritchie says.

After a few more jobs at navy headquarters in Canberra, the then Captain Ritchie took command of the guided missile destroyer HMAS *Brisbane* in mid-1990 before her deployment to the Arabian Gulf. Being the commanding officer put him at the pointy end of Australia's first war since Vietnam, and right in the middle of the most powerful and complex naval force ever assembled. *Brisbane* was one of sixty-seven destroyers and frigates from fifteen nations operating in coalition with six aircraft carriers, two battleships, fifteen cruisers, more than a hundred logistics, amphibious and smaller craft, and some 800 aircraft deployed to the Joint Task Force.

The period between the end of Australia's involvement in Vietnam in 1972 and the invasion of Kuwait in 1990 is known in Australian military circles as the 'quiet time'. In bureaucratic circles, it was the era of the so-called 'peace dividend' of budget savings when defence spending fell to historic lows. For the navy, it had meant mainly diplomatic ship visits to Asia and military exercises such as the Rim of the Pacific with the US Navy off Hawaii.

'We spent a lot of time in Singapore and Hong Kong, places like that,' Ritchie recalls.

This all changed when the first Australian task group, under the command of Commodore Don Chalmers, sailed from Sydney for the Gulf in August 1990. It had no time for a proper workup, where ships are put through their paces to prepare for war. Planning began immediately for the second rotation, and *Brisbane* went into Garden Island dockyard in Sydney for an urgent upgrade.

'We had two close-in weapon systems fitted, we had armour protection fitted, we had a lot of communications equipment fitted – a lot of things that brought the ship up to a standard that you could expect it to fight with,' Ritchie recalls. 'And then we worked up. That work-up went as we continued all the way to Diego Garcia, in fact. Yeah, it was pretty hard actually.'

The second Damask deployment (HMA Ships *Brisbane* and *Sydney*) marked the first time in almost twenty years that RAN vessels had conducted a work-up for a possible shooting war. Ritchie had been a sub-lieutenant on the last ship that had been placed on a war footing – the guided missile destroyer HMAS *Hobart*, when it was preparing to deploy to the Vietnam War in 1971. But she never joined that troubled conflict. The deployment was cancelled a week before she was due to sail because Australia's involvement in the war came to an end.

Ritchie recalls that the work-up for Vietnam was nowhere near as intense as the preparations for deploying to the Gulf. Australian navy ships had not been involved in the Falklands War, which took place in 1982, but some Australian naval people had deployed to the Falklands either through secondments or while serving in the British navy, and they knew what to expect.

'One of them was a bloke called Ted Walsh who was the fleet [nuclear, biological, chemical defence expert],' Ritchie recalls. 'He'd been the XO of a frigate there [Falklands] and he saw what happened so he was really the strength of that work-up. He was the bloke who really made you understand what you might expect if things went bad. It wasn't easy to work up the ship and we had all sorts of extra people put on board. We ended up with about 350 I think. There were people everywhere. They were almost hanging from the rafters! It took some time to get the new culture across, but eventually we did.'

In early December 1990, the Hawke government gave the green light for *Brisbane* and *Sydney* to steam through the Strait of Hormuz between Iran and the Gulf states to conduct operations inside the Gulf. So, the two ships spent Christmas 1990 in the bustling port of Bahrain – home of the US Navy's Fifth Fleet and its Central Command, which includes the combined naval task forces operating in the region. It was also the main base for ships from more than a dozen other nations deployed with the multinational Maritime Interception Force.

In the event, *Brisbane* did not do any war fighting – although during Operation Desert Storm she was placed on alert for a possible mission to shell land-based targets in support of a Marine Corps landing that was supposedly being planned by the US commander, General 'Stormin' Norman Schwarzkopf.

'Schwarzkopf never really intended there to be a Marines thing,' Ritchie explains. 'But he was sold on the idea that if the rumour was there and if ships were seen to be practising, it would be a diversion, bringing Iraqis to the Kuwaiti coast.'

He has no doubt that the first Gulf War was always intended to be predominantly a land campaign. That does not mean there were no risks to the ships.

There were early concerns that the large and quite capable Iraqi Air Force, which had 910 combat aircraft in August 1990, might launch Exocet missile strikes against coalition warships.

'A whole lot of Iraqi aircraft disappeared and went to Iran and nobody knew why they'd gone there. The feeling was that they could possibly fly from the north of Iran down to the eastern side of the Zagreb Mountains, which run down that eastern side of the Gulf. And then they would pop up over the mountain and you would really have [only] about 20 miles in which to see them,' Ritchie says.

The airborne threat never emerged, but there was a big and real hazard to the flotilla – sea mines. The Iraqis released hundreds of free-floating, deadly contact mines into the Gulf, and they remained a significant and unpredictable danger to shipping throughout the conflict. Two United States warships – the amphibious assault ship USS *Tripoli* and the aegis cruiser USS *Princeton* – were seriously damaged on 18 February 1991 when they struck sea mines. No one was killed, but both ships were forced into dry dock for repairs at a cost of more than $20 million. A sea mine costs only about $12,000 – a pittance compared with the costly damage it can inflict.

Brisbane also had a close encounter with half a dozen mines during a patrol in the northern part of the Gulf and was ever vigilant about the threat, with enhanced lookouts and electro-optical sensors used to search for the floating bombs.

'We'd been sleeping all night and we turned around and there were five or six mines floating in the area that we'd just been through,' Ritchie recalls.

Mine protection was a major preoccupation during both the 1991 Gulf War and the 2003 Iraq War when minesweeping and mine-hunting vessels, specialised navy clearance divers, aircraft and even trained dolphins were used to detect and then defuse or destroy both 'contact' and 'influence' mines. This work is highly skilled and horrendously dangerous. Contact mines explode on impact but influence mines are built to detonate in response to a particular ship-type's noise or magnetic signature. This makes them even more difficult to counter.

Although the danger of mines continues to this day, RAN ships deployed to the region are now retrofitted with the latest Mine and Obstacle Avoidance Sonar that allows them to detect and avoid a variety of mines.

Australian navy divers played a key role in clearing Iraq's only deep-water port at Umm Qasr in 2003 where the US Navy dolphins, trained in San Diego, were also employed on the dangerous work. The marine mammals were not very successful, and some simply went native, prompting one memorable newspaper quote from a navy diver that read, 'Flipper's fucked.'

Once it was apparent that the Iraqi Air Force was out of the game in the first Gulf War the Australian warships settled into a routine of patrolling as part of the air defence screen around the aircraft carrier USS *Midway* in the area known as the Central Arabian Gulf.

By mid-January 1991, things began hotting up for warships that were engaged in the Arabian Gulf naval strike force designated Battle Force Zulu.

Early on the morning of 17 January the glowing radar screens in the operations rooms on board *Sydney* and *Brisbane* lit up like Christmas trees when dozens of Tomahawk land-attack cruise missiles and carrier-based strike jets were launched by the coalition against Iraqi forces to kick off Operation Desert Storm. The skies above the Gulf were crisscrossed with smoke and condensation trails; 'happy trails' – American code for 'missiles away' – was announced on the radio network while the weapons streaked towards their targets. More than a billion people around the globe witnessed the spectacle when CNN telecast the bombardment of Baghdad in real time from the roof of the Al Rasheed hotel.

Ten years later, Chris Ritchie had become a Rear Admiral and the Commander Australian Theatre for a new Middle East mission known as Operation Slipper. With Australia's commitment in East Timor gradually winding down, he had taken on the job, thinking it would give him some time to think about future operational concepts. Such a luxury would never eventuate. That year would be the busiest of Ritchie's entire career.

'I had a week to think about that – and then *Tampa* turned up and I never wrote anything,' he says.

In August 2001, the Norwegian container ship MV *Tampa* rescued 438 asylum seekers from their sinking vessel in international waters off the Australian Indian Ocean territory of Christmas Island. The Howard government denied the captain, Arne Rinnan, permission to land his distressed human cargo on the island or at any other Australian port and despatched troops from the elite Special Air Service Regiment to board the cargo ship and enforce the blockade. Then, on 11 September, Al Qaeda terrorists brought down the World Trade Centre in New York and the world changed forever.

'As soon as *Tampa* came we had to put in place a plan to prevent any more boats getting through so that took a good third of the operational navy up on the northwest coast,' Ritchie says. 'Then 10 days later 9/11 happens and everybody is wandering around saying, "Well, what are we going to do?"'

For every senior Australian military officer, the combination of *Tampa* and 9/11 triggered the most hectic period since Vietnam. With the navy fully occupied on border protection operations, Ritchie and his team expected the Americans to request the usual contribution from Australia in the form of SASR troops, RAAF Boeing 707 aerial tankers, P-3 Orion maritime surveillance aircraft, C-130 Hercules cargo planes and a frigate or two. But the Americans asked for more.

'They said, "Well, we want you to send F-18s to Diego Garcia," and we thought, "What for? What are we going to do in Diego Garcia?" "Well, we're going to shoot down aeroplanes that approach Diego Garcia." And we did send planes there,' he says.

So, on 9 November 2001, four F/A-18 Hornet fighters from 77 Squadron took off from RAAF base Richmond bound for the highly strategic Indian Ocean atoll of Diego Garcia.

Visiting Diego is a surreal experience. Even when in transit on board military flights (civilian flights are banned) we were warned against wandering away from the rudimentary terminal facility and barred from taking any photographs. Apart from the strict security measures, it is difficult to grasp that this tiny British territory in the middle of nowhere is a major military facility and that during the Cold War it was a vital staging point for nuclear-armed US strategic bombers in the event of a major conflict. There have also been numerous unconfirmed reports that the atoll was used to 'render' prisoners in the aftermath of 9/11 before the establishment of the Guantanamo Bay prison in Cuba.

The deployment of Australian jets was the first time RAAF fighters had been sent on operations overseas since the Korean War, and many people inside and outside Canberra were perplexed, given the lack of enemy aircraft that were capable of striking the remote outpost.

'Nobody came so they didn't shoot anybody down,' Ritchie says drily.

The frigate HMAS *Anzac* had been on station in the Gulf as part of the blockade against Iraq when 9/11 happened. She was replaced in November 2001 by the first task group under Operation Slipper. By coincidence, *Anzac* was back on duty in the

Gulf in 2003 for the US-led invasion of Iraq. On 20 March, she became the first Australian warship since the Vietnam War to fire on land-based targets when she shelled Iraqi positions during the capture of the town of Al Faw by British commandos.

Anzac has so far made four trips to the region, and the twenty-three-year-old ship's experience – and that of the other nineteen warships to have served there – reinforced the view of many that the navy must be equipped with capable, multi-role, war-fighting ships.

The Maritime Commander during Operations Damask 1 and 2, retired Rear Admiral Ken Doolan, told the 2003 Sea Power Centre conference that the crux of the RAN's Middle East deployments was that Australia could only make a meaningful contribution because it had warships that could 'take the fight to the enemy, defend themselves and win'.

Doolan, who went on to become the national president of the RSL, argued that the operations in the Gulf had finally put to bed the post-Vietnam doctrine of 'low level contingencies' being spruiked by some bureaucrats and academics.

'It would be the most abject folly for the ADF to ever again flirt with the ideas of those who contend that a force equipped and trained primarily for low-level contingencies could be effective,' Doolan warned.

Thirteen years later, he stands firmly behind his claim and as *Darwin* steams away from the east coast of Africa in May 2016 it is clear that the 'war fighting' doctrine is here to stay.

3

At the captain's table

It is the second day of *Darwin*'s new patrol. Everything is quiet as the frigate steams steadily eastwards and the ship's helicopter Orko is aloft for its first sortie on the hunt for suspicious vessels.

My day begins with a welcome cup of fresh Tanzanian coffee at 6 a.m. before I climb up to the wardroom for a hearty breakfast of bacon and eggs with the ship's officers. The CO is not allowed to eat in the wardroom unless invited by the mess, so Phill Henry takes his breakfast, and most other meals during the six-month deployment, in his cabin.

Positioned just below and behind the bridge and adjacent to the armour-plated operations room, the tiny cabin is a sanctuary for the man or woman who has the lives and welfare of some 230 souls and hundreds of millions of dollars worth of military hardware in his or her hands.

A quiet haven where big decisions – including occasional judgements about life and death – are contemplated, made and mulled over, it can also be a place of inner turmoil where the buck finally stops. Many of the calls that a ship's captain has to make are not taught at command school or included in the pre-deployment briefing pack. Each Middle East mission throws up unique leadership challenges.

According to the most experienced sailors, there are broadly two types of commanding officers in the navy – those who spend most of the time in their cabin or the ops room focused on the big picture, and those who, as well as doing that, also make time to interact with their crew. These skippers are generally more popular below decks.

Commander Henry falls into the latter category. During the warship's two-week patrol from Tanzania to the Seychelles he pops up all over the vessel. From serving meals and washing dishes in the sailors' mess to having a coffee in the petty officers' mess, Phill Henry, a bank manager's son, is closely engaged with his crew.

I sit down with him for a cup of tea and chocolate biscuits at his small dining table, and he explains what the mission is, where *Darwin* will be operating and that she will be working closely with the French navy in the waters between Africa and the Seychelles. Prime targets will be fishing or cargo dhows suspected of smuggling illicit drugs or weapons along what is known as the smack track between the sub-continent and East Africa.

Compared with the cramped junior sailors' mess three decks below, the CO's cabin on a guided missile frigate feels quite luxurious. It consists of a small entrance corridor leading into a three-by-four-metre room that serves as an office, dining room and sleeping quarters, with a cramped ensuite bathroom off it. The cabin contains the dining table, a desk and shelves that house a computer, numerous family photos and other personal items and a sofa which folds out into a bed that receives only limited use during patrols. A porthole provides some natural light and a glimpse of the outside world – mostly sea and sky. Beyond the entrance is a small galley where the chief steward, Leading Seaman Anne 'Becks' Becker, organises meals for the boss and his guests. Most of the time that is just a single plate for the captain.

After dinner, the skipper's cabin quickly fills with bodies for the daily heads of department briefing. It is also the venue for operations and command briefings, when up to a dozen people cram inside for the short, sharp gatherings. Intelligence and other sensitive briefings take place in the more secure ops room, where all mobile phones and cameras are banned.

Henry grew up in Dunedin and moved to Christchurch during his teenage years. There he became an apprentice refrigeration engineer and joined the Royal New Zealand Navy Reserves as an engineer sailor.

'I made it to the dizzy heights of Able Seaman Engineer,' he says.

After completing his apprenticeship and working for a year or so in the meat industry, he left to join the navy full time as a seaman officer. There he stayed for thirteen and a half years, following a fairly common path as officer of the watch and then navigator.

'The first time I came to the Persian Gulf was in 95–96 as the navigator in HMNZS *Wellington*, doing the blockade of Iraq operations,' he says. He also saw service in Bougainville and became Operations Officer in the frigate HMNZ *Canterbury*, serving in East Timor. Crossing the ditch in 2001 on an exchange with the RAN, he served in two Anzac Class frigates – HMAS *Arunta* and then HMAS *Stuart*. Towards the end of the exchange he decided he join the RAN.

There was no single reason. 'It was quite a lot of just little reasons. I could see the way that it looked like the New Zealand navy was going at the time, with a reduction in the number of frigates from four to two, a focus on inshore patrol craft and OPVs [offshore patrol vessels] as opposed to a lot of MFUs [major fleet units/big warships] and global operations. They still do the global operations with two ships but there was more opportunity, not only in serving in the RAN but more opportunity in Australia at the time.'

The ginger-haired officer also needed a break after more than thirteen years' solid time at sea. His first marriage had broken down and his former wife had returned to New Zealand, so he took six months off before starting work with the Australian navy.

Once he had joined, he served in the Anzac Class frigate HMAS *Anzac* before moving to the fleet base in Sydney as maritime operations coordinator. Then it was on to postings as XO in two guided missile frigates, HMAS *Melbourne* and then HMAS *Adelaide*. From there he moved upwards, including a year at the Australian Defence Force Academy in Canberra commanding a squadron of second-year cadets.

'It was a year where I felt I was giving back, to be able to help with the training and the shaping of a lot of what would be the junior officers across all three services,' he reflects.

After filling in as XO in the tanker HMAS *Sirius* for six months, he headed to Bahrain in 2014 for eight months with the Maritime Operations Support Group, the official name for the Australian contingent to the Combined Maritime Forces. The Australians worked closely on the planning for operations there.

'At the time, we had *Melbourne* and *Darwin* [in the area] and then transitioned to *Toowoomba* while I was in the headquarters. That was a great experience – working alongside thirty other countries in a united effort to beat smuggling and the anti-piracy operations and [working to keep] the stability in the Gulf under [Combined Task Force] 152.'

Returning to Australia, he took command of *Darwin* in June 2015 from the previous skipper, Commander Terry Morrison.

Ensuring that a ship is ready and capable to return to the Middle East Region is a huge undertaking with strict procedures. After its 2014 deployment, the frigate, which has clocked about 1.2 million nautical miles (2.2 million kilometres), had spent several months in a major maintenance period before moving into her 'system qualifying trial' in May 2015. That is a long and challenging process.

'We make sure all the weapon systems, predominantly, are working as they're supposed to do – so lots of air tracking of targets and firing the weapons systems,' Henry explains. 'That's generally anywhere from three to five weeks. We also do a couple of aviation training-week periods with the squadrons at Nowra and use a ship that's basically dedicated to them, to do the landing and take-offs from the deck so that they are progressing the qualifications of the pilots.'

After that they rolled into a 'unit ready workup' with Sea Training Group, known as the 'green team'.

'They come on board and, progressively over five weeks, make sure that the ship and its people are confident in all aspects of maritime operations,' Henry says. 'It's a very busy period – the ship sails at eight o'clock Monday morning out of Sydney, doesn't get back until four or five o'clock Friday afternoon, and it is put through its paces the whole time. It is a rewarding day when the head sea trainer says, "You've passed." And this ship's company did really well – we passed with nothing outstanding across all avenues. [Jason O'Gorman] and I looked at each other going, "Thank Christ it's over."'

He says the achievement belongs to more than the ship's company. 'It's the Sea Training Group that helped train us to that standard and the support of people at fleet base that kept the ship running while we were out there doing it – you know, we wouldn't have gone to sea on Monday morning if stores people and support people and Thales contractors hadn't worked over the weekend to get the ship ready.'

Then came a further eight weeks of maintenance to add all the systems and self-protection measures needed for the Middle East, as well as to certify the engineering systems to enable her to sail for a long period and remain seaworthy. During this time, specialists from maintenance contractors Thales and BAE Systems swarmed over the ship under a special contract known as the 'FFG Enterprise' agreement.

Unlike past contracts, where blame shifting took centre stage, the 'enterprise' approach focuses on the problem and how to fix it in a fast and cost-effective manner, ensuring that *Darwin's* 100 per cent availability record will be maintained during seven months of hard running.

By November 2015, *Darwin* was ready for her 'mission readiness workup'.

'That was three weeks again with our favourite people at Sea Training Group, doing the training required specifically to come up here – the boarding operations, the increased potential for a tense environment, particularly when transiting in an area where it could quickly go wrong,' says Henry. 'You know, in the Gulf of Aden at the moment there's all the operations around Yemen. There have been tensions between the coalition and Iran throughout the Strait of Hormuz for a long time. We're not planning for anything to go wrong, but you've got to be ready if someone miscalculates, and I believe that our training was at the right level.'

The proof has already been evident on this tour. 'Our operations, where we've had interactions with Iranian Navy and the IRGCN [Islamic Revolutionary Guard Corps Navy], which is the religious side of the military, have been very professional. A couple of times it got a little bit tense but very professional.'

That 'little bit' of tension included a dangerous game of chicken played by several Iranian skiffs during the ship's transit through the strait. Luckily, it did not erupt into a full-blown incident that could have become a disaster.

'We were ready to match [them],' Henry says. 'But they acted not in an unsafe manner. So we were well prepared.'

Each Australian warship deployed to the Gulf region steams from its home base bristling with the best weaponry and equipment that money can buy.

For a civilian fresh from an operations briefing in the ops room, a guided tour of *Darwin*'s weapons and fire control compartments with the fire control and weapons chief, Chief Petty Officer William 'Eddy' Edmondson, is a mind-boggling and sobering experience. After several costly upgrades, the frigate is a lethal fighting ship equipped with millions of dollars worth of state-of-the-art computerised missile and self-defence systems integrated into her three-decades-old framework.

The three missile systems are the SM-2, Harpoon and evolved Sea Sparrow. They, along with the US-made Phalanx Close-in Weapon System (or CIWS, pronounced 'Sea Whiz') and the Italian-made Mark 75 OTO Melara 76-millimetre rapid-fire gun, must all be tested and maintained to the highest levels, ready to swing into action at a moment's notice. So must the six Mark 32 torpedo tubes and a raft of radars, sonars and command-and-control units.

In *Darwin* that responsibility falls to WEEO Lieutenant Commander Jason O'Gorman and his team of specialist 'greenies' – the electrical branch of the navy. *Darwin*'s greenies are led by Eddy Edmondson, and the combat systems chief, Chief Petty Officer Darren 'Swampy' Marshall. They supervise teams of specialists that include electronics and weapons technicians, as well as 'gun busters', or gun maintainers.

Inside the large magazine, immediately below the gun deck, dozens of sixty-three-centimetre-long, seventy-six-millimetre-calibre (diameter) shells are stacked neatly in racks waiting to be loaded into the rotating magazine and fed into the main gun's automatic loading system.

The menacing seventy-six-millimetre gun is mounted amidships just forward of the exhaust stacks. It can hurl 6.3-kilogram shells up to forty kilometres at a rate of 120 every minute. The high rate of fire with pinpoint accuracy, combined with specialised ammunition, means it can be used for a variety of tasks, including anti-aircraft, point or self-defence and ground support. It is difficult to imagine what a Somali pirate in a small skiff armed with an AK-47 assault rifle would make of such awesome firepower.

The CIWS uses a radar-guided, twenty-millimetre swivelling Gatling gun to protect the ship from incoming missiles. It can let rip at up to 4500 rounds a minute. This is a vital piece of equipment because modern sea-skimming supersonic missiles can take as little as thirty seconds from detection on the horizon to impact. After identifying a target's bearing, range, velocity, heading and altitude, the CIWS tracks the outgoing rounds electronically and 'walks' them on to the target.

Also under Edmondson's purview are the Harpoon and SM-2 anti-ship missiles, as well as the evolved Sea Sparrow anti-missile system. The Harpoon and SM-2 are fired from the Mark 13 rotating missile launcher fitted forward of the bridge and next to the Mark 41 vertical canisters for the Sea Sparrows, which are located towards the bow of the ship adjacent to the toilet paper storage cupboard. This is the same 'canister and cell' system seen regularly on TV images during the 2003 Iraq War, when coalition ships in the Gulf launched Tomahawk cruise missiles against targets in Iraq, and in April 2017 against Syria from ships in the Mediterranean Sea.

The powerful arsenal is linked to radars and fire control systems overseen by 'Swampy' Marshall and his combat system technicians. Marshall's domain includes the brains of the set-up, the Mk 92 guided-missile fire-control system and its combined antennae system that is housed in an egg-shaped dome on the superstructure. This allows the ship's weapons to track and engage targets, as does the AN/SPS-49 long-range air search radar that can pick up incoming air threats from 470 kilometres away and up to an altitude of 46,000 metres.

The combat systems also include the state-of-the-art retrofitted Mine and Obstacle Avoidance Sonar. The transducer, located under the hull at the forward end of the ship, can detect sea mines and other obstacles, map the seabed and even track submarines. It automatically locks onto a target and displays how fast and how deep it is and where it is heading. The frigate is further equipped with hull-mounted and towed anti-submarine sonars, and its 'B' model Seahawk helicopter is also fitted with the latest 'dipping' sonar to hunt for submarines. The effectiveness of this kit was later demonstrated during my flight on the ship's helicopter.

Most of *Darwin*'s hugely expensive combat systems have never been used in anger, but each element must be regularly tested and ready for war. So must the operators, who are kept on their toes with regular calls to 'action stations' to test readiness and response times.

When the ship is called to 'action', all on board are focused on their job. Crew members, wearing flame-retardant headwear, move quickly through corridors and along the decks to reach their designated positions. Fire crews and damage control teams man their equipment ready to move in an instant to douse flames or repair damage to vital equipment. Fire and damage control exercises are taken extremely seriously and woe betide any crew member who doesn't meet the minimum performance standards. They will do it again and again until they get it right because out here in the middle of the ocean you can't dial 000 and ask for help. During this frantic period, I am the sole person on board without a job to do, so I just try to stay out of the way.

A constant challenge for O'Gorman's weapons technicians is to keep the 'gates' open between modern-day software and the older hardware on the ship.

After the major refit and arduous work-up, *Darwin* set sail from Australia on 30 December 2015 fully equipped for whatever hostilities the Middle East Region might throw at her. The ship first visited Thailand and Indonesia before steaming to India for the Indian International Fleet Review where *Darwin* was among a group of ninety warships at anchor in the port of Visakhapatnam.

The frigate arrived in the Gulf region on 11 February 2016. First came a few days' briefings and more specialist boarding operations training with US Coast Guard teams in Bahrain. Then, at last, they were into their patrol cycle under Operation Manitou, the Australian government's contribution to the 'multinational combined military force efforts to promote regional maritime security, stability and prosperity'. It was the ship's seventh deployment to the Middle East and the sixty-second rotation of an RAN vessel in the region since 1990.

The first few months of *Darwin*'s 2016 patrols were quite disappointing for the crew. The one exception was a huge weapons haul on 5 March. Since then, they have conducted many boardings but found no drugs or weapons. Now the frigate is more than halfway through her deployment and as she steams further into the Indian Ocean the frustration and disappointment is palpable on the faces of the ship's company.

Henry tries to put a positive spin on it, saying each boarding is worthwhile. 'We're up to about twenty-five boardings – a lot, because of where we are in the season for the smuggling. There's a transition to the southwest monsoon season [rougher weather] and there's a reduced number of smugglers, so we've boarded a couple that were northbound and empty. But even that is a good boarding to do because we're understanding the pattern of life, how they're operating and getting to know them more, to make it easier for a southbound [interception] when they do have drugs on board.'

He says that while these boardings will lead to more intercepts later on, it is not just about getting the drugs. Deterrence is a major component in the fight against the drug trade's funding of terrorism. 'Even boarding when we know they haven't got something is still a deterrent. They know we're out there doing the job.'

Darwin has been working with Combined Task Force 150, which was Australian-led during the first part of the deployment. She has visited Muscat, Bahrain again, and Dubai for a rest and recreation visit.

'We've just done the visit to Dar es Salaam,' Henry says. 'We'll have visits to Seychelles and Muscat before we leave the area and hand over to *Perth* on the 24th of June making our way home via Singapore.'

He explains that the ship is currently engaged on Operation Shirikisho, which means 'unity' in Swahili. It is led in Bahrain by the United Kingdom, now in command of the combined task force, while *Darwin* is operating at sea with the French ship

FNS *Nivôse* and a French maritime patrol and reconnaissance aircraft.

'It is about trying to maximise coverage against the smugglers towards the end of the season down here at the southern end of the distribution track,' Henry says. 'The patrol box is drawn up with CTF-150 in the most likely areas of intercept. So the idea is that it's known tracks that they've been taking or where we expect they may be going. It's constantly evolving so you can't sit in the same spot every year – because obviously as they get pinched in one spot they'll move to somewhere else.'

The areas they are about to enter have been decided by negotiation between four nations. 'We've got the French out here with us; ourselves; the British; and CTF-150 has a multinational staff – there's a Saudi officer as their chief of staff and some Saudi staff in there. So we're all collaboratively working to come up with these patrol boxes and we're adapting them each day, based on where we think things are going and the weather conditions.'

As we chat, the skipper receives numerous updates from the ops room and elsewhere on the ship, as well as several visits from crew. His is a 24/7 job and apart from the occasional respite handover to Tina Brown, Henry is in command and available at all hours of the day and night throughout the seven-month deployment.

Life in a warship during operations is busy for the entire crew, but there is a level of stress for the captain that is only obvious at close quarters. Most of the ship's company can snatch a decent rest at least every few days, but the boss seldom has more than a few hours' shut-eye before he is woken for an update or a decision.

Henry knows that operational command of a major fleet unit will be the pinnacle of his navy career. He also understands that the stresses and strains, the highs and the lows are all part of the job and that his absence from home will pass quickly.

'To be given the opportunity to command a ship, to represent Australia, to lead close to 230 people – every day is Christmas Day,' he says. 'The worst day out here would be much better than sitting at a desk ashore somewhere. That's the mindset you've got to have.'

Meanwhile, *Darwin* is steaming into some reasonable weather in the shadow of Madagascar, but to the southeast *Nivôse* is in a sea-state five with a four-metre swell. 'There won't be any smugglers down there at the moment. They just won't be operating in that. So *Nivôse* is going to move closer to us later today.'

It is also a matter of balancing where they think the smugglers will be with all the operational requirements, including the need to keep the ship's aircraft flying.

'It's hard to get aviation fuel for the helicopter down here in East Africa, and luckily for us the German replenishment ship as part of Operation Atlantic is coming through,' says Henry. 'We're rendezvousing with her on 19 May, and we'll be replenishing aviation fuel from her. So it's constantly evolving.'

At 3 p.m., Chief Boatswain (pronounced 'bosun') or 'buffer' David 'Bowie' Bowden puts trainee boat crews to the test in choppy seas. It is vital to have numerous crews trained and ready to operate the frigate's RHIBs from the moving ship in all sea-states for boarding or rescue operations. The 'L' plate crews are called upon to repeatedly drive the bucking craft in close to the ship's ladders and away again.

For the trainees at the helm and on the ropes in the RHIB, it is crucial that they can instantly respond to the buffer's commands while keeping their vessel out of harm's way.

Manoeuvring a five-metre inflatable boat alongside a large warship steaming at fifteen knots or more in high winds and two-metre seas while soaked to the skin is not an easy task.

Miscalculations or mistakes can be fatal or expensive, so learner crews are put through their paces as often as possible. When boarding operations reach high intensity, the more trained boat crews available, the better.

Each morning at 8 a.m. Henry has a chat with the Commanding Officer of *Nivôse* and every few days has a CO-level chat with the rest of the task force. In an ideal world, intelligence feeds into that planning, the aircraft locates the suspect vessel, and *Darwin* intercepts it and sends in a boarding party. But it doesn't always happen like that.

'Weather conditions may mean that you don't detect it by aircraft – it still might be the ship that detects it,' Henry says. 'There may be no intel to feed into it. We may not know that the smuggler's there and so you may still just run across them using ship sensors. We did a boarding last week where we'd had aircraft up and the weather conditions meant it was difficult for their systems to detect [dhows], when they're trying to maximise the coverage area. We're talking wooden dhows that are sometimes only thirty to forty feet long. It's not something that's easily detectable.'

Darwin's own lookouts, standing on the gun direction platform, saw the dhow first.

'We'd even had the aircraft up flying earlier in the day, the French had had their aircraft up – and it was just the good old-fashioned "Mark One eyeball" [human eye] that spotted it,' Henry says. 'So, we then went and investigated and boarded. So yeah, in the ideal world, early detection by aircraft, ship will then come in and board and we then go through the process under the Law of the Sea to be able to do a boarding, which is effectively establishing the statehood of the vessel. If we can't establish it, then that allows us to then conduct searches.'

4

A close call

Long before the Royal Australian Navy's focus turned to pirates and drugs, Australian sailors were confronting complex and potentially deadly situations throughout the Middle East Region. Iran's fanatical religious Iranian Revolutionary Guard Corps Navy (IRGCN) has been harassing Australian warships ever since the Hawke government gave the green light for RAN ships to move through the Strait of Hormuz.

By far the most dangerous interaction between an Australian fighting ship and Iran's maritime revolutionary guard took place on 6 December 2004 when a boarding party from the frigate HMAS *Adelaide* was menaced by a large hostile force close to Iranian territorial waters.

In this tense and potentially disastrous incident, the *Adelaide*'s boarding team commander, navy clearance diver Petty Officer Andrew Keitley, found himself and his thirteen-member team stranded on a Lebanese merchant ship in the northern Arabian

Gulf with two interpreters, surrounded by a force of aggressive, heavily armed speedboats crewed by Iranian religious fanatics.

Adelaide, under the command of Commander Bruce Victor, was on patrol as part of a combined task force to secure Iraq's two offshore oil terminals, Khor Al Amaya Oil Terminal (KAAOT) and Al Basrah Oil Terminal (ABOT). Situated at the northern end of the Gulf just off the Shatt al-Arab waterway that divides Iraq and Iran, the two terminals generate about eighty per cent of Iraq's total revenue.

In April that year, when the frigate HMAS *Stuart* was on guard duty, a terrorist attack on KAAOT had been foiled when an explosives-laden skiff was intercepted by a RHIB from the US Coast Guard patrol vessel USS *Firebolt*. The skiff blew up, killing three American sailors. A young Australian, RAN Leading Seaman Ben Sime, who was the sensor operator/crewman on *Stuart*'s Seahawk helicopter, was awarded the Medal for Gallantry after he leapt from the chopper to try to save a gravely wounded US sailor. A visit to the ship by Prime Minister John Howard, who was in Baghdad for Anzac Day, was cancelled following the incident.

Two months later, the IRGCN had generated global headlines when, on 21 June, they captured six British Royal Marines and two British sailors in the Shatt al-Arab waterway for allegedly straying into Iranian waters. The British had been training Iraqi river patrol units.

Adelaide had replaced *Stuart* in the Gulf in August 2004 and tensions were still running high when Keitley and his team were ordered to search the Lebanese-flagged vehicle carrier MV *Sham*. The merchant ship, which had run aground in the Shatt al-Arab waterway, was known by the Australians as a 'frequent flyer' because they had boarded her several times already. She was the lead vessel of six merchant ships that had grounded during severe tides and storms in the volatile waterway. Their presence was causing the US high command considerable angst.

Adelaide's GPS and charts clearly showed that MV *Sham* was inside Iraqi waters, which meant that the Australians could board her without interference. But that was not how Iran's Islamic naval guardians saw it.

Andrew Keitley joined the navy in 1988 from his hometown of Warburton just outside Melbourne. Now a Chief Petty Officer, he began his navy career as a quarter master gunner, and his first sea posting was in the guided missile destroyer HMAS *Perth*. After qualifying as a ship's diver, he decided to change streams to become a navy clearance diver. It was in that capacity that he found himself in command of the boarding team on board *Adelaide*.

Divers bring a broad skill set to the boarding role, and most RAN boarding teams include at least one clearance diver who is qualified in advanced weapon skills, close order combat, fast roping and boat handling. Their high levels of agility and fitness enable them to adapt to most situations.

'We are a kind of niche capability that captains can bring onto their ship and rely on, or really lean on when the going gets tough as well,' Keitley says.

As the petty officer in charge of a team that also included a female sailor, he had the capture of the Royal Marines firmly in his mind whenever he was operating close to Iranian waters. He employed great caution as *Adelaide*'s two RHIBs approached the MV *Sham* and began the boarding process.

The threat posed by the Iranians had come into stark focus for Keitley and the rest of the crew when *Adelaide* steamed through the strait to enter the Arabian Gulf in August 2004. It was the first time that many of the crew had gone to 'action stations' when it wasn't just an exercise.

'That was kind of a moment of, "Wow, we've arrived in the Gulf," and things potentially were getting a little bit more real,' he recalls.

The transit was also Keitley's first sighting of the four-to-six-metre-long speed boats, mostly powered by twin outboard motors, manned by between two and six Iranian religious paramilitaries.

After arriving in the Middle East, *Adelaide*'s boarding teams had searched everything from 300,000-tonne super tankers transporting crude oil to twenty-metre dhows carrying cargoes of dates and charcoal. These were 'low threat' missions looking for contraband such as drugs or illegal oil shipments or for people who shouldn't have been on the vessels. They also conducted counter-piracy or constabulary patrols to protect vessels likely to be targeted by pirates, and counter-terrorism security patrols to enforce exclusion zones around the oil terminals.

While the biggest security fears were of a terrorist attack or the ongoing threat of all-out war between Israel and Iran, it was the rag-tag IRGCN that posed a constant and challenging threat. In fact, just a few nights before 4 December, *Adelaide* had gone to action stations in response to the presence of skiffs in the area.

The XO in the Australian frigate was Stephen Bowater. Now a navy captain and in 2016 the CO of the HMAS *Cerberus* training establishment in Victoria, he recalls that the week before 4 December 2004 had been fairly tense due to intelligence reports about a possible attack.

'In a ship's life, a cycle if you like, you get to a point in your deployment where everything's just perfect. It's a sweet spot, it really is,' he says. 'We'd been doing things like refuelling a helicopter off the back of our ship at the same time as fuelling a patrol boat on the starboard side of the ship, while the port side of the ship was putting two boats in the water. That is twice as complex as anything we did in our workup, which we thought was horrific! But we just took it in our stride. We were nailing it.'

On the night of 3 December, a severe storm struck the area and, just after that, US army and navy special forces units flew all-night missions up and down the Iranian border on their way in and out of Iraq. This caused the Iranians to become 'quite edgy', Bowater says. So when a US commander ordered the *Adelaide* to board the MV *Sham*, the Australians were concerned and pushed back against the decision.

'We said, "Look we don't think it's a good idea because they're a bit edgy. You've been flying missions all night and we know she's not a threat, we've boarded her four times in the last three days,"' Bowater says. 'The reply was "No, go and do it." We found out later we were talking to an American reserve dentist who was watch keeping!'

So at 12.20 p.m. the boarding party set off in two RHIBs to cover the 10 kilometres of open sea to the grounded ship, which was located north of *Adelaide*'s position near the oil terminals. The Iranians had an observation post built into a huge crane known by the Australians as 'the crane of death' that had been sunk just inside their territorial waters during the Iran–Iraq war in the 1980s. From that post, which was manned around the clock, they could observe what was going on around the Iraqi oil terminals and keep an eye on coalition ships.

Keitley and his team were tasked to find out why the MV *Sham* had been in the one place for several days and what the situation was on board. The boarding team consisted of fourteen sailors and two Farsi interpreters, with the ship's helicopter, codenamed Sandman, providing overwatch until they had boarded the ship and called 'low threat'. Then the bird peeled away to other duties.

'On our way up there we had to go fairly close to that crane, so they [the Iranians] would have been tipped off,' Keitley recalls. 'Obviously, a helicopter and two RHIBs packed with a boarding party, they definitely would have seen that – which may have been a combat indicator to them, that something was going on.'

The actual boarding was indeed a low threat operation and the MV *Sham*'s crew was compliant. Everything went smoothly as the Australians used the ship's ladder to climb aboard. The boarding party was divided into two-person teams with each team having set duties to perform. For example, the engineering team checks the ship's machinery, the search team conducts a thorough search and the crew control team guards the crew who are normally mustered in the cafeteria.

As the team leader, Keitley talked to the MV *Sham*'s captain and checked his logs and manifest. Because she had been boarded just a week earlier, the process was straightforward. The only issue was the crew's frustration because their vessel was riding so far out of the water that she couldn't access seawater to supply their freshwater maker.

'The crew was also due out for rotation, they were running low on supplies, they didn't have fresh water so they were kind of a little bit weary and wary of us,' Keitley recalls. But despite the obvious strain on the crew he was happy that the situation was secure.

'The boarding party was on board, our RHIBs were in the water with two people in them to keep an eye on things, so if anything unexpected came up then they'd radio us,' he says. 'They were also there in the event that we had to get off in a hurry – worst case scenario jump-off – and then they'd come in and pick us up.'

About thirty minutes into the boarding, the team's communicator on the bridge noticed a fast speedboat heading in their direction.

'That kind of caught my attention and we watched this thing come in at a great speed,' says Keitley. 'As it got closer it was clear that it was coming our way and that there were armed people on board coming straight for us.'

Known as 'Boghammars' after their Swedish builder, the skiffs operated by the Iranian religious forces are modified with weaponry to create improvised naval fighting vessels. Some resemble ski boats, but they have one key difference – they are armed with man-portable missile systems or have rockets or heavy machine guns mounted on board. The skiffs form part of the Islamic group's overall fleet of 1500 vessels that are manned by 20,000 men. The IRGCN has been a constant threat to shipping entering and leaving the Gulf since it swarmed into existence with the outbreak of the Iran–Iraq War in 1980, so the skiff's arrival was an ominous sign.

The vessel initially targeted the Australian RHIBs in a very aggressive fashion, aiming weapons and threatening with rocket-propelled grenades (RPGs) and machine guns as they ordered the crews to surrender.

'They were yelling and hollering and chasing them around,' says Keitley. 'It was, I'm hesitant to say comical, but it just looked really weird because our guys were doing their best to get away from these guys and they just ended up chasing each other around almost in figures of eight.'

A second Iranian boat arrived soon afterwards and his mind turned swiftly to the capture of the Royal Marines. When more vessels converged on the scene it looked to Keitley as if many of the Iranians crewing the skiffs had come straight from a coffee shop – as if they had received the alarm, picked up their guns, and jumped into their speedboats. During the hours to follow he also noted several different types of uniforms and that quite a few men on the skiffs were clad in leather jackets and thongs.

'That really preys on your mind,' he says. 'Just how disciplined are they? What exactly do they want? What is it going to take for them to kick off? These are the questions racing through your head at a million miles an hour while you're down there watching them yelling and screaming and actioning their weapons.'

Keitley decided that attack was the best form of defence and he gave as good as he got, telling the Iranians in no uncertain terms to 'fuck off'. After a short period, *Adelaide*'s two RHIBs were ordered to break away from MV *Sham* and return to the ship. Back on the frigate, the ops room was incredibly busy with calls coming in and out and rescue plans being drawn up and revised. As a former warfare officer, Stephen Bowater, who had joined the navy as a fifteen-year-old cadet, was called in to assist with the planning. This was somewhat unusual because normally the XO, who is responsible for the daily routine of the ship, stays clear of the operations room and lets the skipper, Operations Officer and Principal Warfare Officer get on with fighting the battle.

While plans were being made to extract the Australian boarding party, the replacement merchant crew for MV *Sham* simply waltzed on board the ship and past the Iranians as if nothing was happening. From that moment on the situation became very tense.

The Americans had promised aerial fire support in the form of two special forces helicopter gunships fitted with twenty-millimetre mini guns capable of firing 10,000 rounds a minute. The British also had a chopper in the air that was carrying a sniper armed with a .50 calibre weapon. But like many military plans, the one drawn up by the war fighters on board *Adelaide* for the extraction of the boarding team didn't last long. It was based on aerial fire support but just before launch the ship was advised that neither the American nor the British helicopters would be permitted to fly within fifteen kilometres of MV *Sham* because of the risk from rocket-propelled grenades. They were concerned that the slow-moving helos would be sitting ducks for the Iranians and their RPGs.

'We are not authorised to attempt an extraction,' the Americans said. In addition, American patrol vessels could not get within about four kilometres of the MV *Sham* because of the risk of shallow water.

Frustration was mounting on board *Adelaide*. Australian authorities had direct contact with senior Iranian officials, and a coalition special-forces unit in Kuwait was on standby to respond if necessary. Meanwhile, on board MV *Sham*, Andrew Keitley watched the Iranian flotilla grow. To his horror, he noticed through his binoculars that one skiff even had a twelve-barrel 107-millimetre rocket launcher mounted amidships. The Iranians were becoming more aggressive and demanding that the Australians surrender as they circled the ship in a menacing fashion, probing for a way to get on board.

'They just took up a loose position circling around us,' Keitley recalls. 'To my mind, they were actively looking for a way to get on board, so what I did is, obviously, let all our guys know what was going on. I had them split up in their teams at points where they were hidden but could see what was going on. So essentially we had an all-round lookout.'

He also knew the Iranians had video cameras and he did not want images of Australian sailors being taken prisoner all over global television networks.

Keitley and the team had transformed the ship into a 'citadel'. On many merchant vessels, the citadel is a secure part of the ship, for example the engine room, where the crew can lock themselves in and still operate the vessel during a pirate attack. On MV *Sham* the boarding ladder had been stowed, all entry points were closed and the deck was high enough to prevent easy access from the water. Still, Keitley wondered whether the Iranians would have grappling hooks or would be able to climb aboard using other means.

'I firmly believe they were looking for any chance they could to come and grab us,' he says. 'I don't think they were there just to suss it out, just to come by and observe what we were doing. They were actively trying to get us off the boat; they were actively trying to get themselves onto the boat. There was no way in hell I was going to let any of them on board.'

As they circled the cargo ship the Iranians pointed their weapons at the Australians in a highly aggressive manner. 'One of the guys with a long gun was lying down in the boat in a firing position so he was there the whole time. Every time I walked out onto the bridge to communicate or look around I was very aware that potentially I had a rifle pointed at my head, which is kind of weird. We had a female within the group and she told me later that she was seriously considering cutting her hair off to look like a boy if we got captured. So, there were a lot of things going through everyone's minds.'

The Iranians' constant demands for the sailors to surrender or allow them to board the ship were met with some equally blunt responses. At one point, Andrew Keitley lost his temper.

'These guys were within yelling distance so I yelled, "Just fuck off," you know, "Just get out of here, leave us alone, just go,"' Keitley says. 'In my mind, we had the moral high ground. We're here, we're doing the right thing so just leave us alone.'

Throughout the incident, he was acutely conscious that he did not want to be the one to make a rookie error that would embarrass the RAN and the Australian government and people.

The stalemate had been dragging on for about four hours when the Iranians tried a fresh tactic. They commandeered a cargo dhow and attempted to steer it in close to MV *Sham* so they could leap aboard like old-school pirates.

'Their freeboard was at the same level as ours so all they would have had to do was step across and that just crystallised the situation perfectly for me. It was one of those moments where everything crowds into your mind with all the possibilities at once and it's just, "Right, what do we do? How do we get out of this? What's going to happen next?"'

As the sun started sinking and the cargo dhow was approaching, the tension was building for Keitley. 'These guys are about to come on board. What do you do? Do you fight them? Do you surrender to them? Having a gunfight is just not an option because we're not at war with Iran, there are no hostilities, they're not a declared enemy and it's not a movie or a video game, so if people start shooting, people are going to die. The other option is, "We're all going to get captured and taken back to Iran." So, a lot of shit got real in those couple of minutes.'

Australia, Britain and the US have quite different national rules of engagement (ROE) when it comes to applying military force in the Middle East. The official versions are shrouded in secrecy, but in general terms it is understood that the American ROE are more aggressive than the British, while Australia sits somewhere in between. In this case, the rules of engagement were clear. If Keitley, his team or their equipment were in imminent danger they had the right to defend themselves and shoot first.

'It's an absolute lesson of leadership that I was taught on the spot,' he says. 'Regardless of your ego, regardless of what you think you need to do, regardless of how you see this playing out, you're in charge of people's lives and that has huge repercussions. I honestly thought we were gone. I thought, "You know what, they're going to capture us here and that's it."'

Fortunately, push never came to shove thanks to the low tide and shallow water. The dhow ran aground about twenty metres off the port side of MV *Sham*. The Iranians finally issued an ultimatum that if the Australians were not off the ship by sunset then they would be boarded regardless of the consequences.

Without air support from the Americans or British, the command team on *Adelaide* knew that the only way they could rescue the team was with the ship's helicopter. To do that they would have to shift from coalition command to Australian national command and after a quick call to CTF 633 headquarters (then located in Baghdad) the command shift was authorised.

XO Bowater says the plan was for Sandman to do a dummy run to test the Iranian reaction.

'If you kill five people on a helo it's a lot better than killing twenty people on a helo,' he says of the choice no military officer ever wants to make.

Fortunately, there was no hostile fire on the dummy run so on the second run the bird landed and in two lifts flew them back to the frigate. Once safely back on their ship the young sailors had what Keitley calls their *Top Gun* moment. 'When we had everyone together on board and safe there were just high fives and back slaps all round. It was a massive relief.'

Bowater says it was Keitley's calm professionalism that saved the day for the Australians. If the Iranians had boarded the vessel, the team would have thrown their weapons – two shotguns and their personal nine-millimetre pistols – into the sea and calmly surrendered, so his actions in keeping them at bay without a shot being fired was extraordinary.

For his exceptional leadership in action, Andrew Keitley was awarded the Distinguished Service Medal (DSM), which is Australia's sixth highest military honour. He is the only non-officer in the RAN to be granted the award.

Adelaide's flight commander, Lieutenant Commander Tony Johnson, also received a DSM for his leadership during the drama. Keitley paid tribute to the courage of the helicopter crew who all agreed to risk their lives and run the gauntlet to lift their shipmates off the stranded vessel.

Stephen Bowater admits that he and the rest of the command team – and indeed the entire RAN – were not prepared for a hostage drama. 'It was just shock because we hadn't trained for it, we'd never war-gamed it, we'd never expected our boarding party to be captured by the IRGCN. I mean, we weren't even looking at it – they were not on the radar.'

That all changed after *Adelaide*'s close call. Since then, each crew member deploying to the region has been provided with resilience and conduct-after-capture training.

As the years went on, there would be more incidents in this volatile area. Another group of fifteen British sailors were taken prisoner in March 2007. Like the Australians, they too were searching a merchant vessel when revolutionary guard skiffs surrounded it and claimed it was inside Iranian waters. The humiliated sailors were released eleven days later. In 2016, ten American sailors spent a night in Iranian custody after their two boats strayed into Iranian waters. The Royal Navy and the US Navy were severely embarrassed by these incidents and by the images of their sailors being paraded before the cameras with their hands on their heads.

5

Boardos

Ever since the first Australian Task Group arrived in the Gulf region under Operation Damask 1 in September 1990, boardings, or 'visit and search' operations as they were known, have been the bread and butter of the navy's mission.

The Royal Australian Navy had been boarding foreign fishing vessels in northern Australian waters for decades, but the Gulf mission presented a Pandora's box of boarding opportunities.

Specialist boarding teams began work in the Middle East during the blockade of Iraq before Saddam Hussein's invasion of Kuwait triggered the first Gulf War. Almost all of the twenty Australian warships deployed during the ensuing twenty-seven years have dispatched boarding parties. Their jobs range from conducting crew and cargo checks on 300,000-tonne super tankers to arresting armed pirates and chipping ice from the stinking holds of twenty-metre-long rat- and cockroach-infested fishing dhows that are smuggling cargoes of oil, dates or, more recently, illicit drugs and weapons.

Speeding across an empty sea in a rigid hull inflatable boat and watching a speck on the horizon grow like magic into a massive oil tanker's ten-metre-tall steel side is a unique and never-to-be-forgotten experience. Climbing up a ship's ladder onto a vast deck that stretches for several footy fields also comes as a shock, as does a chat with an Indian skipper about the relative merits of Australian cricket teams. Is there an Indian anywhere in the world who doesn't know who Ricky Ponting is?

Joshua Maher looks nothing like a hardened boarding officer from a navy warship as he sits dressed in civvies at the corner table of a trendy Canberra hotel coffee shop. Appearing very much the professional public servant, he is doing a stint as the 'flag lieutenant', or aide-de-camp, to the Defence Minister, Marise Payne.

It is difficult to reconcile his smart-casual demeanour with the tough navy officer risking his neck scaling the side of a stinking fishing dhow in rough seas on the hunt for drugs or weapons. His reputation as a 'gun boardo' (top boarding officer) was built on board *Darwin* under the command of the no-nonsense drug hunter Commander Terry Morrison during her previous tour of duty in 2013 and 2014.

By then the focus of Australian warships in the region had shifted from counter-piracy operations to the hunt for illicit narcotics and weapons that were helping to fund and arm terrorist groups.

Maher joined the Australian Defence Force Academy as an army cadet in 2006, but just before graduating in 2009 he decided to switch to the navy. His first posting as a junior warfare officer was to the patrol boat HMAS *Armidale* based in Darwin on border protection operations.

'That was my first exposure to boarding operations and some quite significant ones,' he says. They included an incident in late 2009 when seventy-eight Sri Lankan asylum seekers on their way to Australia in an unseaworthy vessel were intercepted by both *Armidale* and the Australian Customs Service armed patrol boat *Oceanic Viking*. They were taken to Indonesia on the Customs ship to be put in a detention centre but refused to disembark. They were later determined to be genuine refugees.

'That was quite a confronting experience. It was my first real exposure to border protection,' Maher says. 'I don't think many people realise the pressure and the mental and emotional exhaustion it puts on sailors.'

He was posted to *Darwin* in 2012. The ship first deployed to Hawaii and then entered maintenance in 2013, beginning her work-up period for the Gulf deployment. By then a lieutenant, Maher began training as a boarding officer.

'I'd seen boardings through my time on patrol boats, but this was the first time I had been there in the thick of it, running a team and starting to read up on what I needed to do,' he says.

The first step for Maher to learn the necessary skills was a trip south to HMAS *Cerberus* for the session of general boarding training at the navy's boatswain's faculty. The week-long course teaches the basics of boarding, including the physical aspects of climbing onto a vessel at sea and simulating fast-roping (descending from a hovering helicopter by rope) onto a moving deck. The course also takes in the legal aspects of boarding including rules of engagement and the use of force.

The second week of training begins with live fast-roping from a real helicopter at the navy's aviation base at HMAS

Albatross. Fast-rope training is vital and it continues as each ship steams towards the Middle East.

'If you tell yourself that that looks scary and you don't think you're going to be able to do it, you're not going to be able to do it and I saw some of my sailors – they went, "Oh no, I can't do that," and they didn't, they couldn't,' Maher says. 'There are techniques in it and you've got to always have your own safety in mind, so if you think, "Oh, I'm not feeling confident today," you've got to step aside. There is no safety rope. Everyone's seen *Black Hawk Down* and if you fall off the rope there's nothing to catch you but the ground. I used to be afraid of heights and I'm not any more.'

The next phase of the training involves boarding and searching a derelict vessel in Sydney Harbour where role plays and various scenarios play out before the boarding team members are certified to join a warship's actual boarding party. Unfortunately, that vessel is nothing like a Middle Eastern fishing dhow so each team relies on the US Coast Guard training facility in Bahrain to familiarise themselves with a genuine fishing dhow.

The US Coast Guard's boarding methods are regarded as the gold standard, and time spent practising on its genuine dhow is regarded as vital by the boarding teams. Given the number of boardings undertaken by the RAN in the Middle East since the early 1990s it is remarkable that it does not have a training dhow. Instead, it has an old Indonesian fishing boat moored in Darwin Harbour that is used by patrol boat boarding parties on border protection duties.

Every RAN ship deploys with two boarding teams, each led by a boarding officer with a senior Petty Officer as 2IC. Once the formal training is out of the way the boarding officers must bring themselves up to speed on the additional aspects of a particular mission. Each ship compiles a post-operational report – a vital reference document for boarding officers and their teams. For example, there are several United Nations resolutions covering the operations of the maritime task groups deployed under the Combined Maritime Forces.

'We looked at reports from ships that were up there at the time, and we spoke to people who had done it before to get an idea about what needed to happen,' Maher says.

Before undertaking boardings, the teams are also run through a series of detailed presentations by the intelligence officer and the principal warfare officer. These presentations usually include detailed slide shows depicting where drugs and weapons have been found by previous teams.

Maher says the key to a successful boarding team is flexibility, and the training must reflect the diversity of the probable demands on the teams.

'Navy can't pigeonhole our training too much because we need to be diverse enough to change our operations quickly,' he says. 'There's a defined set of skills for counter-narcotics, just as there is for counter-piracy. There are similarities between the two but the difference then lies in when you get to a certain point. If it's piracy you've got to be very careful of the legal ramifications. So for the piracy, because they can get prosecuted, it's very much a police exercise as in you've got to get all your evidence and you've got to make sure it's all recorded properly. You do that crime scene stuff, which we got taught a little bit. That's where you bring your police coxswain over. For counter-narcotics it goes down a different path because it's searching for the drugs. They've got those hidden and you have to go looking for them.'

Retired navy chief Vice Admiral Russ Shalders was the Commanding Officer of *Darwin* in the first Arabian Gulf task group back in 1990. Reflecting on his experience in the Gulf he told a Sea Power Centre seminar in 2003 that it had quickly become apparent that the navy needed to develop a capability to board suspect vessels, so as to verify the presence or otherwise of prohibited cargo. From early on it was also clear that the relationship between a ship's helicopter(s) and her boarding teams would be crucial to mission success.

During her first deployment, along with HMA Ships *Success* and *Adelaide*, *Darwin* was directly involved in just five boardings of vessels that were steaming both into and out of Iraqi waters. To put that into perspective, for the same period there were 996 boardings by the multinational naval force that included the Australian task group.

Shalders says the key to successful boarding operations was gaining the initiative early and maintaining it throughout. 'It was necessary to generate a degree of momentum and to keep the opposition on the defensive.'

'Initiative' and 'momentum' remain guiding principles for RAN boarding operations to this day. Many of the tactics, techniques and procedures adopted by the early boarding parties were developed by the US Coast Guard and adopted by the first Australian teams.

Former Rear Admiral Bill Dovers was the CO of the guided missile frigate HMAS *Adelaide* on Damask 1 and he described the American approach as a revelation. 'They recommended that we order shotguns, which we did, as their technique in those days was to fire them into the deck at an angle so the pellets spread out at ankle level. They assured us this would stop people doing things that might be harmful.'

The RAN's approach in those days was to arm boarding parties with high-powered assault rifles and a policy of 'shoot to kill' if anyone became aggressive.

'We had no graduated force for boardings,' Dover told the 2003 seminar.

Another former navy chief, Vice-Admiral Ray Griggs, was CO of HMAS *Arunta* in the Gulf in the post 'Shock and Awe' phase between June and December 2003. This was a crucial time in the evolution of boarding operations following the first boarding of local fishing dhows by HMAS *Kanimbla* in February 2002, when her teams boarded sixteen vessels in one day.

Until then operations had been aimed at larger ships, but the oil discovered in the cargo holds of the traditional wooden vessels and the dates and other illicit cargoes to follow proved that the dhows were part of the smuggling chain and were being used widely to break the embargo. The floodgates opened between June and November 2002 when *Arunta* and *Melbourne* conducted hundreds of boardings, including up to thirty in a single day.

Before the arrival of the Anzac Class frigate *Arunta*, boarding parties consisted of fourteen members or 'sticks', but that was soon scaled back to six, which was more than enough manpower to secure and search a twenty-metre dhow.

'The average dhow carried a crew of between eight and twelve and could be handled by a six-person stick,' Griggs says.

Arunta operated five of the six-person boarding sticks, and that placed considerable strain on the ship's company.

'I knew we were getting close to the bone when my executive officer was the boat coxswain [driver] for one of the boarding parties,' he says.

It was evident that the number of crew trained for boarding party duty was insufficient, and by the end of her time on station *Arunta* had trained up an extra eight sailors for boarding operations. After 2002, all RAN ships deployed under either Combined Task

Force 150 (counter-terrorism) or 151 (counter-piracy) carried appropriate numbers of qualified boarding party members.

Boarding parties are mostly made up of young men and women trained as boatswain's mates who have seamanship skills such as refuelling at sea, berthing and small-boat handling and maritime security – including close range weapons, small arms and fast-roping from a helicopter. They also undertake other general duties such as lookouts, watch keeping and steering the ship (as helmsmen). Sailors from other trades who wish to join the boarding teams are also put through the boarding section of the maritime security course.

Chief Petty Officer Kevin Harris is one of the navy's most experienced maritime security trainers. The twenty-nine-year RAN veteran from Tasmania was posted to HMAS *Cerberus* in 2016 as the senior instructor in the maritime security section of the boatswains' facility at the navy's biggest training school.

'Anybody [including officers] who wants to be a specialist boarding party member will come here,' he says. 'We do deliver the same boarding party courses away from the school on an as-needed basis, but preferably we'd like everyone to come down south.'

Training begins with a comprehensive look at 'use of force' and the legal aspects of how and when force can be applied.

'We cover boarding party theory and what they can expect to see out there, what they should be doing, things they're looking for and how they should move around vessels,' he says. 'Then we go into a practical aspect where there's three days devoted to that and they form up into teams. We take them through how to insert onto a vessel, how to conduct sweep searches and then we slowly ramp that up until they're safe and ready for assessment in three days.'

The final day's practical training and assessment takes place on vessels such as workboats that are attached to the seamanship school. All trainees are qualified to conduct different types of boardings and are also trained in fast-rope insertion from a helicopter. Kevin Harris says there have been very few instances where a boarding was not completed because the RAN team was unable to insert.

However, he says that nothing can prepare a person for the real thing, and each sailor has a clear memory of his or her first boarding operation. 'I don't think you ever forget that first time you smelled the dhow. We do as much as we can to prepare them with photos but it pales in comparison to the real thing.'

All non-officer navy recruits spend three months at HMAS *Cerberus* before moving into their specialist trade courses such as marine or electrical technician, cooks, stores, writers or clerks, stewards, communicators and of course seaman boatswain. The latter includes fourteen weeks of intensive training. Harris himself has done three postings to the Gulf region on board HMA Ships *Perth*, *Brisbane* and *Stuart*. He says that one of the most important assets for any boarding party member is an ability to communicate effectively.

'You quite often find that your best boarding party members are simply those who are most personable, those who can sit down and have a chat or spin yarns and just talk to people one on one,' he says. 'That's probably the most important asset for a boarding party, so the more of those you get the better, regardless of what your trade is. You want people who just have that natural gift of getting along with others. There is a saying that, "The happier the crew are of the vessel we are boarding, the easier the boarding is going to be." We say from the outset that you're there to put everyone at ease, make them happy so that it makes your job easier and you can depart as quickly as possible with the least inconvenience.'

PIRACY

6

Skulls and crossbones

Unlike Captain Jack Sparrow from *Pirates of the Caribbean*, the modern-day version of the high seas criminal drives a fast boat, carries a satellite phone and is armed to the teeth with rocket-propelled grenades and AK-47 assault rifles.

As another tinsel town production, *Captain Phillips*, portrayed vividly, the twenty-first-century pirate has none of the swashbuckling mystery but all of the cold-blooded menace and desperation of the killers who roamed the high seas causing mayhem under the skull and crossbones of the Jolly Roger.

By 2005 piracy in the Gulf of Aden and off the Horn of Africa had become a major global problem when brazen gangs of heavily armed Somali pirates routinely attacked cargo and passenger ships. This is one of the busiest and most important seaways on earth and is the gateway to the Red Sea and the Suez Canal.

In 2008, the Royal Australian Navy decided that it should beef up its capacity for dealing with the desperate pirates who had shown a willingness to kill to achieve their goals. Lieutenant Jace Hutchison was the man they turned to.

The navy clearance diver and former special-forces commando had precisely the skill set required to stand up what was to become known as the Enhanced Boarding Capability brick. 'Brick' is an Australian term used to describe a group of military personnel (usually army but also navy) formed into a specialised fire team.

Hutchison's job was to man and train a 'level four' boarding team made up of navy clearance divers who were capable of using lethal force if and when necessary. That meant not only training to a much higher level than a standard boarding party, but also finding a group of nine clearance divers to make up the team.

'Because of my experience, I was designated as the person to build that capability and to form the team and to take the first team over to the ship in the Gulf,' he says. 'I was the right fellow with the right qualifications in the right place at the right time.'

Hutchison initially requested a fourteen-person unit but was given only nine. He was also able to use his contacts in 2 Commando for help with training facilities.

'We've only got a small special-forces community. They are so busy that when it comes to things like that, unless they're definitely going to get some gold out of it they're always going to say, "It's over to you, navy, it's a navy problem,"' he explains.

The divers were already well equipped with weapons and other specialised gear, but the navy had no close-quarters weapons ranges, for example. 'We've already got radios; we've already got the right dress. It's things like – to go and do close-quarters shooting you need specialist facilities, and so that's where we leant on them [commandos] a little bit and formally requested support and they were happy to do that. You've got to have the right training, experience and resourcing and equipment to be able to do it, so it was specifically then noted for the divers to do it,' he says.

Navy clearance divers are the special operations branch of the senior service and are trained to undertake a variety of roles from explosive ordnance detection and clearance to counter-terrorism and covert operations. There are two full-time teams of clearance divers. Team One is located at HMAS *Waterhen* at Waverton on the northwestern shore of Sydney Harbour and Team Four is based at HMAS *Stirling* south of Perth in WA. Team Three is the war team and is formed up only as required for specialised missions overseas, such as the 1999 East Timor crisis and the 2003 Iraq War.

As well as being very fit and well trained in close-order combat and weapons skills, navy divers use the latest technologies such as handheld personal sonars, robots and blast suits to complete their missions. Hazards abound. A video clip from a diver's personal sonar shows what is clearly a large shark passing close to the diver in low-visibility conditions. Sharks are an occupational hazard for the divers, who have been used as guinea pigs to trial an array of anti-shark measures over the years, including electronic, acoustic and magnetic devices, special wetsuits and even chemical repellents.

The most famous navy diver of recent years is Paul de Gelder who lost an arm and a leg in 2009 in a fight to the death with a bull shark in Sydney Harbour during a counter-terrorism exercise just ten metres from the steps of Sydney Opera House.

Divers also served extensively in the explosive ordnance disposal (EOD) role alongside the army in Uruzgan Province in landlocked Afghanistan using robots and blast suits to defuse insidious improvised explosive devices. This broad skill set made navy divers ideal to fill the enhanced boarding capability role for counter-piracy operations.

Hutchison and his team were deployed in the Anzac frigate HMAS *Toowoomba* as she was departing for the Gulf in mid-2009. Once in the area of operations they began boarding skiffs and other suspect vessels that crisscrossed the ocean between Africa and Yemen.

'We were able to build up a pretty good picture of the patterns of life because if a forty-foot skiff had three people in it then you knew they weren't pirates because they didn't have enough people,' he says. 'They would probably be doing a run between Yemen and Somalia to trade fuel for fish. Maybe with the small skiffs normally it's just fuel, but the bigger dhows would be trading fuel for fish so they take fish over and bring fuel back in the same hold.'

During one boarding, the dhow was simply a floating bomb with a hold full of fuel and the deck covered with drums of fuel. 'It's just like, "Don't let any of them smoke while we're on here. Let's get off!"'

Another time they spotted a skiff with about sixty people on board speeding towards Yemen. The passengers had paid about a hundred dollars each to escape from Somalia in search of a better life.

Their first real pirate boarding occurred as they were training on the flight deck of *Toowoomba*. A merchant vessel about thirty kilometres away reported that it was under attack by armed men in a skiff. A helicopter from a German warship had intercepted the vessel and by the time *Toowoomba*'s RHIBs were on the scene the skiff was not moving.

'We approached them guns up because we had reports that they were armed,' says Hutchison. 'There's only really a couple of ways you can approach a boat on the ocean. We were out zooming ahead of the frigate and then we just came at them from two different angles, guns up ready to go. I had two snipers in the front of my boats so they were always on them. We told them to put their hands on their heads. There were eight of them but we couldn't see any weapons so a couple of our guys got in there, secured them and had a quick search. The next thing you know we had eight weapons – an RPG, six AK-47s and a G3 German assault rifle.'

Even the most desperate and foolhardy pirates seldom push back when confronted with heavily armed professional sailors who are dressed to kill. Prowling in the background is a modern warship that could reduce them to pink mist and their skiffs to a smoking memory in just a few seconds. Even so, intercepting criminals at sea is a dangerous and fraught business. Anything can happen at any time and lives are always on the line.

Once on board, the team secured the pirates' guns and disposed of the ammunition, but because of a lack of international law covering piracy on the high seas in 2009, and no country where they could land the pirates, they had to set them free.

'Our procedures aren't to get in a gunfight and win that gunfight,' he explains. 'Our procedures are to defend ourselves, break contact and then get under cover. It's all about applying force to the appropriate level and if it's going to be a fight then we'll just defend ourselves and get out of it. But there is a point when you close a contact where you must commit ... because trying to get out of it is worse than going through with it. So, there's always a point where I, or the 2IC, are going to commit the force. We trained and trained and trained to make sure our command team knew that. Everybody understood that if it was a worst-case scenario and we couldn't break then we would go through with it and commit to the job.'

They left the pirates with enough food and water to get home across about a hundred kilometres of ocean, and that was it. 'The only problem was that we couldn't do anything with them and there were no consequences for them really.'

They could have detained the pirates but that would have meant transporting them back to Perth to be prosecuted under Australian law.

'That's never going to happen,' Hutchison says.

The Australians were authorised to destroy one of the skiff's two engines but because they were so far from shore he did not think that was a good idea. 'We left one engine but we took all their oil and destroyed it and we took all their intel from phones and their handheld GPS.'

All the weapons except for the G3 German-made Heckler and Koch assault rifle were cut up and disposed of in a 3000-metre-deep part of the Indian Ocean. The G3 was sent to the navy's historical collection housed on Spectacle Island near Cockatoo Island off Drummoyne in Sydney Harbour. This collection is a treasure trove of naval memorabilia ranging from muskets to heavy guns and missiles, from uniforms to glassware. A large, secure armoury at the facility contains weapons from all conflicts of the past 200 years, with special emphasis on recent operations in the Gulf.

Later, Hutchison happened to be on the island for a leadership conference and during a tour of the armoury he noticed the G3.

'They told me it was from [HMAS] *Arunta* – so I had to straighten them out and give them a stern talking to,' he says with a smile.

By 2012, it was estimated that maritime criminals were costing the global shipping industry about $6 billion a year in lost earnings and additional costs such as security and longer journeys as vessels sought to avoid pirate-infested waters. Between 2005 and 2011 Somali bandits had captured thirty-two vessels and held 736 hostages.

The last of these – twenty-six Asian men detained for almost five years – were freed in November 2016. At the peak of Indian Ocean piracy in 2011 there were 151 attacks on merchant vessels and the estimated 5000 pirates involved in the trade earned $146 million, or $4.87 million per ship held.

In 2013, thanks to a concerted multinational naval operation targeting pirates, the number of attacks fell to just nine without a single successful hijacking.

Royal Navy Commodore Guy Robinson is the commander of the Bahrain-based counter-terrorism Combined Task Force (CTF) 150. Speaking on the sidelines of a major Indian Ocean piracy conference in the Seychelles, in June 2016, Robinson said many of the navies engaged in the Combined Maritime Forces (CMF) had mandates to target only pirates. Those countries include Germany, Japan, the Netherlands and South Korea, while others such as the US, UK, Australia, Pakistan, Canada and France focus on more aggressive counter-terrorism operations. Other European Union and NATO countries also contributed to the counter-piracy mission but they tended to operate in the affected countries rather than at sea.

The thirty-one member nations of the CMF are Australia, Bahrain, Belgium, Canada, Denmark, France, Germany, Greece, Iraq, Italy, Japan, Jordan, South Korea, Kuwait, Malaysia, the Netherlands, New Zealand, Norway, Pakistan, the Philippines, Portugal, Saudi Arabia, Seychelles, Singapore, Spain, Thailand, Turkey, United Arab Emirates, United Kingdom, United States and Yemen. They operate in three Combined Task Forces: CTF 150 for counter-terrorism, CTF 151 for counter-piracy, and CTF 152 for Gulf security.

Robinson said it was understandable that some nations focus only on counter-piracy operations rather than narcotics or weapons smuggling. Under current international law, pirates detained on the high seas in international waters can face prosecution, whereas drugs and weapons smugglers cannot be prosecuted so are set free once their illicit cargo has been confiscated.

When it comes to drugs or weapons it is the responsibility of the flag state to deal with a vessel's owners and the crew, but when a vessel is stateless, as is the case with most smuggling boats, then no country is responsible and they fall through a large legal crack.

'It's not an international crime such as piracy is, and of course we ended up interdicting narcotics through the participating nations,' Robinson said. 'Different countries all have different domestic law to deal with narcotics and weapons and so understandably people have a different perspective on it. I think generally people recognise it's a bad thing, but within CMF we have to recognise the mandate that allows nations to come here and participate, and respect that.'

The combined forces operate under United Nations Security Council Resolutions 1918 (piracy) and 1988 and 1989 (the funding of terrorism) and numerous articles of the United Nations Convention on the Law of the Sea (UNCLOS) pertaining to piracy, illicit drugs and fake flags.

The small island nation of the Seychelles lies about 1500 kilometres east of Kenya. The country is 99 per cent ocean and 1 per cent land, has a population of just 90,000 and stretches across 1.3 million square kilometres of the Indian Ocean. A large chunk of its livelihood depends on tourism and especially cruise liners. So the impact of piracy on the tiny economy was catastrophic. The tourism Mecca saw its vital cruise ship trade fall from about fifteen ship visits a year to zero.

Seychelles Foreign Minster Joel Morgan believes that UNCLOS should be tightened up to close the legal loophole that allows drug and weapons smugglers to go free unless they are caught inside a country's territorial waters.

'If they are not caught within our territorial waters, it means that we have no jurisdiction over them and even if we were to bring laws into place that would give us that jurisdiction it could be contested internationally because there is no definite mandate arising under UNCLOS,' he says. 'This is why all of the navies have to operate on a "catch and release" principle while they can seize the arms, but there is no country that will be really in a position to prosecute unless the flag state takes responsibility to prosecute. Very often you find that the flag states of some of these vessels are not willing to take on that responsibility in the first instance.'

The Seychelles is leading the way with the first ever prosecution of an Iranian skipper and his crew caught with help from *Darwin*. Their dhow was caught carrying a cargo of illicit drugs inside Seychelles territorial waters. The captain, who had already been caught three times smuggling drugs in his fishing dhow, finally lost the boat and was facing twenty years in prison and the likelihood of never seeing his family again.

In his office in a lovely colonial building in the Seychelles capital, Victoria, Morgan tells me there should be a UN Security Council resolution that deals with the problem of illegal activities on the high seas, specifically arms and drug trafficking, just as there is for terrorism. Like many political leaders, he feels confounded about the legal loophole given that most of the drugs are funding terrorist activities by organisations such as Al-Qaeda, and all of the smuggled weapons end up in the hands of terrorist groups such as Al-Shabaab in Africa or ISIS in the Middle East.

'I think it will come, it's coming, but we just need to give it the momentum it needs,' he says.

Seychelles Minister for Finance, Trade and the Blue Economy Jean-Paul Adam says the success of counter-piracy operations is a double-edged sword because it has driven those involved to other illegal activities such as drugs, arms or people smuggling.

'A lot of the forces that were driving piracy were economic so people are turning to other things such as people trafficking, they're turning to drug smuggling and these are, while perhaps less sensational, as disruptive to our economy,' he says. 'In Seychelles, we have a rising drug problem among the young people in the country which leads to issues of productivity.'

Adam says that nullifying piracy means that a major source of funding for the criminal networks has been cut off. 'We have to make sure that we're dealing with the other parts of these criminal networks. Unfortunately, the criminal networks are globalised these days, you know they operate like global conglomerates. If one part of their business is not successful they will diversify and they'll go into others but using often the same assets. So precisely when you catch a vessel doing something illegal it has to be impounded, it has to be seized or it has to be destroyed and you have to take out the capacity to continue to operate illegally.'

Like his colleague Minister Morgan, he says that the international community must act to take responsibility for the shared space that is the ocean.

'The challenge really is to bring law and order as we know it on land to the ocean,' he says. 'It's harder because of problems with jurisdictions, problems of capacity. Not every country can afford to have navies that can crisscross the ocean and so we need better networks [not just] in terms of intelligence sharing, of coordination, but a willingness. One of the things that has been missing, and maybe we're going in the direction where they're starting to be much more willing, is to take responsibility for that shared space. I think piracy has opened our eyes to how much trouble there actually is.'

Piracy shone a light into the dark world of maritime criminality in the Indian Ocean region, which includes not only drugs and guns but also charcoal smuggling, the ivory trade, fish poaching and people trafficking.

'These criminal networks make the most of the fragile states like Somalia where there are large parts of the country not necessarily under sustained governance in terms of law and order,' Adam says. He says Seychelles is very grateful for Australia's involvement in the fight against high seas crime. His country could never match the bigger nations when it comes to deploying naval assets to hunt down the criminals. However, his tiny country has shown the way when it comes to using the courts to tackle piracy, with about half of all prosecutions taking place there.

At the Seychelles piracy conference, there was a strong sense that while piracy had been nullified in the short-term there was a grave risk of a resurgence should the Combined Maritime Forces ever take the pressure off pirates while pursuing other criminal enterprises.

Not all the blame for the piracy epidemic lies with the criminal gangs. Fish poaching by foreign vessels and the dumping of toxic waste in the waters off Somalia, triggered by the civil war in 1991, all but destroyed the incomes of local fishermen along the Horn of Africa. With their fish stocks and livelihood gone, poverty pushed them into the arms of criminal networks, which forced them to form armed groups to intercept foreign ships and hold them and their crews for ransom.

According to those who worked on the issue at the time, the desperation of the Somali fishermen was accurately portrayed in *Captain Phillips*, as was the US Navy's rescue of the central character played by Tom Hanks.

Captain Richard Phillips was the skipper of the Danish container ship *Maersk Alabama* when she was hijacked in the Gulf of Aden in April 2009. He was rescued from one of the ship's lifeboats by US navy SEALS, who killed two of his three Somali captors. The third remains in a US prison where he is serving a thirty-year sentence.

On 29 May that year the Australian government, under then Prime Minister Kevin Rudd, agreed to join CTF 151, which had been established to counter the piracy attacks. The navy frigate HMAS *Warramunga* and an RAAF AP-3C Orion maritime patrol aircraft were sent to the mission.

The RAN's first taste of counter-piracy operations had occurred earlier that month when HMA Ships *Sydney* and *Ballarat* were transiting the Internationally Recommended Transit Corridor in the Gulf of Aden on their way to the UK for Exercise Northern Trident via the Suez Canal. Thanks to the close links forged between Australia and the US Navy in the post-World War II era it was a simple matter for Australian warships to be used operationally where possible as they steamed through one of the world's most enduring trouble spots.

On this occasion, the two ships were attached to CTF 151 for the duration of their transit and on 17 May they responded to a call for help from the oil tanker MV *Dubai Princess* steaming about thirty kilometres ahead. When they arrived on the scene, two pirate skiffs disengaged from the tanker. A lethal attack was averted and the Australian task group handed the incident over to a US warship and continued on their way.

The CO of *Sydney* and the task group commander, Peter Leavy, said in a Sea Power Centre paper that neither warship had

had the benefit of a work-up period or any special counter-piracy training, but the core skills on RAN ships allowed them to deal with a tricky encounter.

'The dynamic nature of the situation is perhaps best shown by the ships being at action stations, covering a skiff that had reportedly fired upon a merchant ship, while at the same time making internal plans on how to deal with a SOLAS [safety of life at sea] issue should that same skiff have subsequently become unseaworthy or if those on board needed rescuing. Both ends of the spectrum were being covered, Leavy said.

The experience of *Sydney* and *Ballarat*, he said, proved the value of a visible presence in deterring piracy and the inherent value in the flexibility and versatility of warships.

Bill Waters, who later commanded HMAS *Melbourne* on a Gulf deployment, was the Executive Officer in *Sydney* at the time and he recalls spending a lot of time on the radio back to Fleet Headquarters in Sydney discussing the possible ramifications of the incident. 'We spent a number of hours radioing back to Australia saying, "Right, what do you need us to do with it now? What are our rules of engagement going to be? What are the legal implications, should we seize them?"'

By the time Waters returned to the Gulf region as CO of *Melbourne* in August 2015 all the legal and operational issues were resolved and the counter-piracy mission was clear.

7

Under the not-so-Jolly Roger

The navy's deepest foray into the brutal world of Somali pirates took place in October 2014.

The guided missile frigate HMAS *Melbourne*, under the command of then Commander Brian Schlegel, had arrived in the region and was attached to Combined Task Force 151 for counter-piracy duty off the Horn of Africa. Following a quiet initial patrol, the ship's second patrol began with a bang on 13 October when she was tasked, along with a Dutch warship, to steam about 650 kilometres south at full speed to the scene of a reported pirate attack.

Even at twenty-eight knots that was a twenty-four-hour transit, and by the time they arrived on site the pirates had left. However, soon afterwards a second attack by the same gang, dubbed the 'Pirate Action Group' (PAG), took place to the east of *Melbourne*'s position, which was about 500 kilometres east of the Somali coast in calm seas.

Schlegel says he could never understand why the pirates didn't make a run for home after the first failed attack, but surmises, 'They were clearly under instructions not to come home unless they were successful.'

As it was his first deployment to the region, he was fortunate to have an experienced Executive Officer, Lieutenant Commander Andrew Hough, who had deployed to the Middle East on four previous occasions. The command team established a search pattern that resulted in the ship's helicopter locating two suspect pirate skiffs.

With a helicopter above, a warship nearby and two RHIBs packed with heavily armed sailors surrounding them, the nine Somali pirates had little choice but to surrender without a fight. The pirates were transferred to the warship, and Schlegel was ordered to gather as much evidence as possible from their boats before destroying them and steaming west to land the pirates back at home in Somalia.

The pirate vessels had several large drums of fuel on board to feed the powerful outboard motors. The Australians emptied the gasoline into the boats before the ship's .50-calibre and the helicopter's Mag 58 machine guns strafed them. The skiffs quickly burnt to the water-line and sank. *Melbourne* then made a beeline for the African coast with the prisoners held under shelter on the ship's forecastle (bow area) behind the Mark 13 missile launcher.

Because of the lack of a piracy agreement at that time with the nearest country, the Seychelles, and the on-going stalemate under international law, the Combined Maritime Forces headquarters in Bahrain had decided to send the pirates back to their homeland.

As she steamed westwards, *Melbourne* conducted a replenishment at sea with a British tanker before she set sail for the coast of Somalia.

Under international agreements the pirates could not simply be dumped in the desert. Two likely 'safe' locations were agreed for the transfer in the Hobyo region, northeast of the war-torn Somali capital Mogadishu and close to known pirate camps.

At the first landing spot, *Melbourne*'s RHIBs and a Zodiac found the surf conditions too rough to get ashore so they returned to the ship. The next day a suitable site was found and the RHIBs, under the command of Andrew Hough, towed the Zodiac carrying the pirates towards shore. Then the heavily armed boarding team drove the flat-bottomed Zodiac up onto a sheltered beach.

Schlegel viewed the entire operation in high resolution from the ops room on the ship's powerful optical sensor from about 1600 metres offshore. He kept *Melbourne*'s main gun pointing away from the beach, but the ship's Seahawk helicopter provided overwatch using its powerful Wescam camera and with its machine gun ready to roll at the first sign of trouble.

Suddenly, local militia vehicles bristling with heavy machine guns and RPGs appeared above the beach.

Says Schlegel, 'It was always a line-ball decision – do we just pull back and wait and find another venue, do we have enough time? My worst-case scenario was if they had all jumped in the cars and gone screaming towards the beach landing point, at which stage it would clearly be a choice of – can we get the boats out quickly enough so they're outside their range?'

It was an extremely tense situation. Commander Schlegel split his time between the bridge and operations room, monitoring the action, the ship's position and, crucially, the depth of water.

'I was as close as I dared get with not much water underneath me. All I needed was a mechanical breakdown and I was going to drop the anchor in Somalia and that's the last thing I wanted,' he says. 'Every captain in the navy must have half a dozen stories, if they're honest and open, where they say, "I made a decision on this day, I planned for it, I did everything I could but it could have gone wrong." In a guided missile frigate, all you need is something to go wrong with the plant and you can't move and you can't control that. I cannot control if there's an immediate breach in a hose or a line or anything like that. It's only in hindsight, when you pull away you go, "Gee, that went well." And then you think, "But it could have gone so badly."'

In the event the prisoners went ashore without incident and an hour later the ship was steaming quickly away from the African coast.

The nine pirates were on board *Melbourne* for almost four days and during that time Schlegel noticed that some of his sailors on guard duty were beginning to feel sympathy, almost like reverse Stockholm Syndrome, for the high seas bandits. Some provided them with extra 'treats' and there were even mumblings about whether sending them back to Somalia was the right thing to do.

'In the movie, Tom Hanks initially said the pirates were "only fishermen" and that was something we had to manage,' he says. 'When they all saw the movie during that visit in Dubai a lot of them came back and subsequently said, "You know what, Sir, I didn't realise that this is the sort of people they are."

'There is some merit to the fact they are only fishermen, but they're also fishermen who will kill you in a heartbeat and not bat an eyelid and that was lost on some of my crew, not in a negative way, just in an educational way.'

An old-school navy officer, Schlegel joined the service in 1983 as a sixteen-year-old boy with his best mate straight from Scotch College in Melbourne. They went in under the junior recruit scheme at the HMAS Leeuwin campus in Perth, and Schlegel's initial plan was to eventually become an airline pilot. However, when he began private flying lessons he quickly discovered that he had a fear of heights.

He began his career as a radar plotter and, like many who join the navy, he suffered terribly from seasickness. It took him years to learn how to manage the problem. In 1990 he transferred to the officer stream and worked his way up to reach what many regard as the pinnacle of their navy service – operational command of a warship.

His first command was *Darwin* and in August 2013 he was 'crash posted' to the frigate *Melbourne* just as she was about to deploy under Operation Slipper. He had been about to hand over command of *Darwin* to Terry Morrison when he got the call to join *Melbourne*.

When the father of two young daughters told his wife about the job she burst into tears.

'Why are you crying?'

'I'm so proud of you,' said his wife, who also came from Melbourne.

'To be CO of HMAS *Melbourne* and to deploy to an operation in the Middle East, it's crème de la crème,' he explains. 'It's why I've been in the navy for thirty years.'

Schlegel concedes that he had travelled to the Gulf with 'minimal to zero' expectation of conducting counter-piracy operations, so he was very pleased when the training kicked in and the crew behaved so professionally. He was also comforted by the fact that wherever he was, there was always another coalition warship within about twelve hours of his position. That confidence was enhanced after he saw *Captain Phillips* in a Dubai cinema. He had not heard of the movie before it was mentioned in a news report about *Melbourne's* successful counter-piracy mission to Somalia.

'That movie is an incredibly good portrayal of the circumstances of piracy in the Middle East and I've done a lot of research since, it's actually quite factual and follows the story well,' he says.

As well as the piracy operations, *Melbourne* seized more than three tonnes of illicit drugs, including in excess of 1000 kilograms of heroin, valued at more than $1 billion.

Commodore Bruce Kafer is another Australian naval officer with an interesting perspective on the real *Captain Phillips* incident. He was Commanding Officer of Combined Task Forces 158 and 152 in the North Arabian Gulf when *Maersk Alabama* was hijacked.

Kafer came to national prominence in 2011 when he was Commandant of the Australian Defence Force Academy (ADFA) during the infamous Skype sex scandal. He was cleared of any fault but became a convenient scapegoat for then Labor Defence Minister, Stephen Smith. Kafer is held in high esteem across the ADF and wider community. He retired from full-time service and joined the active reserve in December 2013.

Born in Newcastle NSW in 1959, Kafer spent his younger days messing around in boats on Lake Macquarie. He was keen on joining the navy all through high school and became a cadet midshipman at HMAS *Creswell* in Jervis Bay in 1977.

'I keep saying to people now it was like going to Mars back then. I had no idea,' he says. 'These days I think the recruiting processes are so good, where you can get interactive videos and you can attend the base. You have open days and you can try before you buy.'

Kafer had always had an interest in geography so he trained as a hydrographic surveyor.

'You're actually mapping the seabed. You're mapping the depths of the ocean but you're also gathering a huge amount of oceanographic information as well,' he says. 'Part of my role in the Middle East was gathering what's called military "geospatial information" which is information about the depths of the ocean. We determine ocean currents, so we made tide gauges or current meters [to measure] the nature of the seabed. About ninety per cent of the world's oceans are still uncharted and so every now and then you'll hear about a merchant ship striking a sea mount.'

The work of the hydrographic service is often unsung, but during World War II it was among the most highly decorated of all navy units.

'They were in under the guns of the Japanese surveying the approaches to beaches and so forth for amphibious landings in New Guinea and Borneo,' Kafer says. 'Some of our folk were deployed into the Royal Navy [and] doing clandestine surveys of the Normandy beaches before D-Day.'

In 1988 Kafer went on exchange to the Royal Navy survey vessel HMS *Herald*, which was conducting mine clearance and hydrographic survey work in the eastern Arabian Gulf. Iraq was a British ally in those days, and many of the sea mines in the Gulf had been sown by the Iranians, who were targeting Iraq's vital oil exports.

'It was a mix of hydrographic surveys in support of military operations so for example surveying what we call replenishment at sea corridors where the tankers and the warships could come in and safely undertake RAS [replenishment at sea] operations,' he explains.

The ship also carried the Royal Navy's mine counter-measures command team and deployed with the western European Union mine counter-measures force, comprising the Royal (British), Belgian, Dutch, Swedish, Italian and French navies. Floating mines in the Gulf had taken out numerous tankers and even a US frigate, USS *Samuel B. Roberts*.

'We were deployed into mine danger areas where mines were sighted or believed to exist and at the same time we were escorting convoys in and out of the Gulf as well,' Kafer says. The convoys consisted of several super tankers steaming to and from Iraq's two vital offshore oil terminals, 'KAAOT' and 'ABOT', fifty kilometres southeast of the Al Faw Peninsula.

In 1988, the twenty-nine-year-old Bruce Kafer had, of course, no idea that two decades later he would be back and actually living out in the shallow waters of the Gulf on board the KAAOT facility as the commander of two coalition task forces. During the *Captain Phillips* drama, Kafer was in his headquarters on the oil platform and watched the entire incident play out while his American boss in Bahrain witnessed it in real time and high definition. Because it was a US Navy mission and not a coalition operation parts of it were restricted to 'US eyes' only.

He said the experience was 'memorable' as he observed the might of the US Navy in action with the American admiral able to call on the Navy SEALS and any number of warships to resolve the impasse.

'What I learnt, though, is that our processes and procedures and doctrines are as good as the US Navy,' he says. 'But in the end it was only the US Navy that could cobble something together like that to make that happen. The [American] admiral was under an incredible amount of pressure right through that process even though he had the benefit of those resources.'

Kafer felt privileged to have witnessed the incident first-hand. 'I was like a kid in a candy store because it was just an incredible learning experience. It was just fascinating even though we were doing real world stuff.'

HASH HIGHWAY TO SMACK TRACK

8

Seizing hash and saving lives

Commander Terry Morrison was the skipper of HMAS *Darwin* for her previous foray into the troubled region in late 2013 and the first half of 2014. It was an eventful tour that culminated in the biggest single haul of hashish made to date by an Australian ship on the hash highway: a massive 6248 kilograms – more than six tonnes – of the oily brown drug, found on a dhow during a gruelling twelve-hour boarding on the evening of 29 June 2014.

Morrison assumed command of *Darwin* in August 2013 at the tail end of Operation Slipper and it would prove to be a high point in his distinguished and varied naval career.

Born in Penrith in 1972, he was raised and educated in western Sydney. He, his wife Maridy and their three children still live there, and Maridy is a cardiothoracic intensive care nurse at Westmead Hospital. Morrison describes them as 'a mad rugby family'. None of his forebears were sailors but his older sister, Jenny Daetz, joined the navy before he did.

'She's currently the Deputy Commander at ADFA, as a Captain,' he says proudly. 'She outranks me – but she was senior to me anyway in birth, so she seniors me in navy.' (He was promoted to Captain during 2016.)

In 1988, when Morrison was about sixteen, Jenny managed to get the family tickets to the HMAS *Watson* base in Sydney for the bicentennial celebrations. While they were there he saw some other teenagers walking around with the Naval Reserve Cadets banner. 'So I looked into that and then I ended up joining a cadet unit out at Penrith called TS *Nepean* [Training Ship *Nepean*].'

His year in the unit gave him weekends on real ships and a realisation that he was interested in joining the navy. He took a break from cadets while he studied for his Higher School Certificate and then enrolled in ADFA in 1991 as a naval officer cadet.

'When I did my training courses, I thought at one stage I would become a diver and I was in that mindset until I really got my teeth into ship driving and as an officer of the watch,' he recalls.

It was in HMAS *Hobart* that he was awarded his Bridge Warfare Certificate in 1995. 'I really enjoyed the warship mentality and the fight and what we were there to do. I said, "No, I don't want to become a diver." It is good in its own sense but it's a small team type stuff.'

He consolidated his training in the destroyer escort HMAS *Swan* the next year and, after completing the air intercept controller's (AIC) course, he returned to the *Hobart* for three years as AIC.

He and Maridy, his childhood sweetheart, had stayed together throughout the three-year separation of his stint at

ADFA in Canberra while she studied nursing at the University of Sydney. 'When I graduated from ADFA, we were going out at that stage and I thought, "Well, if she can stick by me for three years she's going to stick by me while we're separated – I think this relationship is going to keep going." So I proposed on my grad night at ADFA.'

In December 2002 he was promoted to Lieutenant Commander and was given his first command – of the Fremantle Class patrol boat HMAS *Geraldton*. For this period of his career, based in Darwin on border patrol duties, he went 'unaccompanied' for the sake of maintaining family stability back home in Sydney.

'I think I was fortunate to meet Maridy early because she has known navy all her life so she's used to it. We do stay here in Sydney. I don't drag the family around everywhere. When I was up in my patrol boat I left them here and I went unaccompanied, which is hard on the family. But her family is in western Sydney as well and the support is there and her family is very close.'

To him, having both career and family is a balancing act. 'I got asked to consider going to the States for a course which would have been a great course, but my daughter was doing her Higher School Certificate at the time and I thought, "No, we're not going to do that, we're just going to stick with the family stability."'

In the end it worked out quite well. 'My wife has put her neck out so much over the years and supported me, whereas a lot of my friends who met their partners after [joining the navy], they've all said, "No, I don't want you to continue at sea, I want you to be home." They haven't had the opportunities, whereas I've been fortunate enough to have a wife who says, "You go and do what you need to do and I'll look after the kids."'

They often joke about an old T-shirt of hers that says, 'How can I miss you if you don't go away?' He says it became so worn out that she turned it into a pillow. 'So the pillow ends up on the bed.'

After relinquishing command of the *Geraldton* he experienced his first stint in the Middle East, deploying to Iraq for Operation Slipper in command of the Australian Navy Training Team, based in Umm Qasr. This job was all about rebuilding and training the Iraqi Navy and for this he was awarded the Commendation for Distinguished Service. He had a team of thirteen Australians. It was a four-country operation led by the Royal Navy. In addition to the Australians there were US Marines and the Royal Netherlands Navy.

'We worked there to rebuild and retrain the Iraqis and to take them out on their patrol boats and teach them. We finished that in November 2004,' he says. 'We'd achieved our mission. It was nice to achieve that element, where they'd got their boats up and they were working, they were going to sea and they'd started to patrol their borders and stuff like that themselves.'

That job was largely land-based for Morrison. 'I'd go out on the patrol boats for a day or so but the other times I was doing road convoys up to Basra and down to Kuwait – just for logistics and moving people around and bits and pieces. That was a little hairy because there were people trying to blow us up and take us out but we got through all that. It was a unique naval experience.'

Returning to Australia, he rejoined his family while serving as Principal Warfare Officer at HMAS *Watson* in Sydney before joining the Sea Training Group with a core role of preparing ships for operations, including for the Middle East.

'We'd train them first and then we'd go back and become the evaluators and we'd certify them, essentially, that they were fit to go on operation. So I knew all the criteria that I had to go through and it was good, it was good to have that [experience].'

In addition, he was deployed on a number of short-term operations, including the evacuation of Australians from Lebanon in 2006. Then it was back to sea as the XO of the frigate *Newcastle* and, from there, on to a number of shore-based jobs before taking command of *Darwin* in August 2013. He took over the command from Brian Schlegel, who had switched to command *Melbourne*.

All but the last twenty-one days of *Darwin*'s 2014 deployment came under the 'war-like' Operation Slipper; the last twenty-one were the beginning of the 'non war-like' Operation Manitou.

The Australian frigates in the Middle East had already started to come across drug smugglers, but until then the focus had largely been on oil security and piracy. Of the earliest drug finds made by ships such as HMAS *Parramatta*, Morrison says, 'Yeah well, I think they stumbled into it! It was [a] maritime security operation, so it was looking at the whole gamut of things and they stumbled across the narcotics. Back then they weren't well hidden so they were just out and about and they came across them. But there are the legal concerns of how you deal with it and the legal framework on how that all works. Back then, [the Australians] were going over just to talk to them to see if they had any information about bits and pieces – and then they stumbled across the narcotics. The Canadians were probably the first to actually really finesse the search and finds. They were getting quite a bit.'

When Brian Schlegel handed over command of *Darwin* to Morrison, he had provided a great deal of helpful information and ideas about tactics and procedures.

'But even then, the way we trained and the way we approached it was in a different mindset,' Morrison says. As for the narcotics smugglers, he says, 'I guess these guys doing the transportation got to a point where they were getting intercepts so they then had to go and hide [the drugs]. They hide it such that your average boarding [party] that you can send over could last about five or six hours of time of extreme [conditions] and then, that's it, you're out. We found on average about eleven hours, ten to eleven hours, we'd get a narcotics seizure. We'd find it.'

Early on he had to develop techniques for how to maintain and to keep going. 'There were a couple of boardings early that were really easy. When it's an open skiff you can see it there, it's easy but it's when they're hidden inside these dhows, that's when it's more difficult.'

So they developed a method for searching the dhows. They found it was sensible to have two boarding parties that they could rotate 24/7. 'When we'd go into a boarding, we'd get our on-call boarding team. They'd go in and the off-call team would go to bed, get their heads down, try to get as much rest as they could because they're going in in six hours. Then we'd just keep rotating every five to six hours depending on the environment, the weather and stuff like that. By doing that we were able to sustain it. The longest boarding I did was twenty-two hours; recently [Australian ships] have had boardings that have gone for three days.'

Under Morrison's command, *Darwin* sailed up to Diego Garcia and then into Muscat. From there she went out on patrol just off the Gulf of Oman and then up into the Red Sea. They also went to Kochi in India. On 1 March, ten days into their first patrol, they came across a group of thirteen Iranians – eleven men and two boys – floating in the water.

'That was an interesting situation,' Morrison says. They first sighted the group at night, via imagery sent back from the helicopter. 'We were looking at it at about two in the morning going, "What is it?" and the best we'd come up with at that stage was, "It looks like a couple of guys on jet skis!" And then [we saw] these big box type containers which we thought were big narcotics tubs or something that they were towing out.'

So they thought, 'Right, this might be a narcotics transfer.'

Morrison continued reviewing the imagery and the more he saw the more he became concerned about it. He thought, 'No – this is something else, something is going on here.' He told everyone ashore what was going on and he then made a decision. 'There's no use going in at night, I'm going to come in at first light and investigate.'

In the morning they planned it, briefed the team and then he came close in at first light. 'As soon as I got there I realised that this was the guys whose trawler had been hit by another ship five days previously. They had tubs that they'd cut in half, and they'd got into the tubs and tied them all together, and there was one little dinghy.'

They had been floating there for five days waiting desperately for someone to pick them up, but nobody had. 'I think ships had been sailing past and they didn't want to get involved because if you get involved then you end up with all sorts of issues. They were Iranian, and they were just outside Pakistan's territorial waters so they were in the Pakistani SOLAS region. I had a difficult situation, where if I brought them on board there were legal ramifications.'

The main thing, he decided, was to look after their safety. He sent *Darwin*'s RHIBs out to take them some water, food and minor medical supplies such as Panadol. 'At the same time, we'd gone through our headquarters, which had Pakistanis in it who called in Pakistan Search and Rescue. And they came out to the vessel and were able to then take them back. Because if you think about it, obviously when they get to Pakistan there are cross-border diplomatic channels that allow them to transfer people back and forth for that sort of thing. Whereas for us, if we board them, then we'd essentially have them on Australian soil and we'd have to take them somewhere. How do we get them into Iran? It was a complicated issue, so I resisted as much as I could bringing them on board, although at one stage we were considering it. But we went, "No, no, no." I had all my backup plans. I had mattresses and everything down in my hangar and stuff ready to go, but my main aim was to try and get them to Pakistan so I could then get them across to Iran. So that was the first one.'

Occasionally the lines between international law, diplomacy and morality can be blurred. A major moral dilemma occurred for then Lieutenant Commander James Lawless during his deployment as XO in HMAS *Melbourne* in 2010.

Primarily based off the coast of Somalia conducting counter-piracy operations in the internationally recognised transit corridor (IRTC) between Saudi Arabia, Yemen and Somalia, the ship did not conduct as many boardings as other vessels. On one occasion the ship's helicopter was on patrol and watching a suspected smuggling vessel when suddenly the large coastal dhow exploded and disintegrated.

'The imagery showed people donning life jackets before a large hose, that we suspected was a fuel hose, was inserted into the bilge,' Lawless recalls. 'One person lit a match and there was a blinding white flash and a fireball. All the people were thrown into the water and incredibly no one was killed.'

Melbourne rescued the men, many of whom suffered serious burns. A Pakistani officer was at that time commanding Combined Task Force 150, under which the Australian ship was operating, and fortunately a Pakistani warship was nearby. The rescued sailors said they were from Pakistan so the decision was taken to hand them over to the Pakistani ship and to treat the incident as a SOLAS matter rather than smuggling. Many of *Melbourne*'s crew, including James Lawless, were concerned about the fate of the men, given that under Pakistani law drug smugglers faced the death penalty.

'I struggled with the idea and it took a long time for me to rationalise that incident,' he says. 'It didn't sit very well with me and it was raised internally, but at the end of the day the captain made a call that was sound. That is the hard thing about command. The decisions are not always easy, they are not always black and white. There is a moral element.'

9

Not just coffee

Darwin's first patrol in 2014 proved to be an action-packed couple of weeks. After rescuing the shipwrecked Iranians, the frigate went up into the Red Sea, where on 7 March she seized 650 kilograms of hash from a skiff. Nine days later, on the night of 15–16 March, they made a huge haul of a further 3012 kilograms of hashish, also from a skiff, up in the Gulf of Aden.

It started when the ship's Seahawk helicopter spotted a dhow that was manoeuvring suspiciously. The ship started shadowing the vessel.

'So I ... sprinted out, intercepted the dhow and pretended I was just passing,' Morrison recalls. 'I just kept on a steady course of speed when two ships are passing and actually we were doing normal stuff like PT so he wouldn't think I'm manoeuvring around him. I just went right past him and then I just sat over the horizon, so he can't see me but I can track him. He stopped,

I came in and then – this was at two in the morning – started manoeuvring around him to work out what he was doing.'

At that time, the helicopter wasn't up because Morrison had used up all the flying time he was permitted. They kept watching the dhow from the ship and at about 4 a.m. it suddenly turned around and started going back the other way.

'I realised, "I think I've witnessed a sea transfer here!"'

But he had no other information to go on. He suspected that drugs had been moved from the dhow to a skiff, but they had not been able to actually see the transfer.

'Skiffs are very small so they're very hard to [see]', he explains.

This was an important development because *Darwin* was not just there to intercept narcotics. The higher command had asked Morrison to try to work out how the smugglers were transferring narcotics to shore. The theory was that they were using skiffs, but they did not know where the small boats came from and where they landed the drugs.

Morrison checked out Google Earth and various maps and looked along the coastline until he spotted two little ports on the coast of Yemen that he thought were likely places.

'The skiff would come out of Yemen and meet a dhow to then take [the hashish] into Yemen,' he says. 'And then it would go across the land in Yemen, which is very much lawless and at war, and then across the Red Sea into Sudan and then from there it's distributed.'

He did not know which of the two small ports the skiffs would head for, but he strongly suspected one of them. He plotted a course that could intercept a vessel that might be heading to either port. *Darwin* was sprinting as fast as it could on one turbine so as to conserve fuel; the radar operators were scouring the ocean and at last he got a call saying, 'Okay, we're just crossing the contiguous zone [twenty-four miles out in international waters] – and we've just picked up a high-speed vessel doing eighteen knots.' It was, indeed, a skiff.

'So I went, "Excellent," put on my second gas turbine and went in, and then I had to keep manoeuvring around him to stop him from getting into the territorial sea,' Morrison says. 'In the end, he stopped when I still had nine miles to run. He was trying to get away from me, just kept turning and so I just kept manoeuvring around. When I realised that he was going around in circles I thought, "Eventually he's going to run out of fuel before I will," and I just kept doing that. And then I requested warning shots, got warning shots, did the warning shots and he stopped.'

The firing of warning shots was in itself something new for drug interdictions. Morrison had routinely used warning shots and escalation of force during the patrol-boat people smuggling operations north of Australia. During preparations for *Darwin*'s tour he had asked whether it was likely that they would need to fire warning shots to stop narcotics smugglers and whether they should train accordingly.

'Everyone said, "No, you won't need to do that." And I was the first after many years to request warning shots – and it took a long time to get it because I hadn't trained [for it]. I kicked myself in the end for not training it! But that's all right, lesson learnt. Whilst we were doing that operation I just had to carefully monitor and orchestrate the whole activity.'

They used the Steyr 556 rifle. 'The warning shots are all about escalation, so you start with the smallest weapon, just because it's making a noise. Eventually I could have gone up to the 12.7 mm or the 50 cal – that makes a lot more noise – and shoot the water. Rules of engagement [for] the operation would only probably permit warning shots. We wouldn't be shooting people for narcotics.'

If Morrison had not been given permission to shoot, he says he would have just kept manoeuvring around the skiff to stop him getting into territorial waters. *Darwin*'s RHIBs were in the 'cradle' ready to go. 'I got two "burst fires" out and he stopped and we were on him, boarding him in two minutes. Three thousand kilos of hashish.'

There were four crewmen on board, all Yemeni. The aim was just to talk to them at first. 'The narcotics is very well packaged and quite often you'll see them in rice bags or coffee bags. These were in coffee bags.'

The Yemeni crew indicated, 'Oh no, it's just coffee.'

'Okay, no worries. We'll just test that coffee'.

'And obviously, it was hashish,' Morrison says. 'Then we got approval to seize it.' It was packed in twenty-kilogram sacks – 151 of them altogether.

'[The master] was obviously very concerned for his livelihood – it's very much a matter of life and death so he requested some sort of recognition. I said to him, "Yeah, no worries." So I wrote him a receipt for 3000 kilograms of hash and signed that and gave it to him. Back then, it was before the Maritime Powers Act changed. [The Act] now requires us to do that anyway; it changed when I was on that patrol. At the end of the day he's paid to go out there, intercept or rendezvous with a vessel, take on narcotics and sprint back and that's all he does. He's not a big player. I don't think he's getting paid very much. I hope that the receipt note was able to assist him, and the people there could understand that he didn't sell it on to someone else.'

Nowadays, the Australian Government certificate that is handed to the skippers of the boats that have been intercepted is a much more official looking document than Morrison's improvised receipt. 'Hopefully that helps them and maybe even prevents them from wanting to do it but it also tells their kingpins that they're not on-selling it, they're not doing anything that is bad.'

He is well aware of the ruthless nature of the drug lords when it comes to protecting their trade and the vulnerabilities of the crews of the smuggling vessels and their families back home.

'But you can only do so much,' he says. 'I guess I have thought about that and other things and in the end I've just put that aside. That's a part of doing business, the business that we're in and hopefully that would put a dent in some of that transfer, which may prevent more people getting involved in it and more narcotics on the streets and all that sort of stuff.'

Overall it was a twenty-two-hour operation, starting with sending the aircraft out, and he says there were lessons learnt. 'But I was pretty happy and probably the most important thing, [and] one of the big reasons why I was there was I was able to show direct evidence of how they offload the narcotics on to the skiffs and which port that they were going to in that skiff.'

That intelligence was vital to establishing where the hash highway led, and also the route of the smack track. 'We've become much better at it.'

He says it was a matter of building up a picture from the intelligence that had been gleaned from the many boardings from 2008; working with people, finding information, sitting down and analysing it and bringing it all together to come up with the theories. 'And then we were there to try and intercept but also prove those theories in some regard. It's a lot of years of painstaking work to do that.'

The action-packed tour of duty continued. On 11 April 2014, *Darwin* provided aero-medical evacuation assistance to a fisherman who had suffered a heart attack on board a French fishing vessel, *Cape Saint Vincent*, approximately 300 nautical miles off Tanzania. They airlifted him by helicopter to *Darwin* and from there he was evacuated to Dar es Salaam, again by helicopter.

The next day, *Darwin* detected a dhow and after shadowing it overnight conducted an eleven-hour boarding on 13 April, resulting in the seizure of 188 kilograms of heroin.

'That was our first heroin seizure that was hidden,' Morrison recalls. 'There were probably a couple before that where we had the one boarding team out and they couldn't find anything and they said, "Oh there's nothing here," and we pulled out. But there was enough what we call tripwires, enough intelligence there, enough things there.'

'Tripwires' are indications that drugs are on board. The first step is to get on board and establish the bona fides of the vessel. They try to find out where it originates; where it is sailing from; where it is going; and what stories the crew tell.

He says a recurring theme is, 'Where are you going?'

'We're going down to Tanzania.'

'Oh yeah, what are you going to do?'

'A friend has broken down, down there, and we're going down to help him.'

'Right, okay, so whereabouts is he?'

'We're not sure.'

'Right, so where are you, how are you going to get that?'

'Oh, he's going to call us on the phone.'

They try to conduct interviews in English but where necessary they bring an interpreter, or 'terp', onto the dhow. *Darwin*'s terp was a civilian who spoke both Farsi and Arabic; Morrison was always conscious of his safety. 'Obviously one of the things we had to look after is that we're sending these guys on these boats that are rickety, and rough seas, so we are always worried about that person because he's not as well trained at the maritime domain. But they were invaluable as far as that information flowed. So we were able to work that out.'

Whenever the fishermen's stories did not add up, the Australians would know there was something suspicious going on.

'It's like any sort of policing,' says Morrison.

At first when they started their searches they tried to find physical features on the boats that were unusual. 'The training that we had here was, you looked for things that were unusual. So we'd go, "Oh look, there's new fibreglass here," so we'd go and we'd drill there and, "Oh there's new fresh paint there! We'll go and do that."'

But Morrison started to realise that this in itself was suspicious. 'I can't conclusively say this, but I'm of the view that they were deliberate. These guys set that up.'

He soon noticed that whenever they found drugs beyond those places that had obviously been repaired, the hiding spots looked deceptively grubby and old. 'So we came up with another method which was not to jump at the areas that [seemed to] need it, but to search methodically through each compartment.'

Because he had previously been Fleet XO he had had the responsibility for ships' damage control. 'We have these ships' layouts. On all our ships, when we do fire-fighting and suchlike, we mark it all out.'

So he said to his crew, 'Right, make me a dhow DC [damage control] board.'

'What do you mean?'

'I want to have a board, just a layout of a dhow.' That was because they all had similar layouts. 'I want to be able to draw on it and map out exactly where we've searched and what we're searching, so they can tell us and we can monitor it from [the ship] so they can move through methodically.'

So that is what they did. 'And we'd go through the wheelhouse and the captain's cabin and we'd go down into the engineering spaces and move through the fish holds and all that sort of stuff and we'd search through that way,' he says. 'By doing that and rotating our people through we became successful.'

Their success was due both to the methodical search and better understanding of where the smugglers were likely to hide the narcotics. 'The methodical search allowed you to not jump at those shadows, so you followed through. Their modus operandi, their tactics, in my opinion, is to set up these areas that you go and expend all your energy on. And you go, "Nothing here to see – I'm getting off," five or six hours later, which was what they did.'

By rotating teams and using other tactics such as fibre-optic cameras they were able to achieve greater success. 'So that's where we started – with [our first 188-kilogram heroin haul] and then, from there, we kept going on to get much more successful.'

10

The River Phoenix

Next came 24 April and a fourteen-hour boarding that yielded a big prize – the seizure of the largest single haul of heroin captured from a vessel on the high seas in Combined Maritime Forces history. It was a huge quantity – 1032 kilograms.

'A lot of people got excited about this one,' Morrison says drily.

The enormous seizure also resulted in the invention of a novel contraption that would go down in naval folk history first as the 'River Phoenix' or 'the Garbinator'.

Darwin had sailed to the region expecting to be engaged mainly in counter-piracy operations, but by now it was clear that illicit drugs had become the main game. Due to the Syrian conflict and the rise of the ISIS terrorist group, an increasing amount of heroin that had previously been moved overland to Europe through Turkey and Iran and via the Balkans was now being shipped southwest on fishing dhows down the Indian Ocean to East Africa on the smack track.

Before the navy had begun seizing narcotics, the hierarchy had taken steps to ensure that sailors could safely dispose of the high-value contraband by donning protective suits and pouring it over the side of the ship. That was fine for 'small' quantities – a hundred kilograms here and there – but the biggest haul was the game-changer. Now, with more than a tonne of heroin to get rid of, there had to be a better method.

Navy learnt the hard way on the eve of Anzac Day in 2014.

As *Darwin*'s then chief boatswain ('buffer'), Chief Petty Officer Neil Lacey, explained, 'The hash wasn't too bad because it's pretty moist. It's very hard to breathe it in. You get it on your hands, it stinks, and that's about the end of it. But with the heroin being so pure, because it hadn't been cut at this stage, as soon as you open the bag and ditch it, it just forms into a dust. If we were doing more than twelve knots then it would end up on the flight deck. There'd be dust everywhere, so it was very hard.'

The chain of custody is vital when it comes to narcotics. The drugs have to be recorded, weighed, photographed and tested prior to disposal.

As *Darwin*'s then XO, it was one of James Lawless's jobs to process the drugs once they had left the dhow. He and two navy divers set about cutting open and shaking out more than 1000 bags of coarse powder in the desperate forty-five-degree heat. It took more than six hours standing on the steaming steel deck plates in full protective equipment including an S10 respirator (a military grade gas mask), disposable plastic overalls, gloves and boots. Dehydration and dizziness were the constant companions of the disposers as they proceeded to dissolve almost $1 billion worth of high-grade heroin in the Indian Ocean.

'We took the bags of powder to the flight deck where they were cut open with a knife and emptied into the turbulence created by the ship's propeller,' Lawless recalls. 'Unfortunately, a by-product was that occasionally the powder would get thrown up and coat us and the flight deck. It wasn't always visible and was like a fine dusting of icing sugar. I went to the front of the flight deck to get some water and took off my mask and ingested the powder.'

After showering and changing his clothes Lawless went to the wardroom for lunch and a chat with the dive team officer who had also been on drug disposal duty.

'I was a bit light headed and asked him how he was feeling. He said, "Fine," and that we are just highly dehydrated,' he says. 'I was sitting there by myself and the engineer came and sat next to me and I remember just looking at him and grabbing his beard and making a "grr" sound at him. That is a bit out of character for me and for most XOs. There was a knock at the door and the buffer was there and he said my eyes were just pinpricks. He couldn't get any sense out of me.'

Neil Lacey says that Lawless was definitely not himself. 'We were supposed to do a Dawn Service for Anzac Day,' he recalls. 'And being the buffer, I have to talk to the XO fairly often in regards to ceremonial things. So I went to see him after they'd been ditching the heroin all day. I remember knocking on the wardroom door and he [Lawless] basically floated through the doorway and I thought he'd been on the piss, originally – and then I noticed that his pupils were just about gone.

'I said to him, "Are you all right?" and he just made a joke and floated back into the wardroom. So I went down and said to the doc, "You might want to check out the XO." And the next thing, we saw him in the chiefs' mess having a urine test and [it] went off the scale for heroin. He was away with the fairies for about thirty-six hours.'

Before taking the urine test Lawless had looked in a mirror and realised something was seriously wrong. When he began stroking a female officer's face and saying something weird and totally out of character, his shipmates also twigged that he wasn't well and accompanied him to the sick bay.

During his thirteen-year navy career, the former Canberra boy and ADFA graduate had never acted so strangely. 'The doctor said I had tested positive to opiates. I was incredibly tired and dozed off for the rest of the day. I was escorted to dinner and restricted until lunch time the next day.'

Fortunately, the ship's doctor had all the necessary remedies on board, including Narcan, in case the effects had to be reversed. It was not needed. According to Terry Morrison, the ship's doctor said Lawless's ingestion of heroin was a relatively minor dose, similar to the effects from a large dose of Panadeine Forte.

'But it was but still enough for us to say, "Whoa, we need to analyse this,"' Morrison says. 'I'd asked early on, "What sort of precautions do I take? What masks do I take?"'

From the ship he spoke to some people back in Australia to explain the new problem. 'I described it as the dust – that it covers them with dust. Obviously, I've got decontamination stations, but to prevent the dust they said, "You need to put it in the water." And I said, "Obviously, but how do I do that when there's a five- to-six-metre drop to the water?"'

So Morrison went to the ship's engineers and said, 'I've got an engineering challenge for you. I want you to make me some sort of trough that I can pour heroin in to make it wet so that it doesn't blow back.'

It was Chief Petty Officer Tony Walsh who came up with the original idea for a heroin disposal unit. According to Walsh, James Lawless had eyes 'like piss holes in the snow' when he was contaminated, so after his discussion with the boss Walsh went to sleep that night wrestling with the problem in his head.

'The biggest thing was we had to be able to use what we had on board, which was limited,' he says. 'I didn't want to go wrecking something that was new so I went and asked the buffer if he had a spare wheelie bin, and he said, "Yeah I've got this one here," which I think had all the wheels broken on it, and I said "Oh, that will do."

'I managed to get another set of wheels for it and then I used that as basically the main bit and cut the bottom out of it. And then I came up with the idea of how I was going to dispose of it.'

Walsh's eventual design was inspired by the concept of a water-jet eductor, to mix and dispose of solids and liquids inside a casing. He had the casing in the form of the wheelie bin, and he used galvanised steel tubing with holes drilled into it and fixed to the inside of the bin about thirty centimetres below the top, connected by a fire hose connector to a water supply. He also made a stand to hold it on the stern of the ship.

The creation took an entire day to put together. 'I welded the pipe so it came out through a plate that was bolted to the inside of the bin and then put another plate on the outside. And then that pipe came to a fitting where the fire main connected to the top of the bin and then to the spray jet inside it.'

Unfortunately, there were no more heroin hauls in the days following so he went to the galley and asked the cooks for some flour to give it a test run.

'I set it up at the back of the ship and poured a bag of flour down it to see how it would go and it seemed to work all right,' he says. 'I had to make a few modifications and just drill some more holes in it in different places and when we did get a bust and they set it up it seemed to work really well.'

Tony Walsh originally named the unit the 'River Phoenix' after the American actor who died from a heroin overdose. Later versions came to be called the 'Garbinator' and during *Darwin*'s 2016 deployment the ship's chippy, Chief Andrew 'Goonga' Sims, further modified and improved Walsh's invention. It then became the 'Goonganator'.

Whatever it is called, the simple, low-cost solution has been central to the disposal of billions of dollars worth of heroin in the Indian Ocean.

'The guys who dispose of it said it eliminated the dust factor and two people could operate at once because they could stand on either side and pour the bags in. It all just got rinsed away with the seawater over the back of the ship,' Walsh says.

The simple invention became well known across the navy after it won a fleet safety award.

'It was a unique solution to a known problem,' says Morrison.

Once that was sorted out, the navy wrote a standard operating procedure for disposing of narcotics.

Chief Petty Officer Neil Lacey deployed twice to the Middle East on board *Darwin*. He regards the 2014–15 trip as the most rewarding experience of his thirty-one-year navy career and not just because of the record drugs haul.

It is his job as the 'buffer' to liaise between the executive department sailors, including the boatswains, combat systems operators and communicators, and the command team, namely the XO and CO. Lacey says that navy sailors today do not deploy as often as their predecessors did, so having the opportunity to work with a group of young people who had never been at sea for seven months before was fantastic.

'They're all unsure of the future,' he says. 'They're scared of the unknown – and then as the deployment progresses you notice [that] they've got confidence, they're more interested in what they're doing and they're basically doing the job they joined up to do. If the ship can work well together and you've got that teamwork and everyone's got trust in each other, then you can overcome basically anything, I think. Some of those boardings went for twenty-plus hours through all conditions, through the night, and unless you can rely on each other you just wouldn't be able to achieve it.'

The buffer's job on a warship is incredibly diverse, ranging from knowing whether there are enough life jackets to ensuring there are adequate weapons.

'There is also a lot of stuff that we had to do on the fly,' he says. 'Like – when you come across six tonnes of drugs, how do you get it out of the boat and back on board the ship? The first bust we had was a couple of hundred kilos and trying to haul that up the side of the ship in mail bags was fairly hard work in the conditions.'

With experience in port services where cranes are crucial, he realised that the davit used for launching and retrieving the ship's RHIBs could lift the cargo nets containing the narcotics. But the drugs also had to be weighed.

'Weighing each individual bag on a set of bathroom scales just wasn't effective, so on the next port visit we got this digital scale which we attached to the crane, and then it was just a matter of lifting the drugs out in the cargo nets, deducting the weight of the net and, bang, weighing done. So, you weren't ginning around in the heat trying to get an accurate weight. Thinking outside the square came into it a fair bit.'

The buffer is required to do a lot of organising to bring the team together to launch and recover boats; weapons training, including live shoots; providing numbers and training for boarding parties; force protection; and moving the ship in and out of harbour.

'You have to be able to talk to different regulators throughout the ship to get personnel from other departments and train them all to do the jobs of the Seaman Department,' he says. 'It takes organisational skills and being able to get on with people. If you can't do those two things, then yeah, you struggle.'

Lacey found there was great sense of satisfaction involved in holding a $600,000 bag of heroin that was worth more than his house and watching it go over the side. 'Oh well, that's $600,000 you [terrorists] are not going to get, that's not going to find its way to the streets of New York, London or Sydney, and someone's kids are not going to be whacking all their money on this and ending up dead.'

Around this time, they had also started noticing more unusual types of vessels sailing on the smack track. The dhow from which they removed the record heroin haul on 23 and 24 April was about double the size of the smaller 'jelbut', or trading and fishing dhows, that they were used to seeing. This one was a 'sambuq', or large cargo dhow.

'So that opened up another Pandora's Box,' says Morrison.

He says it was only by sheer happenstance that *Darwin* was the ship to snare the record haul. The Canadians had provided intelligence that the dhow was on its way down the smack track. They would have conducted the boarding themselves, but tragically they had lost a sailor overnight in Tanzania.

'They stopped and went into mourning, to remember their shipmate who had passed away ashore,' Morrison recalls. 'They were just off the coast, so they got the intelligence and they passed it to us. So we went up and intercepted that guy. And we probably wouldn't have intercepted him normally but [because] we had the intelligence that they'd given us we went, "Let's look at this one."'

The Australians boarded the dhow immediately, overnight, off the coast of Africa. 'We were obviously well outside territorial waters on the high seas and well within our legal rights to do what we did.'

The heroin was packed into bags that were supposed to be carrying powdered cement, hidden underneath concrete in one area of the dhow. 'My boarding team were able to go down and look underneath, and they saw something sticking up that got them interested and they went and looked and found the heroin.'

The drugs had been packed in one-kilogram bags labelled as either coffee or rice, bound in bundles, wrapped up together and stashed in other bags that were hidden underneath pieces of concrete. Other typical hiding places include kitchen areas or underneath and inside the hull.

'That's part of our intel that we pass on – where we find it and how we find it and that sort of thing, so places for others to look at.'

Then there are the chain-of-evidence requirements.

'As soon as I discover it, I have to prove it. I do a test on it and then I pass that back. I get permission to seize from the CTF commander … CTF 150 has got thirty-odd countries involved [which is] part of the reason why we don't bring them on and prosecute. There's a whole bunch of things I have to go back to do. If I find something then I can request permission to test it and seize it and then bring it back on board. Then we weigh it, we put it straight into our torpedo magazine on an Adelaide Class and I then obviously keep the key until I'm ready for permission to dispose of it. I had to get permission to dispose as well.'

Daily inspections of the torpedo magazine were required

to ensure the right conditions were maintained, including the temperature.

'The sailor would come and knock on my door and say, "Sir, I need to do my torpedo magazine," and I'd go, "Yeah, no worries," so I'd go down and open it up and stand there while he checked it all and no way I could maintain full custody of it. The last thing I want is for someone to try to take some of the drugs! I was making sure that we had it all the time. So that was the big one.'

Darwin's next haul came from a huge cargo dhow that was carrying fifteen cars. During a seventeen-hour boarding conducted on 11 and 12 May, the boarding parties seized another huge haul of 449 kilograms of heroin. Once again, they had boarded almost as soon as they found the dhow. But it was a difficult one, Morrison says, because the vessel was so big that he was concerned about how long it would take. 'We had to talk to the crew a lot, which gave us indications of where it was.'

It was only through questioning the crew throughout the operation that they were able to search in the right spots. 'This [dhow] in particular was just massive – it's just huge.'

The bigger the dhow, the greater the risk, especially in a tricky sea state, for the boarding parties who clamber up by means of a Jacob's ladder.

'Tricky sea states can be a reason for me to say, "No, not doing it." I didn't have to do that but I'm pretty sure, pretty confident that my command chain would have supported that assessment,' Morrison says.

Fortunately, he never had any of his boarding party members drop into the water. 'I had one girl drop about a foot into the boat. She started to climb up and it was backwards and she went "No!" and she came back down. I saw that she didn't have the upper body strength with all the weapons and [gear] and it was one of those difficult ones too because of the high freeboard. On the radio I said, "Leave her off, take her off." I only wanted the guys or girls with the good upper body strength. So she didn't get into that boarding, we rotated her out.'

He says the safety of his own people is paramount. 'There's no use doing this and losing people over narcotics,' he says. 'So the safety of people is number one. It's a priority and that stops some people doing it. You have to stretch yourself a little bit to get the success. You can't be overly conservative all the time – if you are, you're not going to do it. So, there's an element of risk that you have to take but it's all managed risk and I think through my experience [at sea and with training] that I'm reasonably good at understanding and managing that risk and not pushing people beyond. You've got to push them, but not beyond safety.'

May 2014 continued to be eventful. On 18 May, a twelve-and-a-half-hour boarding of a dhow resulted in the seizure of a further five kilograms of heroin. The next two days would provide a large bounty, 786 kilograms of hashish found during their longest boarding – twenty-two hours on 19 and 20 May.

'We found the 786 kilograms in the first hour we searched,' he says. 'But we ended up looking more because we had further intelligence that there was more than just hashish. They were talking about East Africa and Tanzania, where we knew the heroin goes to, so we had to make a conclusive search to make sure there wasn't any heroin. And that was just [from] talking to the crew. Some of the crew were saying they were going to Tanzania. Another was just going, "No, we're going to Yemen." Something's not right here – so that was one of our tripwires but we found this fairly quickly.'

Their last haul – and the really big one as far as hashish was concerned – came on the evening of 28 June 2014 when *Darwin* detected a dhow and after shadowing it overnight conducted a boarding on 29 June. That was the search that resulted in the seizure of a record 6248 kilograms of hashish.

Morrison says, 'There were six tonnes of hash – and that one was very well concealed. It took us twelve hours.'

The hash was packed into 315 bags, each containing twenty kilograms of the drug. The sacks were stashed in a secret area underneath the hull, in the bilge areas. At first all they saw were floorboards. 'The guys went in and they could crawl in underneath and it was wood all the way along. They pop out the other side and they go, "Well there's nothing here." Then one of the guys stuck like a rod in through a hole, stuck it in and pulled it out, and there was hash on it. "Something's interesting underneath!"'

'So we got permission to do a destructive search, which means that we cut a hole, and we had to cut through several layers. It was like a big layer of foam and then there was wood and then there was metal. You've got to cut through all that to get in to get it and then once we've cut it all open then the locals, the crew showed us a little tiny passage in through here, which they could fit in – we couldn't get in and get it out. They'd send one guy in and he'd push it all out and same on [the other] side. So that was the six tonnes – and they came in and helped us get it all out, and then we went in and checked it and made sure we got it all.'

It was the ship's twenty-third boarding on this deployment and the eighth that had yielded narcotics. *Darwin* stayed in theatre until 20 July 2014 before steaming home after a record-breaking deployment. In all, the ship seized twelve tonnes of illicit narcotics valued at more than $2 billion during her six-month deployment. This included 1674 kilograms of heroin and 10,696 kilograms of hashish.

11

Eye on the prize

Commander Catherine Hayes was well armed with tips from Terry Morrison when she became the first woman to 'drive' an Australian navy warship in the Middle East Area of Operations – the Anzac Class frigate HMAS *Toowoomba*.

Under her command, the ship took over from *Darwin* in August 2014 at a time of high-intensity operations. Counter-terrorism narcotics interdictions were well underway and Australian naval boarding and search tactics and procedures were well honed.

Toowoomba's area of operations was roughly the size of Australia's land mass and stretched from the Horn of Africa down to the northern part of Madagascar. The ship's tour of duty coincided with the monsoon season, making it especially difficult. Nonetheless, *Toowoomba* did exceptionally well with three major interdictions, the first of which nearly equalled *Darwin*'s record single haul of hashish.

They had sailed out of Muscat in Oman and were just off the Makran coast.

'It started out as this guy in a fishing dhow who was a bit suspicious, so we tracked him for a while,' she recalls. 'The guys went on board and they said, "He has this weird brand-new fridge, like a freezer. It's got a false floor. Can we drill a hole?" So they put in a little hole, had a look, nothing in there, and then [the master] said, "Oh, my engine is broken." He was hanging around as if everything was broken.'

The boarding party left and returned to the ship. 'We went away from him for a while, just to watch what he was doing. We knew there was something wrong and we went away and boarded some other dhows.'

She had realised that it was important for her team to gain boarding experience early in the patrol. 'You need to get your first go at it under your belt. So my theory was, we board to get rid of all of the "firsts" and then we can get on with doing our job and we did lots of boardings really quickly.'

This gave them experience in verifying the dhows' paperwork and fulfilling the UN requirements, but they found nothing by way of drugs during those boardings. They kept an eye out for the original dhow.

'We just kept watching him,' she says. 'The weather was turning a bit warm. We had our aircraft, so it would go and check on him and update where all the vessels were in our area. It only covered so much in the area and we lost him for a little while'.

They even turned back into Port Muscat to look for him. 'And then he reappeared and we were like, "Oh, hello my friend, and where are you going now?"

He started sailing south and *Toowoomba* followed. The weather turned bad, but the frigate's crew kept asking, 'Boss, can we board him?'

She had to hold them back. 'We can't get you on board – I'm going to end up with you all in the water. That's just a disaster. We're just going to follow him.'

They tracked him for five days.

'Every morning without fail, I'd go to the bridge. I'd get up in the morning and have my coffee and hope the weather's better,' she recalls.

And every morning the boarding team said, 'Can we go today, boss?'

'Sorry, guys, no.'

They were so eager that they started to suggest boarding by the more adventurous methods in their repertoire, including fast-roping from the ship's helicopter onto the dhow.

She said, 'Have you seen [the sea]? You'd fast-rope yourself into the water. That's not happening.'

'They were just so keen,' she says. 'And I remember talking to the bosses – the Pakistanis were our boss ashore – and saying, "I'm just going to tail this guy."'

As commander, she knew that she had to hold back. 'You want to go too but you have to wait. And the thing is, he wasn't going anywhere. We were so close to him. He must have been looking over his shoulder thinking, "They're still there." Every morning, "I wish this warship would go away." We could predict where he was going to go and he came all the way down.'

After five days sailing south he turned to the right and starting heading north towards the Yemeni island of Socotra, which sits between Yemen and Somalia near the Gulf of Aden.

'I thought this was our chance,' she recalls. 'If he gets into the lee that's created to the north of Socotra Island he will get a bit of abatement in the weather and we're going to get on board. I said,

"Right, let's predict that." So we started working it out and all the moons aligned. He did what we imagined.'

As he headed towards Somalia they were able to keep him in international waters. 'So, that morning we got the guys on board and they did all of the requirements to verify his flag or otherwise. Once that was completed I could get authorisation to do full searches, and we started searching. They went straight down to that refrigerator and said, "Someone's patched the hole, right."'

When they had first boarded the dhow he must have gone into the Makran coast to load his cargo, which he then stashed in the gap under the fridge.

'Someone had sealed it. It was perfect – perfectly fibre-glassed in, a very good job.'

Even if they had not previously boarded the dhow and spotted the gap, she thinks they would have twigged that that was the hiding place. 'I think the guys would have searched because it was, "There's a gap – why is there a big gap?" And if you look in, you expect insulation, not a void.'

They asked, 'Can we put in a hole?' So they did. Then, 'There's something here now!' So they cut a bigger hole. Then, 'No, no, we need to cut a bigger hole.'

Finally, they could reach in with their bodies. 'There are hessian bags in here!' First one hessian bag, then two – 'Oh, there's something!'

It tested positive for hashish.

'Okay, this is a decent find,' she says. 'And then the boys started pulling the stuff out and it was, "How many bags now?" They kept coming and coming and they were saying, "This is awesome, we're pulling out all this stuff." The gap was probably two feet and some of the big boys were getting down on their bellies and having to push through the fibreglass, which is really bad, to pull the bags out. They were covered in the stuff.'

They kept pulling it out and piling it up. 'I'm saying, "How many now? Oh God!" They just kept going and going and going and the bags were twenty-kilo bags so they were quite hefty. And they didn't finish pulling them all out until quite late in the evening. I'm thinking, "It's going to take us forever to move this stuff from there to our ship."'

The two boarding teams, led by lieutenants Kane (Stephan) Stuart and Neil Partridge, swapped over during the process.

'And then at night we pulled them all off,' she says. 'I said, "Everyone needs to get their heads down because tomorrow's going to be a big day. We've got to process all this stuff."'

She ordered six hours' rest and put a holding team on the dhow to keep watch on the narcotics and the crew. It took the entire next day to bring the bags back to the ship. 'We just ran the boats backwards and forwards and brought the stuff back and laid it out. The entire flight deck was filled with it.'

Meanwhile the crew of the dhow kept to themselves, which was typical behaviour.

'Most of the time, they were the guys who were just moving cargo so they were quite compliant,' she says. 'Sometimes some of them will tell you [information] but most of the time they don't say anything. They're trying to make a living and obviously they get big money compared to what they would normally do for fishing or their normal trade ... I often wonder how they feel when they go home – are they going to have these guys come and find them? But I guess they know that's part of the game.'

Once the haul was on board *Toowoomba* the next step was to unpack every bag and, weigh, photograph and catalogue it as evidence. Samples were also taken.

'Yeah, a long process,' she says. 'It's really hot and then everyone is so excited – the whole ship's got a buzz.'

It came to 5.6 tonnes of hashish. Naturally, they all wanted to see what such a huge haul looked like, but for obvious reasons the general ship's company could not be allowed to walk among it. So her officers said, 'Okay, you can all go up the back, on top of the hangar, and look down on it.'

By that stage most of the boarding party had their heads down and the disposal team took over. Because hashish is oily, they first had to drain it before throwing it overboard so that it would dissolve in the ocean.

'I went down there and helped them out,' she says. 'They're down there putting one kilo at a time [overboard] yelling out "One Ferrari, ha ha ha!" Or "This is my house!" This plant material is worth so much money. I don't know what it would be worth if you broke it down and sold it in Australia.'

They had to follow strict evidentiary processes before disposing of the drugs.

'Obviously, evidence of packaging indicates where it came from and what source it is,' she says. 'So they do all the processing as they normally would with any police operation and try and collect as much evidence as they can.'

Considerable effort had been made to disguise the bags.

'It's really well packaged,' she says. 'So it's quite interesting. You go, "I'm holding a kilo." It's bizarre – "This is twenty kilos of hashish."

Police officers back in Australia were stunned to hear of such an enormous haul. 'Some of the police are like, "How much? I haven't seen that much in my entire career!" But it's obviously a different part of the supply chain.'

At the end of the operation her boss said to her, 'That was excellent tactical patience.' It was the first time she had heard the term. The sense of satisfaction was tremendous and the crew could hardly wait to do it all again.

'When's the next one?'

'Okay, slow down, everyone go and put your heads down, it's quiet time now.'

Then they headed back to Dubai for maintenance, but first they caught up with the Australian cricket team, which had arrived to play one-day matches.

'We did their opening ceremony,' she recalls. 'They came on board, which was good. The boys loved that.'

She gave a speech, saying, 'We judge our successes by how many hundreds of tonnes of narcotics we've interdicted and at the moment we're in the thousands. I hope that the successes of the Australian cricket team are measured in hundreds of tonnes too.'

The coach, Darren Lehmann, joined the banter.

Although that was their first and biggest haul, she thinks the most rewarding aspect was the way they tracked the dhow for so long.

'It wasn't just a, "Look, there he is." Our planning worked. Whether it was through luck or good planning, it worked.'

Cath Hayes is a modest, straight-talking yet quietly spoken officer who joined the navy aged eighteen after a classic family upbringing in Diamond Creek on the outskirts of Melbourne.

Her mother had always had a romantic vision of the navy, borne of memories of her own older brother, Carl, dressed up in his smart naval uniform. So when, after an exciting 'digger for a weekend' visit to Puckapunyal, Cath announced she was going to join the army, her mother demurred.

'Oh, how about we look at the navy – they have nice uniforms!' her mother said, reminiscing about Carl arriving home 'in this lovely uniform with these lovely young men'.

'Oh dear,' Hayes says with a laugh. 'I think as a young teenager she would have remembered that! I think that I always wanted to do something that's a little bit outside of the box and something a bit adventurous.'

After some research, she went into the navy's recruiting office in St Kilda. To her amazement, she had just sat down when all the recruiters got up and left the room. Bemused, she popped out to the car where her mother was waiting for her.

'What happened?'

'Well, they all ran away,' Cath said.

'Oh, I don't know whether this is a good idea any more,' said her mother. 'Maybe it's not as romantic as I thought'.

But the recruiters soon returned. It was 17 January 1991 and the coalition had just bombed Iraq in retaliation for Saddam Hussein's invasion of Kuwait.

'So here I am in their recruiting office, and our navy was potentially out there alongside their coalition partners in the Gulf,' Hayes recalls. 'This was navy involved in the biggest show in town at that time and they were, I think, quite excited and apprehensive. They were very typical of sailors – "Wow, there's actually conflict going on and our ships could be there." And funnily enough, less than fifteen years later, I was in that same location doing operations, because navy had been doing operations ever since.'

Hayes completed a science degree as a naval cadet at ADFA in Canberra. She threw herself into life at the academy and approached it as a big adventure.

'I loved the whole team environment. You had good friends there and there was lots of sport and there were so many things you could be involved in,' she recalls. 'I was busy just getting into the military life. The academic piece of it, while it was important, certainly wasn't my favourite part.'

She does not recall any unsavoury experiences of bastardisation or harassment. 'I think I would have remembered if there was something that really turned me off, and nothing did.'

She became really hooked on the navy at the end of her first year when her class went to sea for the first time. The usual training ship, the old HMAS *Jervis Bay*, was being used as the 'Mogadishu Express', ferrying supplies and troops to the Somalia campaign. So instead of training in Australian waters the entire class was flown to Diego Garcia and from there to Singapore for ten days – the biggest adventure any of the new midshipmen had ever had.

'I think that was a fantastic introduction for our whole year to travel and the opportunities and new sights,' she says. 'And the opportunities didn't stop from there. There was a challenge all along the way, but I guess that's part of the enjoyment – you get challenged and you succeed or fail or get tested and get tested again.'

Her first full posting was in *Darwin* for two and a half years. The frigate spent six months in southeast and northeast Asia. She found it exciting. 'I lived on the ship as well, so you can imagine. For the first ten years of my career I either lived on the base in a little cabin or on board the ships. It was a little team and we'd often go to movies and go out and enjoy the weekend together and that was fun. It's like being in a dorm I guess [and] a good way to save money.'

She made her way up the ranks and postings, including as a gunnery officer in the frigate HMAS *Sydney* in the Arabian Gulf in 2003. That was the year of the US-led invasion of Iraq, and *Sydney* was heavily focused on protecting the two key Iraqi offshore oil installations at the head of the Gulf. The job then changed to helping to enforce the UN-sanctioned blockade against Iraq and prevent the smuggling of oil and dates on dhows and tankers.

'So that was very exciting and our teams conducted lots of boardings then,' she says. 'They worked really, really hard to try and hinder that smuggling.'

The key maritime threat was the danger posed by waterborne attacks from small vessels after the terrorist attack on USS *Cole*.

'Certainly, that was high on everyone's minds,' she recalls. 'Most of the threat within Iraq from the heavy missiles had been neutralised [and] it was all about the risk of guerrilla warfare at sea.'

Any small vessel might be carrying explosives that could be used to sabotage coalition ships. 'It's not always a threat that's easy to see. You just don't know what's a threat or not a threat, so you have to be suspicious of everything until you prove that it's not a threat.'

The boardings and quantities of contraband were markedly different from the drug hauls that would come later.

Returning home around the middle of 2003 Hayes was posted to the amphibious ship HMAS *Kanimbla* for a number of operations, including providing humanitarian assistance off Aceh after the 2004 Boxing Day tsunami – a rewarding but extremely sad experience.

'It was disastrous and catastrophic and lots of people lost their lives, but we felt that we were doing good,' she says. 'To see people who were just happy to be alive – it's very humbling to see that they just survived with simple things and a smile when they'd had their whole lives taken away.'

After a few months they returned to Singapore thinking they were on their way home. The ship's company had packed up everything, stripped it all back, gone through the quarantine procedures and were all out celebrating when they were suddenly recalled to the ship. At first, they thought it was a joke but they soon discovered that there had been an earthquake on the North Sumatran island of Nias.

'We had a whole heap of medical staff and equipment flown in,' she says. 'We had two helicopters and then we went around to Nias and at six o'clock in the morning we had decided to leave the aircraft in, doing some reconnaissance.'

Then, at 4 p.m. they received a call saying that one of their aircraft had crash-landed.

The crash of the navy Sea King helicopter designated Shark 02, caused by a maintenance fault, claimed nine Australian lives – six navy and three air force. It was the first time Hayes had ever lost colleagues on an operation.

'So, you know, there was a job to be done and we kept doing that,' she says. 'We stayed, obviously, to do a lot of the work, body recovery, all those sorts of things and we continued to provide aid. And then, when we got the word, we headed home.'

She stayed with *Kanimbla* for a further five months. Her next move was her first command, in 2006 – as skipper of one of the new Armidale Class patrol boats.

'Patrol boats are a unique team environment where everyone has to pull their weight or the boat doesn't do what it needs to do.'

This was a significant period in her career.

'It doesn't matter whether you're in command as a lieutenant, lieutenant commander, commander or captain, you know that you have that boat or ship at sea and in the end the decisions you make are yours,' she says. 'So I guess the weight of that doesn't change. The environment changes a lot and the challenges with people change a lot too because there's more of them, not less of them.'

Hayes was selected to command *Toowoomba* in 2012 and joined the ship in 2013. After two short but intense operations – one on border protection and the other in the search for the vanished passenger aircraft MH370 – it was off to the Middle East.

After her record haul of hashish, *Toowoomba* headed south away from the hash highway and down the smack track off Dar es Salaam. She soon came across suspicious-looking dhows.

'During some of these boardings, the guys do all of the paperwork at the side of the wheelhouse while I get approval for a detailed search,' she explains. 'Sometimes they're searching for a long time. We sit there and they send photographs, so we're going, "Check under that board," or, "Is there anything there? Is there space under that?" So, we're all trying to see because they're very, very inventive. You know they're not hiding it in simple spots.'

Some searches lasted for twenty hours. 'At some stage you have to say, "Enough's enough."'

On one dhow, the skipper told them where a package of drugs was hidden, but it was only a small amount. They kept searching and in the end they found about 300 kilograms of heroin.

'The guys were very, very keen,' she says. 'It used to make me smile because they'd come back and they'd be dirty and filthy and stinking like fish, because they'd made [the crew] pull out all the fishing nets. It would take four hours and they'd search everything and they'd get down on their bellies.'

Another dhow, on which they found nothing, was carrying crates of mangoes and bales of straw.

'So they're wading through the mangoes,' she says. 'I thought, "I don't want to eat a mango ever again." They're pushing bales like a game of Tetris, squishing through the bales like little worms, one line then another line. "Oh, we've found a little hole" and they'd go in there and check it out. They came back filthy and exhausted, stinking like fish, straw, whatever they'd been searching through.'

But they would still say, 'Is there another one?'

She would say, 'Can you have a shower first? You've got to stop.'

The thrill of finding smuggled narcotics was immense.

'I think what we used to say is, you get addicted to finding the drugs, not for taking the drug,' she says. 'They were addicted to the success of that.'

They picked up a total of 713 kilograms of heroin from two dhows. It was now November, getting towards the end of their tour, but they did one final boarding before they left, after an aircraft reported a dhow that was coming south.

'It was a fair way north of where we were,' she says. 'We only had so much fuel and we had to get to Seychelles and I only had so much aviation fuel as well, so I could only fly so many hours.'

The command of CTF 150 had just switched from the Pakistanis to the Canadians. 'That night we're all in the ops room saying, "Okay, let's calculate if we can make it up there." We drew circles around the Seychelles. "Can we get this boarding in? How many hours can we go on board before we have to go to the Seychelles?" And, "We can't run out of fuel, we're going to run too low on fuel," and all this sort of stuff. We're all in there with this plan and the boys were getting excited and they're saying, "All right, let's go for it." And we said, "Okay, we're going for it and we're going to get on board – c'mon, we've got to find this thing."'

It was their first boarding under Canadian command.

'We had this whole little plan about how we were going to find it and track it. We found it, we got on board and we only had so many hours we could spend before we had to go. I think we got to eighteen hours but we couldn't find anything. So if he had something on board obviously he'd hidden it well. We'd thought we were going to get one more bust.'

Then they had to head to the Seychelles. 'But the good thing was, it was challenging like the first one when we had to orchestrate this plan. And the guys loved doing the plan and loved how we were operating on the margins of our fuel, how we had to calculate it. I'm watching the principal warfare officers and all the guys in the operations room had their radars, going, "Oh, I can see it, no it's not there, no ..." The [birdies] were hanging out because they wanted to be the ones that sighted it first. Part of it is that once you get the taste of success you want a little bit more and a little bit more.

'It's almost like a puzzle – you're out there and we're trying to solve the puzzle. We are adults playing hide and seek because the supplier is hiding somewhere and we've got to work out how he's thinking, where he's going, what his speed is, how is this affecting that, and it just shows the training that the guys do. To me, that was them coming up with a plan and I just needed to tick off on it. And then they executed it and they found the dhow and they got the final boarding, so I think it was a good way to finish.'

Toowoomba handed over to HMAS *Success* and headed for home, arriving just in time for Christmas on 23 December.

Reflecting on the Middle East tour of duty, Hayes says, 'I like to be proud of what my team achieves, what they do and how they handle it the right way. I think that's inspiring.'

She admits that there is always unofficial competition between the ships but says she and Terry Morrison never talked about who found the most drugs.

'It doesn't really matter. And the nice thing is that when we got a bust Terry said, "Well done, really good, well done you guys." And when the next frigate up there got [their hauls] I did the same thing because you know what their team is feeling.'

The financial value of the narcotics to terrorist organisations was sobering. 'It's not just some guy trying to make a buck out of a bunch of dates. It's really big money if you consider how much is involved in 700 kilos of heroin.'

The boardings can also be hazardous. 'It's not all beer and skittles,' she says. 'Some of the things we do, they're risky. When the guys are boarding those vessels, there are always moments. As a CO we watch what they're doing and it's usually the moments when they're getting on board and they're securing that vessel and they're climbing up a ladder onto a dhow, which looks like a little Noah's Ark. The sides on these things are a good twenty feet high and the boat's moving around and the little boats are moving around and they're trying to climb up with all their gear on up a rope ladder.'

She used to sit watching them on the ship's television camera and every few seconds she would count them. 'How many are on board? One's on board, two's on board,' she says. 'And because we had someone drop in the water your heart goes in your mouth. You want them on board, secure and safe.'

Boarding parties climb aboard the dhows fully equipped to deal with any threats.

'They go on expecting danger but the reality is that these guys are there just to courier the stuff, so we weren't finding huge amounts of resistance,' she says. 'When you drive a big warship up alongside a small fishing dhow, and I've got five-inch gun and I'm sending a boarding party who are fully kitted and spurred with their ballistic vests on and weapons and the whole lot, I think it would be a suicide mission for them to do anything. They're not there for that sort of thing. They're there to make money.'

MAKING IT WORK

12

Tonnes of guns

Darwin was only a week and a half into her first patrol of 2016, steaming 170 nautical miles or 313 kilometres off the coast of Oman, when on 27 February an officer of the watch spotted a dubious-looking dhow that appeared to be heading for Somalia. The vessel was tracking towards the Yemeni island of Socotra – hardly a known fishing ground, which made it one of the key 'tripwires' or indicators that something was amiss. The Socotra area was where *Toowoomba* had seized 5.6 tonnes of hashish in 2014.

'We initially suspected it was drug smuggling,' Commander Henry recalls.

As usual, *Darwin* had two boarding parties – one on, one off. The 'red' team was led by the lanky and plain speaking twenty-six-year-old Lieutenant James Hodgkinson. His second-in-command was the no-nonsense forty-one-year-old Petty Officer clearance diver, John Armfield. In charge of the 'black' team was the more reflective red-headed and bearded clearance diver Lieutenant Robert Kelly, with the witty and extroverted Petty Officer David Herrer as his 2IC.

Hodgkinson says, 'It was the first boarding that we'd done since in-chopping and we actioned the boarding party late the night before, around 2300 or 2330 [hours], based off a cold hit. We didn't have any intelligence on this particular dhow [but] it met all the tripwires for us to board. It was heading south, it was a fishing-style dhow which was outside of fishing areas and things like that.'

It was not a small boat. At forty or forty-five metres long, searching the 'jelbut' dhow was never going to be quick and easy. By the time the boarding party got on board it was after 2 a.m. They first secured the vessel and then transferred over US Naval Criminal Investigative Service (NCIS) agent Paul Lerza and his Baluchi language interpreter.

Australian vessels deployed to the Middle East Region carry an NCIS agent when possible and an American-employed interpreter who works with them.

'It was a flat night and we had a little bit of moon but the ocean was incredibly calm,' Hodgkinson recalls. 'So it was relatively easy to get on board. Once we did get on board and the crew were secured we went up to the wheelhouse with the master and the interpreter, [and Lerza] went through his paperwork. [The master's] paperwork was incomplete and also his fishing licences didn't match up with his registration paperwork, which didn't match up with the crew manifest that he had. He had an odd number of people on board and everything just didn't add up.'

As soon as they had collected the evidence that his registration was not correct they recommended to Phill Henry that he declare the vessel stateless.

'He did that in consultation with headquarters ashore in Bahrain,' Hodgkinson says. 'And from there we started searching the vessel.'

It was about 4 a.m. before the search got underway. Armfield says that after discussing the various tripwires they picked the areas they wanted to target first, leaving the fishing nets until later. 'On this particular vessel the nets are quite large. We like to bring the nets out last because it takes up too much space, so we'll systematically search front to back, top to bottom [first].'

Hodgkinson explains, 'The structure of these dhows is that they've got an area all the way forward, they've got a little bit of deck here and they hit the anchor there. Then immediately behind that they have a net well or a net hold. Behind that they've got a freezer hold and behind that, engineering space. You've got the wheelhouse up higher and below that living quarters and stuff like that.'

They started searching at the bow. 'There was a fair bit of stuff down there which we had to pull out, but that took us through to 0500,' Armfield says. 'At 0500 they usually like to do a prayer. You can't really work around them, so we do prayer from 0500 to say 0530, however long it takes, and mostly everyone will do it one at a time. And then from there we went into breakfast, which was about another half an hour, fed the crew and by that time everyone had finished completing the searches that we wanted to do.'

When they finally came to the nets there seemed to be some confusion. The boarding party wanted the crew to take the nets out; the crew, who were generally quite a friendly lot, tried to put them back in as fast as they could.

'So the interpreter had to come down to get them to start taking the nets back out,' Armfield recalls. 'And that went on for about five to six hours.'

Hodgkinson says, 'There was something in the vicinity of seven to nine miles of nets that we took out in varying states of repair. So obviously those nets hadn't been used for fishing because we had new nets, we had old nets, we had nets that were patched together and, in hindsight, the way that they handled them was not the way that other fishermen handled them. So I'm not convinced that they were fishermen. And right when we got near the bottom of these nets they started going really slowly pulling them out, but we kept pushing. In fact, I was pretty close to being over it, after having pulled out nets for something like six hours.'

The 'black' boarding team had arrived on board to take over just after breakfast, around 7 a.m. or 8 a.m. Their 2IC, David Herrer, recalls, 'You guys were pretty fatigued by that stage. You'd been up all night then we came on with our fresh set of eyes.'

Almost everyone was ready to give up. 'Command was very close to wanting us to get off – we'd spent a lot of hours on there and were coming up fruitless,' Herrer says. Agent Lerza and the interpreter also both thought there was probably nothing there and that it was a legitimate fishing dhow. But John Armfield's internal alarm bells were ringing.

'Petty Officer Armfield was keen to keep going just to see what we had under there,' Hodgkinson says. 'The rest of us were ready to walk out. We were ready to go. He said to me, "Sir, I really want to get in here and find out what's under this," because I was ready to up stumps.'

Herrer too thought they should keep going. 'I was like, "No, all we have to do is finish with the nets. It's crazy to leave now, we've gone this far."'

'So I decided we should stay and continue with the nets,' says Hodgkinson. 'But I still wasn't convinced that the crew were anything but innocent fishermen. And it's as we were doing our handover that we started to see a few white bags, sacks and cases poking out from underneath.'

Herrer says, 'They're looking, and I'm like, "What's all that white stuff through the nets?" And then one of the ABs – one of our EOD [Explosive Ordnance Disposal] techs – jumped down and opened it up and straight away we knew. And that's when we found them all.'

Meanwhile, the others prevented the crew from continuing to pull out the nets and pushed them inside the wheelhouse so that they would not be able to see what was going on. The EOD pulled out the first case to make sure it was not booby-trapped and took it all the way to the top of the vessel. He opened it up and brought out two RPG-7s and then the launchers. The initial estimate was that there were about a hundred bags; the final count was closer to 500 filled with weapons.

To this day, those who boarded the dhow are not certain whether the crew knew the full story of what was going on.

'I don't think the crew knew,' says Hodgkinson. 'I think the master had some indication of it. While the search was happening, the NCIS agent, the interpreter and myself were questioning the master and questioning the crew and going through and finding the inconsistencies that existed in their different stories, and then hammering home on those inconsistencies. There were a few holes [in their stories] but nothing too revealing.'

While the weapons were being transferred onto *Darwin*, they kept the crew isolated so they could not see what the Australians were doing.

'The skipper, when we took him forward to show him and explain it, he was shocked,' Hodgkinson recalls. 'Whether it was feigned or not he was very shocked and he went down on his knees and started grabbing our interpreter around the legs, which we found out later was a humiliation thing. He was showing how humiliated he was and turning his face away, and he said that he had no idea and he was disgusted. But he didn't look at us then for the next few hours, sort of looked away.'

The interesting thing about the weapons was the way they were packed, Hodgkinson says. 'They were packed in an equal weighting, so that they provided an even balance at the bottom of the ship. When you looked at it you could see that it had a load but it was so well balanced that the ship still rode properly. It didn't unbalance it at all which, if it had been an amateur job, it would have done.'

Instead of loading the weapons on the RHIBs to ferry back to *Darwin* it was decided to bring the dhow alongside the ship for a direct transfer. 'It was just easier to bring it alongside and use our boat crane to crane it all off in a big cargo net.'

The total load on the dhow was about seven tonnes of weapons and five tonnes of nets. Once the sailors started pulling out the weapons and stacking them on one side they started to unbalance the dhow.

'We induced a list,' says Hodgkinson, 'and [so] we had to modify how we were doing that, and that was part of the deliberations as to why we brought [the dhow] alongside – just realising what a large quantity of weapons we had. We would have been there for another twelve hours [otherwise].'

An added difficulty was that it was hard to 'clear' the weapons, to ensure they were not loaded with ammunition, because they were all wrapped in packages.

Kelly says, 'You couldn't walk on top of it because you didn't know what you were walking on, so we got our guys to clear all the packages and then individually check them, make sure that they were not connected to anything [and] make sure they were free of EO [explosive ordnance] before they were passed up, so it was a long process.'

Every single weapon was cleared as 'safe' before it was brought on board.

Positioning the dhow alongside *Darwin* was unusual and quite an operation in itself. After shutting down the dhow's engine they used both the RHIBs as if they were tugboats to push the vessel alongside the frigate. 'I think one of the big things to come out of it that really impressed me was that it wasn't just boarding party doing all this effort. It's great that the whole ship got involved. Everyone got up, formed stores parties, got involved down there unpacking the weapons, helping clear them and then packaging them up to get them onto the ship and again counting them in the hangar.'

Each serial number was recorded as part of the counting process. It was a long job. The total count came to 1989 AK-47 assault rifles, a hundred rocket-propelled grenade launchers, forty-nine PKM general-purpose machine guns, thirty-nine PKM spare barrels and twenty 60mm mortar tubes.

'So it was quite a significant find,' says Henry. 'Because we were able to deduce that he was tracking towards Socotra and then to Somalia, that gave us the authority under the UNSCR Resolution to seize the weapons, which we did.'

Agent Lerza thought the shipment was heading into Somalia, from where it would be on-sold throughout the local region, but it was not possible to be certain whether it was an organised single shipment going to a particular group or just a general part of the arms trade. Either way, Hodgkinson believes it was a professional operation based on the fact that the weapons had all been oiled and were wrapped in plastic then wrapped again in a sack and all numbered. 'Certainly to my mind it was not an amateur operation, just purely from how it was packed.'

But they think lot of the weapons would not have functioned properly, particularly the AK-47s, some of which had mismatched bolts or had not been put together properly. Some dated from the 1970s; others were newer. The RPG-7 launcher tubes, for example, were brand new but not of good quality.

The weapons haul was especially lucky for Able Seaman Pete Irvine – it was not only his boarding party who found it, it was also his very first boarding.

Irvine hails from Bateau Bay on the central coast of New South Wales, and was privately educated at the Central Coast Grammar School. He joined the navy from Newcastle in 2010.

'My reason for joining was my grandad was a doctor in the army and my nan was a nurse in the army, the British Army,' he says. 'My grandad started in the Gurkhas for Nepal and went to the British Army. My dad went to military boarding school – so it just came through the family and I ended up in the navy.'

An electronics technician by trade, Irvine joined *Darwin* in 2014 and took his boarding party courses and his ship's diver course before coming on this trip.

Of the weapons haul boarding he says, 'That was a long one. It went for … like two days. So that was a bit of an eye-opener for what was ahead of us. I think we went to boarding stations around midnight and then it was unexpected, so we didn't know it was coming. We boarded around 1 a.m. and then we didn't get off that dhow until about 10.30 in the morning. By then we'd found the weapons and [the 'black' team] were just coming on for the next thirty-six hours. But yeah, that was full on.'

The haul made a big impression on him. 'It was 2000 AKs – it's like a little army. They could take out a lot of people. Some of the AKs, they're year-printed so 1967, 1981 and all that, so you know these guns have been around the world before. I don't know what they've been involved in but it's pretty cool to see that we just took that ability off someone.'

Navy boarding parties are not just a boys' club. *Darwin*'s 228 ship's company includes thirty-nine women, several of whom are members of boarding parties. Able Seamen Lisanne Hyland and Emily McNeill were both on board the dhow for the weapons haul.

McNeill, aged twenty-two, joined the navy in 2013 aged nineteen and is a combat systems operator.

'My job is to work with radar or sonar to detect the surroundings,' she explains. 'And if we find things, we classify them [as to] whether they be friendly or suspect.'

Born in Longreach in Queensland, she moved around a number of small rural towns as a child because of her father's work as a teacher and shearer. The family settled in Goulburn in New South Wales where her father now works as a wool agent, and that is where she attended high school. After leaving, she did a personal training course and, keen to get away from the small town, worked part-time as a waitress at the local Soldiers Club while waiting for enlistment day.

Once in the navy, she set her sights on joining a boarding party.

'I've always been a hands-on type of person,' she says. 'So I always wanted to be a part of the boarding party ever since I joined. I wanted to find a job where I could easily become part of the boarding party. So I do like my job as a combat systems operator, but I feel that I'm more suited to boarding party just because I like the physical aspect of it rather than just sitting in an operations room looking at the console. And what I love about it is that this is what we're up here for – this deployment. I feel really accomplished being part of the boarding team. It's very rewarding. It's the best feeling I've ever had.'

Not only was this her first, but it was also a night boarding. 'We were always told the ships before us never did night boardings, and [friends] said to us, "Oh you'll never do a night boarding, they'll just wait until the morning." But my very first boarding I was woken up at midnight and we had fifteen minutes to get ready. It was just so surreal and we ended up having that massive weapons haul as well, so I don't think anything else will be like that.'

During the ship's work-up period, Emily McNeill had been in the operations room and had not been part of the boarding team, so she had not been given the extra training for it. That meant she learnt on the job. 'It was [my] first exposure to it and it's been our best haul, so I'm very happy with that.'

Lisanne Hyland, twenty-two, is a boatswain's mate. She was born in Ireland and her family moved to Adelaide when she was aged eight in 2002 'for a better lifestyle', joining her aunt and uncle who had already migrated to Australia.

In 2014, three years after leaving school, she followed in her cousin's footsteps and joined the navy. 'He made it sound really good,' she says. 'I've always wanted to do something active, didn't really want to have a desk job, so the navy was the job for me, I think. My mum was a bit iffy, thinking it's a military job, but they were happy for me to do it. They knew I wanted to do it.'

Before the weapons haul, Hyland had been on two 'approach and assist' boardings that did not involve any contraband. 'It was pretty much just to get us into it, see what it's like, see how boardings work.'

She loves it. 'It's exactly what I joined up to do. Boatswains usually do boarding party gigs [and] when we join at recruitment they say, "Yeah, you'll be boarding party, you'll drive the boats and stuff," so pretty much the exact reason that I became a boatswain's mate was to do boardings. It worked out perfectly.'

She joined the ship just after the work-up and at first she, too, wasn't supposed to be part of a boarding party. 'But they ended up putting me in, which worked out well.'

Being there for the weapons haul was 'pretty cool', she says. 'We had no idea how many weapons were there when we saw the top bit of it, and then we started getting lower and lower into it, just crazy … I was just by the nets when we sighted the first bags. We were there for most of the weapons they pulled out.'

She is not deterred by her experiences of searching filthy, stinking dhows. 'I enjoy it all. I can't really think of anything that's difficult about it.'

Emily McNeill says the hardest part for her is the actual boarding – climbing up on the ladder.

'Especially in the sea state we've been having,' she says. 'Getting on and off is quite challenging, especially when we have to try and time it with the movement of the waves to jump on, but that's what I love so much about it. I love how challenging it is and I love getting involved. And because we're obviously smaller than a lot of the guys, they put us into the spaces where they can't fit in to search to see if they hide anything in there.'

Hyland admits the length of the boardings can be quite testing. 'You get pretty tired towards the end of them. At one point our team was over there for about fourteen hours. So towards the end of that you're just like, "Oh, I just want to go to bed."'

At the end of the operation, the master of the dhow, a Baluch from Baluchistan between southern Iran and Pakistan, was given an official receipt and an HMAS *Darwin* ball-cap and sent on his way. Hodgkinson is still uncertain about how much the skipper knew about the cargo he was carrying.

'I think the way in which it happens in the port that they come out of [is that] a lot of these masters don't have a regular run or they may not have a regular run. They sort of hang around the port looking for work and then an owner will say, "Hey, I've got a job for you," or, "I want you to take my boat and go down and do a two-month fishing trip down off Africa and then come back."'

The owner will provision the vessel, provide the registration, pay for all the bribes and charges, and then the master picks his crew from among itinerant workers and fishermen.

'Then they form that crew and so off you go,' says Hodgkinson. 'So this particular vessel had been in a re-fit period where the owner had said, "Hey my ship's just come out of re-fit, I need you to take it down south and go and do this trip for me because I can't go. I've got some other business here in country, I can't leave but I need you to go and take it for me and I'll pay you well for it."

'So the master then took it and went, and the whole time he said that he never does anything illegal, he hates illegal activity and he'd never do anything to jeopardise his family and so on and so forth. But certainly to my mind if someone had come up with this awesome deal and said, "Hey I just need you to go and do this run for me I'll pay you well," you would have the questions in the back of your mind ... He may have known that he was doing something bad but he had plausible deniability and he wasn't told so therefore he just went, "I'm just doing this for my family."'

Looking back on the many boardings they have conducted since then, Herrer says, 'It's just funny, because that was our first boarding. And when you look after all the fishing ones, see how it's done, there's a huge difference in the type of person that's a fisherman. Their hands are callused, most of them don't wear shoes, their feet are all callused because they use their feet in the same way as their hands with the nets [for] repairing them and stuff. And you stand there and watch them on a legit fishing dhow, they are incredible the way they pull the nets, they work perfectly as a team. They're pulling them out, they're working on them, they're really efficient whereas all the ones that are a bit suss, whether we've got something or not, don't look like fishermen. They don't have the hands or the feet. And when you watch [real] fishermen pulling nets out, they're working in shifts almost, pull, pull, pull – they just keep going, it doesn't stop. I know a lot more now, now that we've been doing it. Straight away a tell-tale.'

Apart from several souvenirs for the RAN's historical collection the weapons were handed over to the United States Navy for destruction.

ABOVE A bird's-eye view of the guided missile frigate HMAS *Darwin* on patrol in the Indian Ocean in June 2016, taken from the ship's Seahawk helicopter 'Orko'. PHOTO IAN MCPHEDRAN

LEFT The navy's Middle East Area of Operations covers a vast slice of the Indian Ocean.
IMAGE ADF

RIGHT Then Petty Officer Andrew Keitley leading a boarding operation in the Gulf in 2004. He was awarded the Distinguished Service Medal (DSM).
PHOTO ADF

BELOW Navy clearance diver and enhanced boarding team leader Lieutenant Jace Hutchison (left) during a training mission on board HMAS *Toowoomba* in the Gulf in 2009. PHOTO ADF

RIGHT Never before published photo of Somali pirates swarming onto a beach in heavily armed 'technical' vehicles after their comrades were landed ashore from the RAN guided missile frigate HMAS Melbourne in October 2014.
PHOTO ADF

ABOVE These Iranian fishermen were rescued by HMAS *Darwin* five days after their boat sank in a collision in March 2014. They were adrift on makeshift rafts and cut-down plastic containers. PHOTO ADF

ABOVE Previously unpublished photo of high-speed Iranian Revolutionary Guard Corps Navy skiff, with a heavy machine gun mounted on the bow, harassing Australian navy sailors. PHOTO ADF

ABOVE High-speed skiffs from the Iranian Revolutionary Guard Corps Navy, armed with machine guns and rocket launchers. PHOTO ADF

ABOVE Boarding teams from HMAS *Darwin* prepare to board a suspect fishing dhow in the Indian Ocean. PHOTO ADF

ABOVE Sailors from HMAS *Darwin* interviewing the crew of a large cargo dhow in the Arabian Sea. PHOTO ADF

ABOVE A major haul of illicit drugs by HMAS *Darwin* during her 2014 deployment. PHOTO ADF

ABOVE Australian sailors from HMAS *Melbourne* detain a group of Somali pirates off the African coast. PHOTO ADF

ABOVE Commander Catherine Hayes 'drives' the Anzac frigate HMAS *Toowoomba* into a wharf from the bridge wing. PHOTO ADF

ABOVE Before the invention of the 'River Phoenix' or 'Garbinator' drug disposal system the illicit powder was simply scattered over the side, placing sailors at risk of contamination. PHOTO ADF

ABOVE The 'River Phoenix' heroin disposal system, developed by engineers on board HMAS *Darwin* after an officer was contaminated by heroin powder. PHOTO ADF

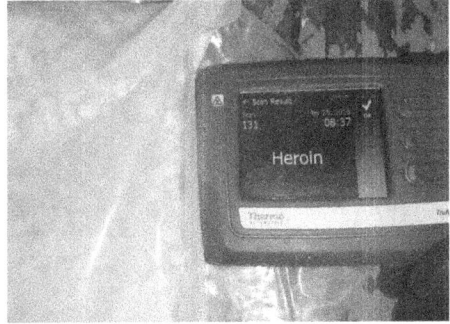

LEFT Illicit drugs found on board a fishing dhow test positive for heroin using the TruNarc tester. PHOTO ADF

ABOVE AND INSET Some of the thousands of weapons, including more than 2000 AK-47 assault rifles, uncovered deep in the net hold of a fishing dhow by HMAS *Darwin* off the coast of Oman in February 2016. The haul weighed in at seven tonnes. PHOTO ADF

ABOVE An Australian sailor from HMAS *Darwin* is dwarfed by dozens of bags of weapons in the net hold of a fishing dhow in February 2016. PHOTO ADF

ABOVE Security personnel at the ready as HMAS *Darwin* departs from Dar es Salaam harbour in Tanzania on 16 May, 2016. PHOTO IAN MCPHEDRAN

RIGHT A suspect fishing or jelbut dhow in heavy seas, seen from HMAS *Darwin* off the west coast of Africa in May 2016. PHOTO IAN MCPHEDRAN

RIGHT US Naval Criminal Investigative Service (NCIS) agent Paul Lerza boards a rigid hull inflatable boat (RHIB) from HMAS *Darwin* in rough seas off the African coast in May 2016. PHOTO IAN MCPHEDRAN

ABOVE Commanding officer of HMAS *Darwin*, Commander Phill Henry, with the ship's heroin haul in the Indian Ocean in May 2016.
PHOTO IAN MCPHEDRAN

LEFT HMAS *Darwin*'s Executive Officer, Lieutenant Commander Tina Brown, oversees the disposal of illicit heroin in May 2016.
PHOTO IAN MCPHEDRAN

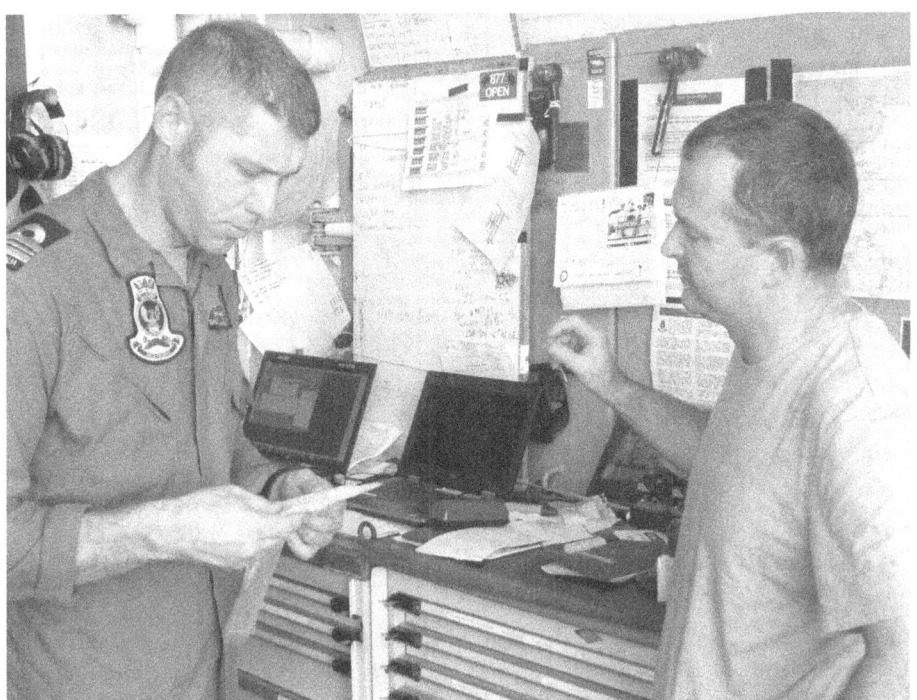

ABOVE Flight commander on board HMAS *Darwin*, Lieutenant Commander Kye Hayman, discusses the engine emergency with maintenance boss Chief Petty Officer Nathan Blanch.
PHOTO IAN MCPHEDRAN

ABOVE The chiefs in their mess on board HMAS *Darwin* on patrol in the Indian Ocean in May 2016. Left to right: Chief Petty Officers Darren 'Swampy' Marshall, Colin 'Stores' Benbow, Andrew 'Goonga' Sims, Nathan 'Birdie' Blanch, David 'Bowie' Bowden, Michael 'Muz' Murray, William 'Eddy' Edmondson, Robert 'Turbo' Pearson, Denis 'Swaino' McKenna, Joy Newman, Saul McLean, Ty 'Sparrow' Davis, Tim 'SWO' Brading and the veteran Nick Scarlett. PHOTO IAN MCPHEDRAN

ABOVE A very happy group of officers with chaplain Richard Quadrio (second from left) as HMAS *Darwin* enters Sydney Heads. From left: Lieutenant Commanders Kye Hayman, Trevor Henderson and Chris Duke. PHOTO IAN MCPHEDRAN

ABOVE 'Cheffos' Able Seamen Simon Betts and Trevor Bird hard at it in the galley sweat box aboard HMAS *Darwin* in the Indian Ocean in May 2016. PHOTO IAN MCPHEDRAN

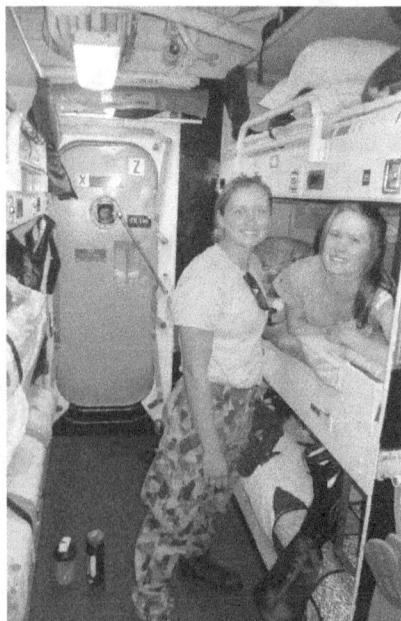 

ABOVE Boarding team members Able Seamen Lisanne Hyland from Adelaide and Emily McNeill from Goulburn in the cramped female sailors' mess on board HMAS *Darwin*. PHOTO IAN MCPHEDRAN

ABOVE Leading Seaman chef Cameron Acreman, who died tragically in Muscat near the end of HMAS *Darwin*'s 2016 deployment. PHOTO ADF

ABOVE A dangerous business as a team from HMAS *Darwin* prepares to board a suspect dhow in a high sea state in the Indian Ocean. PHOTO IAN MCPHEDRAN

ABOVE Anxious moments for HMAS *Darwin*'s navigator Lieutenant Scott Benstead and XO Lieutenant Commander Tina Brown as they watch a boarding operation underway in the Indian Ocean in May 2016. PHOTO IAN MCPHEDRAN

ABOVE Large cargo or 'sambuq' dhows like this could take more than 24 hours to search for illicit cargo. PHOTO ADF

ABOVE HMAS *Darwin*'s 'red' boarding team, led by Lieutenant James Hodgkinson (second left in front), on board a smuggling dhow with NCIS agent Paul Lerza (front centre) and some of the heroin uncovered during a successful boarding. PHOTO ADF

ABOVE HMAS *Darwin*'s Seahawk helicopter 'Orko' fills the window of the control officer's shack as it makes a safe landing during an engine emergency in the Indian Ocean in May 2016. PHOTO IAN MCPHEDRAN

LEFT Aviation Warfare Officer Lieutenant Clare Nickels following the engine emergency on HMAS *Darwin* that really focused her mind. PHOTO IAN MCPHEDRAN

ABOVE Officer of the watch on HMAS *Darwin* Lieutenant Casey Green during a replenishment at sea (RAS) in tricky sea conditions. PHOTO IAN MCPHEDRAN

ABOVE The guided missile frigate HMAS *Darwin* approaches Victoria Harbour in the Seychelles after a successful 14-day Indian Ocean patrol in May 2016. PHOTO IAN MCPHEDRAN

RIGHT The joy of homecoming shows on the sailors' faces as HMAS *Darwin* berths at Garden Island, Sydney, in July 2016, after seven months away. PHOTO IAN MCPHEDRAN

RIGHT Family and friends of the crew of HMAS *Darwin*, including Chief Petty Officer Andrew 'Goonga' Sims, at the welcome home on the wharf at Garden Island after seven long months. PHOTO IAN MCPHEDRAN

ABOVE The author with bags of heroin on the flight deck of HMAS *Darwin* in May 2016. PHOTO IAN MCPHEDRAN

13

Dunnies, drains and dinners

Darwin's sophisticated weapons make it a lethal fighting ship, but there is far more to keeping it in top condition than meets the eye.

Almost every day brings fresh demands on Chief Petty Officer Andrew 'Goonga' Sims, a 'chippy' (naval shipwright) who, with his team of technicians, is responsible for keeping the warship seaworthy and fully functional. Nothing can be taken for granted.

'I'm the manager of all auxiliary machinery on board,' Sims explains. 'That involves the sewerage system, freshwater-making systems, all our air systems on board, whether it be high-pressure or low-pressure air, our main system for fighting fires and also providing cooling to machinery.'

He is also responsible for the air-conditioning units, refrigeration units and all the damage-control equipment on board, and for rectifying defects around the ship.

'In other words dunnies, doors and drains,' he says with relish. Then there is the 'material' state of the frigate. 'That's the integrity of compartments – so the whole structure, bulkheads, deck heads, any rust or corrosion throughout the ship.'

Apart from fuel for the ship's gas turbine engines, fresh water is the most important liquid on board. It is provided by two main reverse osmosis desalination units, each producing about 6800 gallons (25,700 litres) a day.

'We're constantly testing the water,' he says. 'Every day we have to make sure the salinity is below its acceptance level. We've got four large fresh-water storage tanks. They hold roughly 2000 gallons (7500 litres) each.'

The desalination units have electric motors driving high-pressure pumps that push the salt water through the filter membranes to extract all the salt and brine. They then treat it with bromine to kill the bacteria and make it drinkable.

'Some people do say it's better than Sydney water when we drink it, because you don't get that chlorine taste,' he says.

In the old days evaporators were used instead of the 'desal' units. 'We were always on water restrictions, shutting down the laundry and scullery, just to try and catch up with the water, and then we'd relax restrictions again.'

Nowadays, water is rarely restricted on the ship, other than in foreign ports – such as Dar es Salaam – where the quality of the local water is either unknown or risky.

Toilets are another necessity. They work on a vacuum system and are flushed using fresh water to avoid any build-up of potentially lethal hydrogen sulphide gas. Many sailors have fallen victim to gas poisoning over the years, so the sewage collection, holding and treatment compartment in the bowels of the ship is fitted with hydrogen sulphide monitors.

Outside the twelve nautical mile (twenty-two-kilometre) territorial limit, the ship can purge the treated contents of the tank into the ocean, but in port the sewage must be stored and pumped into either the local sewerage system or a truck. Two hundred and twenty-eight people generate a large amount of waste so the tank needs to be purged every two or three days. In case the vacuum pumps fail there are three standard gravity-fed flush toilets on board for emergency use.

Toilet blockages are a major issue for Sims and his maintainers.

'The pipework itself is only 50 mm in diameter so we do get blockages where we have to pull pipework apart and unblock them just to get the system back up and running again,' he says.

Preventing the need for this unpleasant job involves education. Newcomers in particular learn that a 50 mm pipe cannot handle what a 150 mm pipe back at home can deal with. Having the guilty party assist with the unblocking process usually ensures there is no repeat offence.

Day in and day out, a warship's company is kept on its toes by a rigorous training regime. They train as if their lives depend on it, because one day they might. Barely a day goes by when the chiefs are not putting sailors through their paces on fire-fighting, toxic hazard or some other emergency aspect of the ship's safe operation. From damage-control teams to weapons-systems operators, every person on board must be ready to act and respond at a moment's notice. Well-drilled emergency responses are vital in a lone floating steel box thousands of kilometres from land with thousands of metres of water below.

The senior sailors – the Chief Petty Officers – and their bosses, the XO and CO, take a dim view of poor performance and often order a repeat performance until the job is right.

For Sims' boss, the Marine Engineering Officer, Lieutenant Commander Trevor Henderson, the *Darwin* deployment was his first on a guided missile frigate and the culmination of a forty-two-year naval career. His only regret was that he did not make the move sooner – Henderson has served on numerous navy ships but regards *Darwin* as the best in the fleet.

'If it's not the best then we must be number two but I think we're the best,' he says proudly.

He jumped at the chance to 'have a drive' on a frigate as the chief engineer before his planned retirement to a beach house on the New South Wales south coast in 2018. 'That would be a good way to finish my career and I've loved it. The fraternity is very tight, senior sailors and junior sailors – very, very tight. It didn't take me long to pick that up. Even though I'm an engineer I had to listen to what they've got to say and I've listened and taken it on board.'

The navy has been like a second family for Henderson, who comes from an Indigenous background and was raised in a tough neighbourhood in the Canterbury-Bankstown area of Sydney. 'I knew that I needed to get out and away from certain people otherwise I'd probably be in jail or worse. I could see that coming, I could feel it.'

For the troubled teenager the navy offered stability, training and a job.

'I thought it was the greatest adventure of my life joining the navy and I still do,' he says. 'Instead of being in trouble and going down a wrong path I was with good people.'

He trained first as a shipwright at the navy's old apprenticeship school at HMAS *Nirimba* west of Sydney, starting in January 1976. It was a different navy in those days.

'When they said "two-minute showers" they meant two-minute showers otherwise you suffered the consequences, you know, physically, and that's just the way it was,' he says. 'I just followed the rules and that meant leading seamen really dominated. You never spoke to warrant officers in particular and chiefs were like gods.'

Henderson, who mixes comfortably across all ranks, thinks the modern navy has become a little bit too 'touchy feely' and the lines between friendship and discipline have become blurred. 'In those days [when he joined] there was a very clear rank structure and I enjoyed it. I was used to that way.'

The structures and routines of navy life, along with his wife of thirty years, Rhonda, also helped him overcome one of his biggest personal problems by giving up alcohol. His marriage was in trouble due to the grog and he was staying with his dad when he told his father that the beers they were enjoying would be his last.

'He said, "You won't last," and I said something very colourful like, "We'll fucking see," and it's only been twenty years since I have had a drink,' Henderson says. 'When I joined up drinking was part and parcel, and one reason I wanted to become a PO [Petty Officer] so quickly was because you could drink during the day as a senior sailor. That was part of the deal – you could go in at lunchtime, stand easy and have a beer. I was a pretty heavy drinker and it does impact and it does impede you. I think it's better that we've got rid of that culture.'

In 2008 Henderson was serving as Senior Marine Technician Warrant Officer on the former amphibious ship HMAS *Manoora* when he decided to move to what sailors like to call the 'dark side' by joining the ranks of commissioned officers. The final straw that pushed him across to the officer corps was the navy's $80,000 retention bonus offer that was given only to chiefs and leading seamen but not warrant officers. 'They still wanted us to do the job and I said, "I'm over this, I'm out of here."'

His first sea posting as an officer was on board the navy's notorious 'sex ship of shame' HMAS *Success*, after she had been the subject of numerous media exposés and a bruising public inquiry. The navy wanted a core of older, more mature officers and sailors on the ship to implement the cultural change required following the scandals.

'We had a new team, new purpose, new focus you know, and I enjoyed my time on *Success*,' he says.

'Goonga' Sims would certainly be regarded as a fully qualified member of the 'tight' guided missile frigate community that Trevor Henderson encountered when he joined *Darwin*. A laconic and good-humoured sailor, Sims has been in the navy for twenty-nine years and has spent almost twenty-two of those away at sea on board frigates. The 2016 deployment in *Darwin* was his fourth to the Middle East. His first was in *Melbourne* and he remembers when the ship was in Bahrain to protect the ABOT oil terminal on the day Saddam Hussein was captured. In the early days he was also a 'boardo'. Sims was rewarded for his outstanding service with a Conspicuous Service Medal (CSM) in the 2017 Queen's Birthday honours.

One of the biggest changes he has noticed is the boost that comes from being almost always in touch with loved ones at home in the modern age of Wi-Fi and satellite communications. Back in 2003, sailors in the Gulf were allowed just two phone calls home in the entire six months.

'We were actually gone over Christmas and the calls had to be restricted to five minutes,' he recalls. 'You try and talk to your wife and two kids in five minutes when you're at sea. It's really hard to try and fit everything in.'

Being a 'chippy' is one of the most diverse and essential roles in the senior service. On top of fresh water and sewage, Sims says other regular problem areas are the doors and hatches, especially when the ship is at sea and closed down to 'readiness state Yankee'. That involves keeping all of the hatches and doors from 'two deck' (which contains the galley, the café, the chiefs' accommodation and other working spaces) and below closed to maintain water and gas-tight integrity. This means they must be opened and closed each time crew move about the ship, generating high levels of wear and tear.

Other things that require regular repairs include bunks, latches, hinges, showers, taps and sinks. The fire-fighting main and cooling lines use salt water so they are always corroding and in a thirty-two-year-old ship pinholes frequently appear and must be repaired. During the 2016 deployment a tiny leak was discovered in the cooling line to a mission-critical radar.

'We had to pull out the old degraded pipework and manufacture new elbows and pipework to get it back up and running,' says Sims. 'When we've got defects like that it's all hands on deck until the job's finished.'

It takes a special group of cooks to bake vast platters of sweet and savoury pastry scrolls and sticky buns to top up the post-dinner crowd at a charity auction on a navy frigate. For Petty Officer Maritime Logistics Chef Rob Bateman and his team of 'chefos', the bake-up for an auction in May 2016 is their contribution to a successful fundraising effort.

Fitting the task into their frantic schedule of providing 228 hungry sailors with four hot, tasty meals every day for seven months is no mean feat. The wiry and full-bearded Bateman and his seven-person team prepare, cook and clean up after more than 125,000 meals during the deployment – not including 'mornos' (morning tea) and 'arvos' (afternoon tea).

Despite the uncharitable moniker of 'tucker fuckers', navy cooks play a vital role.

'Full bellies are happy bellies,' says Bateman.

He is not only the petty officer chef but also the senior caterer and line manager of the two leading seamen and five able seamen who staff the galley. The leading seamen, or 'killicks', cook and look after the galley and the stores while the more junior seamen cook, clean and man the galley and serving line. One is always rostered on as night chef to bake fresh bread and create desserts and salads for the next day.

They also cater for special occasions and VIP events such as cocktail parties where the canapés can vary from party pies to crocodile croquettes, mini pavlovas and chocolate mud cake. There are 'steel deck' barbecues where 200 steaks, 300 sausages and 100 chicken kebabs as well as salads, coleslaw and dessert are served on the steel flight deck at the stern of the ship – a long way from the galley and its larders and pantries two decks below. And they keep the hard-working boarding parties sustained with toasted sandwiches and other goodies at all hours of the day and night.

A week's typical meals includes roast lamb and veg, spicy pasta and apricot crumble, peri-peri chicken, stir fry, beef vindaloo, chicken cacciatore, crumbed snapper, rump steak, beef rissoles, creamy bacon pasta, teriyaki chicken, cheeseburgers, spaghetti and meatballs, and many more. All meals are served with vegetables, the salad bar is always open and a variety of freshly made desserts, from cakes and custard to fruit salad and jelly, are available.

Another highlight is the ever-popular soft-serve ice-cream machine. Newcomers soon find out that going hard and early is the best ice-cream strategy because the machine does run dry.

'You could leave that on 24/7 and no one would complain, I'm pretty sure,' says Bateman.

A conscientious country boy from Dalby in Queensland, he joined the navy when it became apparent that the family farm would be unable to support him. There was a drought, so he virtually went straight from Year 12 at Dalby High School to the navy's recruit school at HMAS *Cerberus* in Victoria.

He qualified first as an electronics technician, but after a stint in the galley he re-trained as a chefo. 'I love being a cook. I've got to be on the go constantly, I can't sit dormant for too long, so catering and being a cook seemed like the perfect set up for me.'

The father of two school-aged children has been at sea for more than ten of his fourteen years in the navy and the 2016 deployment in *Darwin* is his second to the Middle East. His family lives in Cairns where his wife works as a nurse. They moved north after he was posted to *Cerberus* for three years as an instructor teaching 'baby chefos' their trade.

The chefs' biggest job is trying to keep everybody happy and healthy for up to thirty-eight days at sea with a limited supply of fresh, frozen or canned foodstuffs. The cooks work off a six-week cyclic menu set by the chef with the ship's doctor, and each cook can see what is coming up on the card and create their meals accordingly. One of their biggest pressures is maintaining a high level of food excellence in cramped and often tough conditions.

'It's an extremely hot environment in the galley and you are on your feet the whole time and it's day after day after day,' says Bateman. 'It is a relentless job and it can be a thankless job. We're very, very fortunate on this ship that the crew is very grateful for what my guys produce along the line, so that's been a breath of fresh air and that can make or break a deployment for the chefos.'

There are usually four able seaman cooks on duty from 6 a.m. until about 9 p.m. One preps for the next day, one cooks the next meal, one makes salads and desserts and cleans up in the scullery and the fourth assists the stores 'killick' with supplies and works as a general hand. They might get a break around 3 p.m. for an hour or two, but otherwise are on their feet in their sweatbox deep in the bowels of the ship where the low stainless steel ceiling and walls keep the heat locked in. The fifth cook's night shift starts around 6 p.m. and goes through until 7 a.m., baking about thirty loaves of bread and other specialist baked products.

In the unlikely event that the cooks get bored, there are constant cleaning jobs to ensure that all food and preparation areas are spotless. An outbreak of food poisoning would be a disaster, and Rob Bateman and his galley 'killick' are responsible for maintaining the standards.

'If you [have food poisoning] the crew loses faith in you and you've got to rebuild the reputation that you've built up,' he says. 'That's the worst thing that could happen to a chefo and his team so we stay on top of personal hygiene and galley hygiene and make sure we are adhering to our food safety plan.'

The 'killick' is the linchpin for hygiene and drives all aspects of galley life from peeling spuds to whipping up a chocolate mousse and washing the dishes.

'He'll make sure everything is up to scratch,' Bateman says. 'I come in as the overseer or quality controller before the meal goes through. I'll taste everything, make sure it's all visually appealing as well as tasting good and then we open those shutters and the hordes come through.'

The stores killick monitors stock levels, rotates stock and assists with the ordering. Few people have access to the dry store and the freezers located one deck below the galley. Says Bateman, 'That is so we don't have our Tim Tams go missing or people think, "Oh I'll just grab extra milk," because there's only so much stock we can carry on board so we have to calculate it.'

Supplies are never completely exhausted as the ship must have an emergency food supply in case it has to 'crash sail' or extend a mission at sea and cannot be resupplied.

Waste food is processed in a large unit known as the 'Egor' and pumped into the sea when the ship is more than twelve nautical miles offshore. All other rubbish is sorted and stored until the ship docks in port.

Bateman sets high standards and aims to train his cooks to become better than he is. He also allows them to extend themselves with favourite dishes. 'Our resident Russian, Dennis, has got some amazing dumplings and some dishes that are traditional for him that he thoroughly enjoys making. So when it's possible I'll say, "Okay, sweet, make your whatever-your-dish-is." We've got people who love making curries so it's, "Right, here's all your stuff, make the curry, make it however you want, as long as it tastes good, it's good to go." All they've got to do is put up their hand and say, "I'd really love to try to make this." "Absolutely, go for it." Or if we don't have the stores for it we can't necessarily make it.'

Where they can really show their creative flair is when VIPs and dignitaries come on board for cocktail parties and CO's luncheons. 'It's fine dining, it's dress it up, be as creative as you want, make art on a plate basically and send it up. Because you're working with small numbers of, say, five people for a CO's luncheon, you can put all your effort into it and make something that really jumps off the plate.'

All the skills of the galley would be on display later, after the ship docked in Victoria Harbour, Mahe Island in the Seychelles, when the CO co-hosted a cocktail party with Mauritius-based Australian High Commissioner Susan Coles on the flight deck.

The VIP guests were treated to *Darwin*'s unique version of a 'sunset guard' ceremony complete with a performance by the resident indigenous dance troupe. Under a starlit sky with the Southern Cross blazing above the guests, including many who were in town for a major piracy conference, they consumed kangaroo sliders and crocodile croquettes washed down with cold beer and Aussie wines as the painted dancers and the ship's formal guard strutted their stuff.

Among the crew these events are known as 'cake and arse' parties and there is a usually a rush to try and avoid having to serve as waiters or waitresses or don formal uniform and make small talk with VIPs. However, for the guests they are a unique and memorable sample of far-away Australian culture.

The Maritime Logistics Officer, or 'pusser', Lieutenant Commander Chris Duke, is the power behind the throne. The pusser, which is navy slang for a warship's purser and translates to many as 'punching bag', supplies everything from peas and pens to pumps and potatoes, apart from weapons. Duke and his stores team even supply and maintain spare parts for the ship's helicopter.

Duke was born in the UK and comes from a long line of navy men, both his father and brother having served in the Royal Navy. He joined the RAN as a clerk in 1991, three years after the family moved to Australia. Fourteen years later he transferred to the officer stream.

His is a lengthy association with *Darwin* because he first joined the ship as an able seaman in 1993. He did two further tours on board including one as deputy supply officer before his latest posting as the boss, looking after the supply, personnel administration, chefs and steward departments. The dry-witted father of one son takes great pride in keeping the frigate in tip-top fighting condition.

Duke cops a lot of good natured flak from his shipmates in the wardroom, but the reason *Darwin* is a happy ship is due in large part to his hard work and diligence.

Operating a long way from home and in some exotic locations throws up unique problems. His job is made easier by a shore-based team of RAN supply and logistics experts led by Operation Manitou's Maritime Logistics Officer, Lieutenant Commander Neil Krauklis. Based at the Australian headquarters in Al Minhad Air Base, Krauklis and his team travel ahead of the ship to the next port to ensure that everything from a berth to fuel and fresh food and water are ready for ship's arrival.

One of the most complex methods of resupply is the replenishment at sea. While used mainly to resupply the ship with fuel and water, it can also be an opportunity for Duke to land extra supplies, transferred either directly or using the ship's chopper for a vertical replenishment, known as VERTREP.

'It's a fine art because you've got to take into account how long it will take to get it from where it's boxed and packed out to the ship, and then from the ship to us. You may lose about ten days' endurance with that, so you have to calculate the risk that by the time it gets to me – within twelve to fifteen days – I will be putting a lot of it in the bin,' Duke says.

He also manages the food budget – a strict $2 a person per meal. That is $1380 a day or $250,000 for food alone for the six-month deployment, so the type of food is driven by the budget and time left at sea. Yet his biggest challenge is not food but sourcing the spare parts required to keep the ageing American-built warship operating.

As the ship approaches a port, the list of new supplies grows and Duke's stress level rises accordingly. Thanks to the internet and satellite phones he knows what to expect at the wharf. The navy's sustainment system is reliable and internal supplies can be tracked electronically all along the chain.

Once loaded onto the ship, supplies become the responsibility of the 'storbys'. The six-person team, run by Chief Petty Officer

Colin Benbow and his deputy, Alex Rossi, manages a stores system that supports all of the ship's departments, from electrical to medical, and holds some 35,000 individual items in crowded compartments in the bowels of the vessel.

Stocktaking is done manually so attention to detail is vital.

Rossi says that the need to prioritise often results in conflict between engineering and aviation – the two areas with the most time- and mission-sensitive demands for spare parts.

'Funding is a big part of that,' he says. 'For example, is it priority one or priority three? And do we get it overnight by DHL and spend $20,000 to move a $500 piece of equipment, or go through the sustainment process and have it filtered down to us at a minimal cost?'

In the end, those decisions are above the team's pay grade. Final judgements are made by Duke with the skipper, the headquarters of Task Force 633, and Joint Operations Command back in Australia.

Like everyone else in the warship the storbys have ancillary duties that take them away from the stores department. It might be as a bowman on the RHIB for a boarding or a lineman in the fire-fighting department – for example, as a fire fighter, Able Seaman Louis Mahutariko must do at least an hour's training each day and is on stand-by away from his job during operations such as replenishments or refuelling.

Compliance is another major challenge. Alex Rossi says new rules have seen the administrative workload doubled in the past few years. 'It's always a juggling act, but we do the best we can and it's easier for us now that the tempo is constant. The twelve months leading up to deployment is probably our busiest time.'

Benbow, a jolly and rotund chief who hand-embroidered a detailed cross-stitch image of HMAS *Darwin* for his wife during his downtime on the ship, keeps close tabs on who is buying what. Once a ship is being deployed the gloves come off with regards to replacing stores – especially for the engineering department.

'There's probably 10,000 line items that we [now] have to buy,' he says. 'But our budget did not increase. That includes stationery, cleaning gear, tools, parts, paint, all those things.'

Deciding what they can and cannot afford is a difficult balancing act. 'In the twelve months leading up to the deployment we have a lot of arguments,' he says. 'They like to go for the highest quality, which is good, but with our budget we have to do the sanity check. We get audited on the compliance side of the paperwork. Anything with a financial value has to be correct, otherwise you are held accountable.'

Benbow applies a simple test. 'Okay, what is it actually required for? You don't need to build a car from scratch so I don't need to buy you the tools to build you a car from scratch. We'll get you the tools and the amount of sets that you need.'

This hard-line approach can lead to conflict. Despite his laid-back demeanour the bespectacled Benbow admits to going 'nose to nose' with some angry sailors who reacted badly to some of his purchasing decisions, but he sticks to his guns. 'I've had some roaring matches with some but I can be as pigheaded as they can.'

14

Beating the blues

With their two previous patrols yielding no drugs or weapons, the crew of HMAS *Darwin* are desperate for a change of luck in May 2016 as they set off to chase heroin smugglers coming down the smack track. The woes of these recent empty-handed patrols have been compounded by the ship's early departure from Dar es Salaam.

Military life is characterised by long periods of mind-numbing boredom broken by moments of sheer terror or adrenaline-pumping action. Maintaining high morale, especially during the quiet times, is vital to the success of any naval deployment and requires constant vigilance by commanders.

In all other ports visited during their 2016 six-month deployment, *Darwin*'s crew were allowed to leave the ship, check into a nice hotel, enjoy a fresh meal and a hot shower and even have a cold beer or two. After two to four weeks at sea sharing ablutions with shipmates, sleeping in a 'rack' no bigger than a coffin and lining up and eating meals alongside dozens of other sailors, the simple act of donning civilian clothes or civvies and leaving for a night or two ashore really lifts the spirits.

Adding to the frustrations is the sacking of two shipmates who had broken the strict rules on alcohol consumption while ashore in Dar es Salaam. Sending sailors home under a disciplinary cloud is not just disappointing. It also generates extra work for others until replacements arrive and it can severely disrupt plans for such things as leave. The offenders blew well above .05 after spending their shore leave propping up a bar. Under the strict and well-understood rules regarding alcohol, their deployments were cut short and they were sent home via the Australian Middle East headquarters.

For centuries, many of those who go down to the sea in ships have had a tricky relationship with alcohol. Traditionally, seafarers are renowned as hard drinkers and brawlers; those in uniform are no different. While consumption and fist fighting have been toned down in recent years in line with community attitudes, asking 228 young Australian men and women who have been locked in a 138-metre-long tin can with their mates for weeks on end to confine their shore time to visiting shopping malls, art galleries, museums and tea rooms is unrealistic.

Except during 'warlike' operations, when booze is banned altogether on RAN ships, alcohol is permitted on board at the discretion of the CO. When allowed, the strict limit is two cans – equal to three standard drinks – per person per day and a blood alcohol limit of .05 is enforced. The beer ration is strictly supervised by the Naval Police Coxswain.

For those commencing duty the limit is .02. This restriction also applies onshore in ports such as Singapore on the way home when, for off-duty sailors, the .05 limit no longer applies. The reason for the on-duty limitation is simple – the ship may need to 'crash sail' at short notice and the crew must be ready and able to do their jobs.

Random drug and alcohol tests are conducted throughout each deployment. Commander Phill Henry says the key is responsibility. All Australian Defence Force personnel deployed to the region are paid their salary tax-free for the duration, and on top of that they receive a tax-free 'non-warlike' deployment allowance of $83.75 a day. They are also well aware of the rules and the cultural sensitivities regarding alcohol in Muslim countries.

'All of us knew those requirements before we sailed,' says Henry. 'The days of sailors going completely mad and being renowned for the amount of alcohol they drink are gone. Society's expectations have changed. The expectation of the Australian public is that we are up here representing Australia so you can't come up here and behave like you might do on a Friday night in Sydney.'

Even when the ship has 'out chopped' from the operation and docks in a lively port such as Singapore on the way home, the crew are not just tourists. 'You're there representing Australia, the Australian Defence Force and the Royal Australian Navy so the expectations of behaviour are above that of a tourist. I think really the Australian public would expect us to behave appropriately, but yeah, they can go and have a few.'

Before each port visit the ship runs a compulsory 'visit liaison brief' where the visit liaison officer outlines the highlights and risks associated with that particular port. As well as the best restaurants and dive spots, the briefing focuses on medical risks such as malaria, and the cultural, social and political sensitivities including dangers such as terrorism. They give reminders about the alcohol and drug restrictions, places to avoid and force-protection issues. In addition, the CO makes a general broadcast or 'pipe' to the ship's company before the ship docks to remind everyone of their responsibilities.

Making the recommendation to send the two sailors home is one of those unpleasant decisions that falls to the skipper. Henry admits it has been an emotional time for all on board.

'I've known both of those gentlemen since I joined the ship and developed a close working relationship with them,' he says. 'Would I have wanted them to have stayed? Naturally, because they are very professional, but the rules are there and you can't say, "Well, look you're doing a great job so I'll keep you." The moment that I don't return them to Australia or recommend to return them to Australia then I'm condoning their actions that were in clear breach of our regulations. Dealing with them was difficult – but there are so many other things also regarding welfare issues for crew when you're deployed [that] I think over the years I've mentally prepared myself, but it never gets any easier.'

The ship's Chaplain, Richard Quadrio, sees a lot and hears plenty of home truths. Unlike in the army and air force, navy chaplains – or 'sin bosuns' in navy slang – do not hold a rank and therefore assume the rank of the person they are talking to. Unlike other officers, Chaplain Quadrio can also sit down and eat with the junior sailors in their café, and he does that most nights in *Darwin*. He also spends time dishing up meals to the sailors from the galley servery.

'Every night I sit there and listen to them as we eat dinner … and they always know that they can say stuff to me that's confidential,' Quadrio says. 'I don't have to report them or what they say, but the gist of things I can pass on.'

Phill Henry and XO Tina Brown also spend several shifts in the galley servery and scullery spooning out food, washing dishes and chatting with sailors to stay plugged in to what is going on.

Quadrio might live in the wardroom but he regards his lack of rank as a blessing. He says army and RAAF chaplains, who hold particular ranks, can cop it from both ends because those above them can dismiss them and those below are too wary to speak up.

'To put it bluntly, my career is not on the line. So if necessary I can say some things that are maybe not as popular,' he says. 'Command doesn't want to hear that everything is fine. They want to hear the truth – because then they can manage it, they can alleviate it and they can work around it. Sometimes they agree, sometimes they don't.'

The former Presbyterian minister from Eastwood in Sydney joined the navy late in life after serving for twenty-five years in the ministry that included establishing a chaplaincy at the Easts Rugby Club. Married with three children, he and his wife, Wendy, a schoolteacher, decided that age fifty-two was not too old for such a dramatic career change.

'I went off to the New Entry Officers' Course for six months with a whole bunch of twenty-year-olds,' he says. 'That was a fascinating experience because I was the peer of a bunch of people my kids' age! It was hard work but it was good and I passed, so I got through it.'

His experience was forged during a two-year posting to the patrol boat fleet in Darwin, at the tail end of the high-tempo counter-people-smuggling Operation Resolute. That was the busiest period in history for the Armidale Class patrol boats, when 40,000 asylum seekers attempted the perilous sea journey from Asia to Australia.

'It was very challenging for [the sailors] because they had to deal with psychological trauma dealing with death,' he says. 'But then they also had cultural challenges, moral challenges. They tried to get women and children on first – and the men would fight that and wanted to get on themselves. That is the sort of moral challenge they had to face.'

Quadrio says the rate of post-traumatic stress disorder (PTSD) among sailors from Operation Resolute is much higher than for operations in the Middle East. 'There were periods when they were taking bodies out of the water and as they were taking them out limbs were falling off. I had a young fellow on board one of the patrol boats and he said to me, "You know, the one big problem I have after all this is I can't go to the movies." I said, "You can't go to the movies, what's that about?"

'He said that on one of the patrol boats they had a couple of deceased people in bags that leaked and the smell went right through the ship – imagine how terrible that was – so to mask the smell they'd make popcorn and now he can't go to the movies because the popcorn smell just overwhelms him and brings back all that memory.'

Quadrio's time in *Darwin* is mainly taken up with matters such as homesickness, relationship breakdowns, troubled children and other family issues.

'The chaplain's role is an unusual one and it's an historical accident in some sense,' he says. 'But one of the important things is, I have absolutely no role anywhere in command – I'm never allowed to command anything. I do assist command but my primary job is to assist the sailors and officers.'

Whether the problem is the standard of food, number of days at sea, lack of a proper shore leave or a drama at home, the skipper hears the gripes warts and all from Quadrio, who says that judging morale is an inexact science. He might talk to four sailors who tell him they are having the worst day 'in the history of the ship' while another four say they are having the best day.

Commander Bill Waters, a four-tour veteran of the Middle East who skippered *Melbourne* during the ship's deployment in 2015, says morale was a critical management issue during patrols that lasted up to thirty-eight days between port visits. Two important components were keeping lines of communication open between himself and his crew, and maintaining everyone's physical fitness.

Just like Australian soldiers in remote operating bases in Afghanistan, who spent hours pumping iron and consuming vast quantities of protein supplements to build their bodies and overcome boredom, navy sailors kill a lot of time honing their six packs or pounding the deck or the exercise bike. The ship's gym is one of the busiest places on board. In fact, almost any spare deck space on a crowded warship is used for physical activities ranging from yoga to weights and circuit work.

Sunday sea days are also critical to morale. On those days the crew can relax, play deck games, have a barbecue and even try their luck at fishing if speed can be reduced enough for a lure cast over the stern to stay in the water.

During *Melbourne*'s seven-month deployment Waters was determined that everyone who was able to achieve their next qualification would do so. Training has played an important role in his life ever since the time he learnt to sail and race yachts. His father was in the Royal Navy, and the boy from Box Hill in Melbourne was destined to follow in the footsteps of his dad and his maternal ancestors who also served at sea.

'My father was at one stage an amateur professional yachtsman and so I got a love of being at sea from him and I grew up in boats,' he says.

Waters competed in several Sydney to Hobart ocean races, and after joining the navy he was sent to the UK to represent the navy in yacht racing. That, however, was a one-off and the ADFA graduate and young seaman officer was soon at sea in a markedly different environment.

After some initial resistance to his idea for improving crew qualifications, he says the momentum in *Melbourne* built a head of steam. People were soon training those below them and 'learning upwards' at the same time. 'That meant there was a constant flow of training going on, which was very successful and that kept them focusing.'

Another strategy was to challenge each of the 240 people on board to achieve a personal goal. 'I really didn't care what that was as long as it was legal, appropriate and ethical.'

Personal fitness dominated, but some learnt a language or a musical instrument and others even undertook cooking classes. Fortunately, alcohol was not a major problem and just one sailor was sent home early for blowing over the limit.

Chaplain Quadrio loves the fact that he doesn't have a formal workspace on board the ship.

'If I'm sitting at a computer and a chief walks past me and I say to him "How's the new pup [baby]?" because I know they've got a pup [and] his son's got some issues, the conversation turns out to be a forty-five-minute conversation about his concerns,' he says.

He is also amazed by the capacity of young sailors to spend money. Retail therapy during port visits is a huge spirit booster. One junior rating purchased a $3000 rug in Bahrain, while a leading seaman parted with $13,500 for a Rolex watch. During a charity auction on night eleven of *Darwin*'s fourth patrol in the southern Indian Ocean, $14,000 was raised from the sale of seventeen sporting items, including $3000 for a NSW Blues rugby league jersey. The atmosphere in the junior sailors' café was electric as each bidder was urged on to greater heights with comments about everything from their favourite team's honour to their manhood. Richard Quadrio simply shook his head and laughed along with his competitive shipmates.

Phill Henry rates the incredible depth of support from home as a key ingredient of good morale – from RSL care packages to Jan-Maree Ball's 'Aussie Hero Quilts' campaign, where teams of people make quilts for deployed defence personnel. Henry himself has a quilt on his rack featuring his beloved All Blacks rugby team, and there are some 110 quilts and hand-stitched laundry bags on board the ship. A dozen of the quilt-makers would later be on the wharf at Garden Island to welcome *Darwin* home.

A helping hand for families left at home is also important, particularly when a parent with children has to juggle family life alone for seven months. 'About two weeks out, you notice that the family starts to switch off to dad or mum,' Henry says. 'The walls go up around emotions and you try to avoid conflict – it is tough.'

There is nothing worse than a sailor calling home, only to be told about a long list of problems that he or she is powerless to fix. The navy and the defence force have support networks in place, but such factors can still have a profound impact on navy personnel at sea.

'We can't do it without the friends and families and the people back home,' Henry says.

Social media is a double-edged sword at sea because it can generate operational security problems and feed personal anxieties. The ship runs a Facebook page that relays information and receives messages of support, which can be a big boost to the spirits.

'When we did our weapons seizure early on, within the space of a couple of days there was a couple of thousand "likes" and "comments" about what we did and to be able to relay to the crew some of those messages of support from home is just fantastic,' Henry says.

But XO Tina Brown had an unpleasant social media experience after the ship's departure from Sydney. An image on Facebook of Brown with her husband Ken, two-year-old son Mason and Prime Minister Malcolm Turnbull generated some nasty and unfair 'trolling' about her suitability as a mother.

Comments on the Prime Minister's Facebook page such as: 'Where are your mothering instincts? That poor baby boy! Won't her husband have fun! Why would you even have children if you knew you were going away in a job like this?' were upsetting when she was asking herself some of the same questions.

'It hit a little bit of a sore spot,' she admits. 'It was tough because every other experience I have had with the navy, I have never felt anything but pride from the public.'

Everyone employs different methods to cope with the inevitable down times during a long stint at sea and for Tina Brown that can be a simple flick through family photos on her phone or laptop.

'The best way for me to overcome it is not to ignore it and to acknowledge how I am feeling and to always think about the light at the end of the tunnel and dream of the reunion and the next posting that may be a bit less busy,' she says. 'I really do love my job, and you can justify being away from your family when you love your job and believe in it and the job is extremely busy and is a legitimate distraction. Men have been doing this for a very long time and miss their families as well.'

Women in the navy do have different challenges, the most obvious one being children. Tina Brown finds herself mentoring younger officers and sailors on both a professional and personal level, and many of the personal conversations centre on children.

'I have felt well supported every step of the way,' she says. 'There was no pressure and they [the navy] revisited me when I was ready. I wasn't punished or put behind my classmates due to my maternity leave.'

She does not feel any great pressure from being a female in what was traditionally a very male dominated job, but there are still some expectations. 'There is always the expectation that as the senior female you have to be beyond reproach with everything whether it be your technical mastery of whatever job you are in, or even just behaviour and appearance. Had you asked someone in this position ten years ago they might have felt more pressure than I do.'

A bigger pressure on military families is the need for flexible working hours. For example, her husband Ken is working ashore so that he can care for Mason, but this comes at a cost known as the 'flexibility stigma'.

'He sometimes feels hamstrung because he can't leave Mason and travel interstate for a course,' she says.

The couple spent ten months apart in 2016, and 2017 is looking little better. Fortunately, Ken is a couple of years behind her in the navy's warfare stream. If they were at the same level they would probably both be offered postings at the same time and so one of them would have to sacrifice it in order to take care of Mason. So far, both have been able to keep their careers progressing.

'We have been doing it for quite a while and we are good at communicating. The navy has also helped with leave when possible.'

*

Social media and phone communications are shut down during boardings or other operations – code-named as particular designated 'states' – and that can be a difficult time for crew and families. Other designated states on board a warship refer to various equipment and systems such as 'going black' to shadow a target, which means no lights; 'emcon silent', which means no radar or other emissions for maximum stealth; and 'ultra-quiet' when everything is shut down and all on board remain still for a minefield transit.

Henry's predecessor as CO of *Darwin*, Commander Terry Morrison, says he had first-hand experience of communication shut-downs. 'I had people saying to me, "Oh it's terrible, we don't know if we're coming or going."'

To ward off any strife, Morrison always sent out a pre-formatted email to the families. 'I basically just said, "Look, we're all safe, everyone is safe, everyone is fine but we just need to shut our communications down for the time being because we're going into an operation." Part of it is because of the bandwidth requirement – there will be a lot of data going back and forth – so we can't let someone go on Skype. I have to send back photos of the boarding as well.'

But the main reason is to maintain operational security. 'We don't want the information going to people ashore about something that we're currently trying to wade through methodically,' says Morrison. 'Don't jump at shadows, don't start sending out to people that we've got these narcotics. I need to control that, and also where we are, and all that sort of thing. It's all sensitive. It's all part of our tactics not to give that away.'

The biggest morale setback for *Darwin* during her 2016 deployment would occur after the May patrol, with the tragic death of leading seaman chef Cameron Acreman, twenty-seven, in a hotel room in Muscat, Oman, in June.

It was a crushing blow. Everyone on board knew the popular and outgoing sailor, a chefo 'killick', who kept his shipmates entertained with his lively banter during meal times and beyond. His death affected the ship deeply. He had been *Darwin*'s 'sailor of the quarter' in May 2016 for his 'professionalism, sense of humour and willingness to go the extra mile'. He also beat Chief Petty Officer and Country Women's Association member Joy Newman in a charity scone bake-off in front of a large, hungry crowd in the galley.

For Henry and Quadrio, Cameron Acreman's sudden death was a particularly dark time. Both men left the ship when it arrived in *Darwin* to attend his funeral in Queensland.

'Meeting Cameron's parents Terry and Heather was one of the toughest things that I have ever done,' says Henry.

15

Birdies

It is 19 May and the huge weapons haul of 27 February feels as if it happened a long time ago. Day three of the new two-week patrol dawns fine and sunny with a rising sea state as *Darwin* steams northeast away from Africa inside her patrol box. It proves to be quite an eventful day.

The ship's helicopter, Orko, is airborne and scanning the ocean for smugglers, while the skipper and senior officers make final plans for the replenishment at sea later in the morning, when we will take on aviation fuel from the German navy tanker FSG *Spessart*.

After I have breakfast in the wardroom and chat with XO Tina Brown about the strains a navy career places on family life, it's time to head to the hangar for a visit with helicopter maintenance boss, or 'birdy', Chief Petty Officer Nathan Blanch.

At 8 a.m. we are walking along the main passageway – called The Esplanade after the city of *Darwin*'s main drag – that runs from the ship's 'waist' to the flight deck at the stern. (The waist is the centre of a guided missile frigate, which viewed from above curves inwards like the human waistline.) We have just reached the hangar door when all hell breaks loose. The emergency call 'Pan Pan Pan' erupts over the intercom, or 'pipe'. This is not an exercise. The mood on board switches instantly to 'game on' as the ship's company hurries to their emergency stations. For the visitor, that means quickly getting out of the way and cramming into the back of the Helicopter Control Officer shack attached to the superstructure above and at the front of the flight deck, for a bird's eye view of the action.

The reason for the emergency is that a 'chip indicator' on the Sikorsky Seahawk has caused pilot and flight commander Lieutenant Commander Kye Hayman to shut down one of the machine's two turbine engines. The indicator means that there is the threat of foreign matter in the engine oil, which could potentially cause terminal damage to the helicopter's power plant.

The aircraft is about twenty-eight nautical miles (fifty-one kilometres) away from the ship. Its three crew members are Hayman, Aviation Warfare Officer, Lieutenant Clare Nickels, and loadmaster/sensor operator, Leading Seaman Dan Colbert.

The bird has approximately twenty minutes' flying time towards the only possible landing place in a vast ocean, with two- to three-metre waves and strong winds that would normally mean it would be a straightforward landing but today, with one engine down, it could be anything but.

The ship is in full emergency mode as the Seahawk flies into view. The fire-fighting crews are on red alert. All compartments below the flight deck have been cleared in case of a crash landing and a lethal fuel fire that could quickly spread to the decks below.

Landing a chopper on a moving ship in the middle of the ocean is never easy and with a question mark over one engine it becomes even more dangerous. From the control shack it appears to the novice observer that the rolling flight deck is nowhere near big enough to accommodate the rapidly approaching nine-tonne helicopter. It is a nail-biting moment for the inexperienced observer.

While the bird makes its final approach to its floating landing pad, Hayman decides to restart the suspect engine in case he needs the extra burst of power. With its huge rotor blades seemingly just centimetres from the reinforced shack windows the machine appears to grow bigger and bigger, hovering above the deck before finally thudding aboard in a textbook landing.

'If the engine was going to die we'd squeeze whatever life it had left out of it just to help us arrive to the ship,' Hayman tells me later.

Single-engine operations are highly risky at sea because of the large amount of power that the Seahawk requires to hover and land on a flight deck.

'We generally don't like to hover or approach for take-off and landing to a ship with one engine,' he says.

All three members of the crew are visibly shaken but greatly relieved as they set foot on the flight deck and the adrenaline rush begins to fade.

'You do get worked up and a little bit more critical of the aircraft and how the other engine's performing,' Hayman admits. 'It was a great sense of relief to land, shut the aircraft down safely, get the crew back safely and then sit down and have a cup of tea.'

After emerging from the helicopter Clare Nickels declares, 'That was the longest twenty-eight miles of my life.' She later admits to quietly 'freaking out' and wondering how she would escape a sinking helicopter through the small escape window with all her flight gear on, although she felt reassured when the training kicked in and the team calmly went through their checklists and about their business as per the intense training regime. But she says the loss of two crew when an army Black Hawk helicopter crashed off the deck of HMAS *Kanimbla* off Fiji in 2006 flashed through her mind while Orko was flying for those last twenty minutes across the empty ocean back to *Darwin*. The Seahawk and Black Hawk are virtually identical machines but adapted for different jobs, and Nickels is not the only one reflecting on the 2006 disaster. Many of the ship's company are also talking about how choppers sink when they ditch into the sea. They know all too well how quickly the Seahawk would turn upside down and disappear beneath the waves.

All navy helicopter crews dread having to ditch, even though they are trained to escape from a rapidly sinking, inverted chopper. They all undertake an intense helicopter underwater escape training (HUET) course and must renew the qualification every two years. This takes place at a purpose-built facility at naval aviation headquarters at HMAS *Albatross*.

It is because of their top-heavy design that choppers will almost immediately capsize in water. The Seahawk is fitted with emergency floats but no one is confident of their ability to keep the machine on the surface for long. Hayman says that the last thing a crew does before take-off is to talk about emergency procedures and particularly their underwater escape drills. 'The training we conduct at *Albatross* shows that you can get out within a few seconds, all going well.'

Phill Henry is waiting in the hangar to hear first-hand about the incident and to reassure the crew that they have done a good job. After the bird's rotors are folded up and the maintenance crew have wheeled it into the hangar, Hayman briefs his team of 'birdies' to make sure that only correct information runs along the ship's grapevine. Then he retires to the wardroom for a well-earned cuppa.

'It's not a pleasant thing to do to shut one of your two engines down in flight,' he says. 'There's certainly plenty of other aircrew out there in the Seahawk world who have [done it] but it does get the heart racing a little bit. Fortunately, we were relatively close to the ship but the indications we were getting inside the cockpit suggested that the engine probably wasn't performing as well as it should be and once you see those indications you secure the engine.'

Born in Penrith in western Sydney and raised on the Sunshine Coast, the straight-talking Hayman began his career as a trainee army pilot before transferring to the navy. The former Domino's pizza store boss was too tall for the army's Kiowa training helicopters but could fit safely into the navy's Squirrel machines. He lives at Vincentia in Jervis Bay, New South Wales, with his wife Lisa and four children. *Darwin* is his second deployment to the region following a stint on HMAS *Parramatta* in 2010.

A helicopter is a great force multiplier for a navy frigate. The bird is used for a multitude of missions, including its primary role in anti-submarine warfare as well as search and rescue, 'hash and trash' (cargo), vertical replenishment, personnel transfers, offensive overwatch (sitting above a target with weapons at the ready) and hunting smugglers. It can also 'sanitise' (search and clear) vast areas of ocean in a short time.

Orko had replaced an unserviceable helicopter, and before it arrived, *Darwin*'s flying routine had been below par due to maintenance problems with the original machine. 'The previous aircraft was suffering some gremlins that just meant the availability wasn't what it needed to be,' Henry explains. 'So we were averaging probably only about thirty to forty per cent of the sorties due to those maintenance issues.'

There are two complete chopper crews on board the frigate, and typically a surface search mission takes a helicopter no further than 250 kilometres away from the ship. In *Darwin*, Orko generally flew from 5 a.m. to 8 a.m. and again from 10 a.m. until midday to scan the ocean for dhows and other vessels used by smugglers.

While the warship's sensors are effective for close-in search operations against metal vessels, the wooden dhows favoured by smugglers are difficult to detect electronically. The chopper also has powerful electro-optical and infra-red cameras to assist with searching in often rough seas.

The 'mark-one eyeball' (human eye) and powerful binoculars employed by lookouts on board the ships' gun direction platform above the bridge are also effective against close-in targets, but the helicopter extends the ship's 'eyes' out to hundreds of kilometres. It can also hover over suspect vessels to deploy a fast-roping boarding team or conduct detailed intelligence gathering.

On this patrol Phill Henry is able to coordinate his own flying operations with the French frigate *Nivôse* and its helicopter, as well as a French maritime patrol aircraft operating from the islands.

'We're looking at when the maritime patrol aircraft last flew and noting that our predominant smuggler is a wooden dhow doing five to six knots,' he says. 'So if they've sanitised an area then we'd look at when someone might have got through [and] when's the best time to go up again. For instance the French patrol aircraft was flying this morning and it flew yesterday so we won't be flying today.'

Before the engine emergency Henry had planned to have the helicopter airborne for five hours a day during most of the fourteen-day patrol. Soon after leaving Dar es Salaam the chopper was at one hour's notice to fly, but as the patrol wore on, maintenance and crew rest requirements have widened the gap.

'We try and get into a cycle where effectively they fly in the mornings and are finished – not just the pilots but the maintainers and everyone – by mid-afternoon to be ready again for the next morning,' Henry had said when the patrol started. 'We'll be averaging five hours a day on this patrol.'

Unfortunately the Orko's engine problem now causes two full days of flying to be lost.

The daily flying routine includes a briefing at 3 p.m. to outline the next day's mission. Just before take-off, the Principal Warfare Officer and Aviation Warfare Officer meet in the ops room to finalise the plan, based on any new information. The search pattern is planned in advance but can be altered at any time during the flight.

The Seahawk helicopter is a technically advanced fighting machine. The sensor operator ('senso') sits on the left-hand side facing forward to a bank of consoles and screens. He or she also operates the Mag-58 machine gun when necessary. Stepping up through the right-hand door, I perch on the right-hand side across from the senso and immediately behind the pilot for my flight on day ten of the patrol. Beside the pilot in the left-hand front seat sits the Aviation Warfare Officer.

As the machine climbs away from the ship, the vastness of the Indian Ocean soon becomes apparent. Within minutes *Darwin* is out of sight and there is nothing below but white caps and 4000 metres of deep blue sea. After swooping on a couple of legitimate fishing vessels and a demonstration of the chopper's anti-submarine warfare capabilities, it is back to the mother ship for winch drills and the most challenging phase of the flight – the landing.

Soon the heaving deck comes into view through the open side door while the deck crew stand ready to fix the chains that will fasten the machine onto the deck.

At this point I clutch my harness release mechanism as the pre-flight safety briefing runs vividly through his mind. Fortunately, this is a relatively calm day and the landing goes off without a hitch, but that is not always the case. There is some remarkable vision on YouTube featuring navy helicopters landing on ships in impossibly rough seas. As the chopper settles on the steel deck the ground crew give the thumbs up and I can breathe again.

Like most pilots, Kye Hayman is relaxed when he talks about what to non-flyers can sound utterly frightening. Unlike a fixed landing zone on terra firma, the ship can manoeuvre to give the pilot the best possible wind and sea conditions for the take-off and landing under the so-called helicopter operating limits. Depending on the take-off weight of the machine those limits are roughly four to five degrees of pitch and up to fifteen degrees of roll. The officer of the watch will position the ship into the wind, and in addition to finding the dead centre of the rocking flight deck on final approach, the pilot must also place a probe attached to the underside of the machine into a metre-square trap on the deck.

'We basically fly a three- to five-degree approach to the ship as you would approach a runway keeping that landing point fixed in the windscreen and then we move over the deck and we transition from the approach into the hover,' Hayman says.

The pilot then lines the bird up with white painted lines on the ship. When the Aviation Warfare Officer confirms it is in the correct position, the RAST (recover, assist, secure and traverse) probe attached to the helicopter is positioned directly over the trap on the deck of the ship, where it is hooked in. If there is a major problem with the aircraft or if the seas are very rough, there is another riskier method for getting the chopper onto the deck.

'We can lower a messenger cable out through that probe and a cable comes up through the ship, we join them together then raise that cable up and it hooks into the aircraft and we use hydraulic pressure from the ship to bring us down into the trap,' Hayman says.

For all pilots, most of their flying will be ninety per cent routine and ten per cent gut-wrenching fear. Kye Hayman says the take-off and landing phases are the most intense, and he regards night landings in rough weather as the biggest test of all. 'It's one of those things that you wouldn't tell your mother about because she'd go, "What are you doing?" It's excitement and sheer terror all at the same time and when you recover on the ship at night all the crew breathe a sigh of relief that we're here, particularly after a long sortie when you're fatigued.'

Clare Nickels agrees that night operations at sea are the most challenging for the aircrew. 'When you depart at night you can't wear your NVDs [night vision devices] so you have no idea what's around you and you are glared out by all of the lights from the deck. You lift up from the deck, you slide across the deck, you turn away and the pilot has to put the nose down in order to climb, which is not as counter-intuitive as it seems, but basically you've gone from a whole bunch of lights to complete darkness and you have to make sure that you're watching all of the instruments to make sure that you're climbing away. It's nice when you see the radar altimeter climb through about 200 to 500 feet because then you know that you're definitely very clear of the ground.'

Nickels loves the flying part of her job and through a diverse twelve-year navy career it is the flying that has been the highlight. Born in Papua New Guinea and raised on the New South Wales Central Coast, she wanted to join the military from the age of ten when she thought being a civil engineer in the army would be a great job. After completing Year 12 at Gosford High, she went to ADFA in Canberra, but after six months she had a change of heart and switched to direct entry trainee navy pilot. Unfortunately, she failed the pilot's course so she then convinced the navy to allow her to go back to ADFA to complete a science degree, as well as the aviation observer's course.

Her first job was with 723 Squadron, which flies the Squirrel training helicopter, and she deployed to Afghanistan in a ground job for six months. Upon her return she converted to the Seahawk and joined 816 Squadron as an Aviation Warfare Officer, formerly called 'observers' in helicopters.

'We sit in the front left seat of the helicopter and we control the mission,' she says. 'We do have basic piloting skills. I can fly a helicopter, although you probably don't want me to, but I definitely can. We do navigation and radios and things like that and then we control the anti-submarine warfare mission, we control the anti-surface warfare mission using both the sensor operator in the back and getting the pilot to basically fly us around. It's a neat job.'

While admitting to vertigo if she stands on a chair Nickels simply loves the flying aspect of her job. 'You get to see so many different things. I've flown cross-country from Darwin to Nowra going through Broken Hill and then Coober Pedy and across – you wouldn't do that anywhere else.'

Despite her love of flying her next job will be a non-flying position controlling the large flight deck and numerous helicopters on board one of the navy's two new landing helicopter docks.

Between deployments, Nickels plays classical music (viola) and studies graduate law part-time as well as maintaining a keen interest in offbeat TV drama and comedy. On board *Darwin* she is renowned for her knowledge of pop culture and her eclectic collection of TV show boxed sets. Her navy career has traversed some challenging times for the defence force in terms of gender equity and sexual scandals, but Nickels is adamant that while she has experienced some sexism it has never been a major issue for her.

'If you are female in this organisation and say that you haven't experienced it, it's because you've blinded yourself to it deliberately or otherwise, but in twelve years I've seen it improve,' she says. 'I have been I suppose lucky, insofar as I've never been the target of deliberate sexual harassment or anything worse than that, which is good. In my part of the fleet area, the people there have for the most part, I would say, almost entirely treated you the same regardless of your gender, which is awesome. I've had this conversation a couple of times with some of my girlfriends who happen to be pilots and observers in a fleet air arm and it is also up to us to stand up and go, "No, that's not okay, don't do that."'

Despite the occasional bad egg and some bad press reports, Nickels says she would have no hesitation recommending the navy as a career for young women.

'I would strongly recommend it to any of my friends who have daughters who say, "I don't know if I should let them join the navy." I would recommend it as a place to work,' she says.

Hayman says that once the Seahawk helicopter is airborne and in a steady state flight, it is a stable machine. During surface search missions, where they fly quite high, the environment is benign compared to low-level operations. 'If we're down at 200 feet then a little bit closer to the water there is quite an awareness that if anything goes wrong you've got less reaction time, particularly if it's catastrophic and you do need to enter the water.'

The flight simulator back at HMAS *Albatross* is vital for aircrew training, but Hayman says there is nothing like flying off the ship at sea to keep them on their toes.

Maintenance is a major issue for any machinery operating at sea, but for a helicopter and its thousands of moving parts the challenges are even greater. In fact the chopper provides more maintenance headaches than any other piece of equipment. Chief Petty Officer Nathan Blanch and his team of nine maintainers stay busy keeping the twenty-eight-year-old Seahawk flying. After every sortie they swarm over the bird to ensure that the vital piece of equipment meets the navy's strict airworthiness requirements and is available to the skipper at all times.

'There are some components that wear through more than others that require changing out or repairing or ongoing maintenance,' Hayman says. 'Our maintenance procedures are quite robust. It's all set in stone with the publications and we have a good conduit with the shore base support services, the squadron and the assistance program office back at Nowra. So if we need information or technical support we can always ask for that. Worst case, if we're not sure, we'll stop flying until we get the answer to go ahead.'

That is exactly what happens following the engine emergency. It takes several days to get the go-ahead from HQ at Nowra to resume flying operations.

After the incident the engine is flushed out with a powerful detergent and the oil filters replaced before it is deemed safe to fly. The twin turbo fan engines are then run up on the deck before a maintenance test flight and finally the approval to resume flying is given.

The navy's fleet of S70 Bravo model Seahawks have done sterling service but their time is up after thirty-odd years. They are being replaced by the new Romeo model Seahawk, and most Bravo models will be honourably retired by the end of 2017.

No sooner has the bird been safely stowed away following the morning's drama than the ship's company turns its attention to the replenishment at sea, ironically to take on aviation fuel.

This is a stressful operation for the two ships involved, and when the seas are rough it can be very dangerous. Tina Brown is expecting this one to be particularly challenging. There is a high sea state and the German tanker has only one refuelling point, located amidships. This means the frigate has to steam slightly ahead of it because *Darwin*'s avgas tanks are located at her stern.

The two vessels rendezvous at 11.15 a.m. and Phill Henry 'drives' the frigate from his place on the port bridge wing, where he remains for the ninety-minute operation, concentrating on speed and position and ordering half-knot or half-degree variations to stay the course.

A rope is shot from *Darwin* across to the tanker to guide the refuelling line – a black flexible hose about the size of a fire hose – to the refuelling point. Officer of the watch Lieutenant Casey Green looks through a special set of distance binoculars to monitor the exact distance between the two ships. Every thirty seconds she calls the number, for example 'Sixty-five feet and closing', so the skipper knows exactly where *Darwin* is relative to *Spessart*.

The only incident is a minor fuel spill on the deck at the end of the transfer, and the two ships part company with loud music blaring from *Darwin*'s PA system and some deft dance moves being pulled by the refuelling team.

'That was the most difficult RAS of the trip by far,' a relieved Henry says.

THE SMACK TRACK

16

Truckies of the ocean

Day four of the new patrol begins with no let-up to the frustration of the ship's company. As Petty Officer David Herrer, the 2IC of the 'black' boarding party put it, 'Unfortunately, it's been a dry spell ever since that first patrol. The [rough] weather has certainly been a big deterrent.'

They have realised that the smugglers are becoming much smarter. But they have also gained a lot of experience conducting different types of boardings during the last two fruitless patrols, according to 'red' boarding party commander Lieutenant James Hodgkinson.

'We've got our flag verification boardings,' he says, ticking them off in his head. 'We've also got "approach and assist" where we'll come up to a vessel in the RHIB and just talk to the master. And then if he invites us on board, that transitions into an approach and assist visit where we go on board but we still have no remit to look at his paperwork or start searching the vessel or anything like that. I couldn't tell you how many I've been doing – I've done heaps.'

There is a lot of friendly rivalry and banter between the boarding teams.

As 'black' boarding party boss, Lieutenant Robert Kelly, says, 'We have to clean up after the red team.'

'Yeah,' says Hodgkinson. 'We drill the holes and they fill them up, that's how it works.'

Darwin is steaming northeast on a clear, moonlit night to the north of Madagascar at about 7 p.m. when the ship's radar detects a thirty-metre dhow about seven kilometres away. When the frigate closes on the suspect vessel in a two-metre swell the lights of the dhow are clearly visible from the bridge.

XO Tina Brown is responsible for the safety of *Darwin*'s two RHIBs. The helmsmen sit in the inflatables as they are lowered into the maelstrom created by *Darwin* as it keeps steaming at about fifteen knots throughout the launch. Once the boats are in the water and tethered to the side of the frigate, a rope-and-timber ladder is lowered and in turn the two six-person boarding teams clamber down into the increasingly wet and bucking boats as water sloshes in. They are soon speeding across several kilometres of ocean towards the bobbing lights of the dhow *Seena* to conduct a flag verification boarding.

As I move from *Darwin*'s boat deck into the secure ops room the world becomes suddenly dark, with glowing screens illuminating the faces of the operators who are focusing intensely on their consoles. The imagery on infra-red and optical screens in front of the Principal Warfare Officer, Lieutenant Brett Schulz, is clear as the RHIBs approach the heaving dhow and the boarding teams climb up.

Schulz, who is on his first tour to the Middle East, sits in front of the skipper and continually scans the high-resolution images that show the boarding team herding the nine-man crew into the bow of the suspect dhow. There they are isolated so that the team can secure the vessel before searching it. The sailors are well defined as they move about the deck of the bobbing vessel.

Seena, which departed from the Iranian port of Chabahar on the Makran coast, has form, and was also intercepted previously by HMAS *Melbourne* during her 2015 deployment. This is also the dhow that French sailors from *Nivôse* had boarded without success several days earlier. They had spent twenty-four hours on board and conducted an 'intrusive' search, which included drilling 150 holes into the bulkheads, but they did not have an interpreter with them to glean information from the crew and left empty-handed.

Holes drilled during intrusive searches must be repaired if nothing is found. If contraband is discovered, boarding teams are authorised to conduct a 'destructive' search where bulkheads can be broken down.

Sitting in the raised skipper's chair in *Darwin*'s darkened ops room, Phill Henry – who has a bottle of red with the French skipper riding on the outcome – monitors the boarding and is briefed on all aspects of the operation before he announces his intent. The briefing pack produced for the boarding includes a document from the French ship showing the extent of the holes they drilled during their search. This information is also passed to the ten-person 'black' boarding party.

After information from the dhow is relayed up the chain to the Australian Joint Task Force 633 headquarters at Al Minhad and Combined Task Force 150 headquarters in Bahrain, permission is granted for the boarding party to conduct a detailed search of the vessel.

The warship has been communicating with the dhow by VHF marine band radio, with the interpreter telling the master that *Darwin* intends to board it under articles of the United Nations Convention of the Law of the Sea (UNCLOS).

'Usually we call ourselves *Coalition War Ship 04* simply because we have the big 04 painted on the side and there can be no mistaking us for somebody else,' Schulz says. 'We don't necessarily identify ourselves by our nationality at that stage. It's not until we get on board a little bit later on that we do that.'

They start by asking the master of the vessel some questions, such as:

'What was your last port of call?'

'What is your next port of call?'

'What is your current tasking?'

'What are you doing?'

'They might, for instance, reply that they're fishing,' Shulz says. 'Or perhaps they're a cargo vessel transiting from one point to another point. We'll ask them what their nationality is – as in the nationality of the registration of the vessel – and we'll ask them the total number of people they have on board. If they say what their job has been then we might ask specific questions about that job. They might say that they're fishing. We'll say "Great, how long have you been fishing for? What have you caught? Do you have any fish on board?" We might ask them other questions such as, "Are there any weapons on board that we need to know about before we get over there?" And finally we'll explain to them that we are sending a team over to have a chat to them on board and just to ensure that their paperwork is in order.'

Coalition warships do not board every dhow they encounter on the high seas. If the craft are not suspicious, they are allowed to proceed on their way. Alternatively, they might be subjected to an 'approach and assist' so that sailors can deliver so-called 'maritime engagement products' such as bottled water and energy snacks to the crew.

'We find that they're a great source of information, a great source of intelligence about what's going on in their particular area, especially if they are legitimate fishermen,' Schulz says. 'Legitimate fishermen don't necessarily approve of smugglers and as a result we get over there and we might ask them, "Have you seen any vessels in the area that are suspicious? Have you seen things going on that you know are there or have there been any pirates in the area?" They are more than happy to have a conversation.'

The ship also closely examines the vessel using its own sensors or the powerful cameras that are mounted on the helicopter, if it is aloft. However, the most effective method of assessing a dhow is by getting up close and personal either alongside or on board and the Australians felt that in the case of the jelbut dhow *Seena* a new search might do the trick.

'We were aware that fresh eyes can turn up new things so we were just going to go through the same procedures, taking into account that the French had searched it for twenty-four hours,' Rob Kelly says. 'We had the benefit of having the interpreter that the French didn't have, so could converse more easily with the master.'

Once *Seena* is secure, Paul Lerza and his interpreter are ferried across to question the crew as Rob Kelly leads his team on a thorough examination of the vessel.

'We just went by normal procedures and recorded all the possible void spaces and areas where things could be hidden and they came back to me fairly early on and said, "Look, everywhere we've searched has already been searched",' he explains later.

'Because we'd been burnt before, I was of the opinion that we really needed to give it a good go. So we sent them back to do a thorough inspection of every compartment with a fresh set of eyes and to really go through with a fine-tooth comb to find anywhere that things could be hidden.'

The dhow had a forward hold, a net hold and a freezer hold, as well as the wheelhouse and machinery spaces and a galley area at the stern. The crew sleeping area was a raised platform aft of the wheelhouse. 'It was different to ones I'd seen before and there was a weird void space aft, but it looked unused and it was full of rubbish but we searched it all thoroughly.'

The vessel was also in better condition than many others that Kelly had been on. That is a red flag in itself.

'The wheelhouse was actually spotless and there was not that much stuff in there, which to me is a tripwire that beckons a further search because it's not what we're used to seeing,' he says. 'Maybe this guy takes pride in his vessel and keeps it super clean, but this was the kind of boat where there wasn't excess rubbish or tools or things lying around where there should be. Everything was spotless, which is uncommon.'

Kelly says the crew had an easy-going demeanour and their hands and feet showed all the signs of belonging to genuine hard-working fishermen. Sadly for Phill Henry the search turned up no contraband. Two hours later the dhow was declared clean and the RHIBs returned to the ship. Henry had lost his bottle of red.

Enjoying a cuppa at the wardroom table next to the sole porthole in the officers' mess several days later, Brett Schulz tells me that English is a common language at sea. Many of the vessels plying their trade, both legal and illegal, across the Indian Ocean have masters who can speak some English.

'We only have one interpreter on board and he might be conversant in several languages, but it's not going to be every language that you could possibly get in the Indian Ocean,' he says. 'In the maritime world English is still, just like in the aviation world, the primary communication language. So while we are dealing with very small dhows that are usually traditional fishermen or owned by these guys, a lot of people do still speak English. We can at least establish what it is that we are about to come over and do and then once you're on there of course the procedure of going through the checks is very self-evident and we explain to the masters what it is that we're there to do, once we get there.'

Not all of the dhows operating so far south are engaged in illicit activities. There were some that Schulz and the rest of the crew were sure were carrying illegal cargo that were unexpectedly clean and others that appeared to be clean that turned out to be anything but.

'There have been some vessels that we've come up to and they just meet all of the expectations. Our boarding party has got on board and they've looked at it and said, "Guaranteed, this is absolutely everything we were taught to look for," and at the time that we were on board they certainly weren't doing anything illicit,' he says. 'Other times, you will do a routine stop and you won't have a great hope for it, you think it's going to be nothing at all and that turns out to be a jackpot – a successful boarding. In many ways it is a numbers game. The more people that you can get onto, the more people that you talk to, the more likely you're going to have success.'

Just being in the area, observing patterns of life and engaging with as many vessels as possible allows *Darwin* and other coalition vessels to build an intelligence picture. 'So if fishing vessels always look like this and they're always doing these kinds of things then that's great, and if you find somebody who's not doing that certain thing then that sets off an alarm bell.'

As a first-timer on patrol in the region, Schulz says the biggest surprise for him has been the standard of seaworthiness of the tiny dhows and the seamanship of their crews – not to mention their capacity to hide illicit cargoes.

'These vessels go a very long way and they are well prepared, they are well equipped, they are incredibly savvy about how they disguise their illicit activity,' he says.

Schulz has also been pleasantly surprised by how casual the crews are about the contraband that in some cases would be worth hundreds of millions of dollars. 'They deny, deny, deny until such time as its obviously incontrovertible that, "Yes you're doing something untoward," and then they'll say, "Great, you got us." There's no malice whatsoever on board. It's purely a business. That's probably the biggest surprise for me.'

The fishermen are the truck drivers of the ocean earning an extra dollar carrying something illegal.

'They simply take a consignment and they move that consignment and they're paid for their time,' Schulz says.

Just like a truckie on land, the master of the vessel is responsible to those who have paid him to deliver their product. In the case of a consignment of smuggled drugs or arms this could be a matter of life and death for a skipper whose cargo is confiscated, so the RAN takes its responsibilities very seriously. Each vessel that has cargo seized by *Darwin* is issued with a receipt signed by Commander Henry that explains what has happened.

'It says, "Yes, we've taken this off you. Yes, it's illegal. Here is the proof that we've taken this off you." I am certain that it's important for them to be able to account for the fact that their stuff didn't make it to wherever it was going,' Schulz says.

The official certificates of seizure do seem to carry weight with the smuggling kingpins back at the Makran coast because some skippers whose cargoes have been confiscated do make repeat trips down the hash highway and the smack track.

Before each search operation, a security team boards the suspect vessel to ensure that the crew is unarmed and there are no booby traps on board. It also conducts an initial assessment of the crew to try and establish who might be the most talkative and therefore most likely to give up useful information. Once it is apparent that the captain's story is not credible a search is authorised.

Sometimes the story told by the master of the dhow is so far-fetched that it simply defies belief. During an earlier boarding the 'red' team had been told that the dhow was so far south and well away from the fishing grounds because the skipper was searching for a friend who was lost at sea. He told James Hodgkinson that his mate had disappeared three months earlier.

'All his cousins were on board and they'd been at sea for a little over a week. He'd gone down south and he was showing me on his GPS where he was going and he was basically heading down a hundred miles off Somalia. And then he said he was going to search in this exact pattern back towards the coast,' Hodgkinson says.

Hodgkinson asked, 'Okay, so what was the last thing that you heard from him?'

'He was stopped in this position here,' the master claimed. 'And his engine was stopped and seized and he sent out a distress call to Iran and we've come to get him three months later.'

'I talked about the improbability of actually finding him,' Hodgkinson recalls, 'and he was, "No, no, I'm going to find him."

And apparently he didn't have any means of communicating with him. What he was going to do was go around to every dhow that he saw and say, "Is he on board? Have you guys seen him?"'

It was hardly a convincing story. 'Yeah, this ship was full of intelligence tripwires, fresh paint, new bulkheads, new wood panelling.'

With the master's fantastical story and the other evidence, the team felt certain that there was something illegal on board somewhere but they just couldn't find it. According to Dave Herrer, they drained every single fuel tank, drilled around 150 holes at various points and put the borescope camera in to look for contraband, but after two frantic hours of searching it was to no avail.

Hodgkinson has become known as 'the dentist' due to the number of holes he drills in the bulkheads of suspect dhows during search operations.

'Unfortunately we had some time constraints, which meant that we had to leave the vessel,' Hodgkinson says. 'So it left and continued on its way, and then we had some subsequent intelligence that it in fact didn't go a hundred miles off Somalia and then start its exact search pattern. It actually went another 350 to 400 miles south and then lingered off the coast of Tanzania. So we boarded it again on its way back north.'

When they boarded the dhow for the second time, they realised that a lot of things had changed on board since the voyage south that indicated that it probably had been carrying a drug consignment when they first searched it. There had previously been four large water barrels on either side, each of which had held about 2000 litres of water. Now several of them were drained and one had been moved up to the top of the wheelhouse. A small boat it had been carrying had been flipped over and moved. There was also a broken chimney stack and the forward net hold, which had been full of nets, was now being used as a sleeping space. They had searched as comprehensively as they could on the first boarding and would have liked to have spent another couple of days on it.

Herrer says, 'The problem is, though, if we don't find anything and even if we do, we have to repair and that's the danger. So you could spend three days on there drilling big holes and then you've got to fix it. That's the one thing I guess the Australians are good for. We come up here and we fix it, we don't just destroy it.'

As for the crews, Hodgkinson says, 'The sad thing about a lot of these blokes is that they're either heroin addicts or recovering heroin addicts so when you board it there's little methadone bottles all on board and they'll be speaking to you and they're just drinking methadone out of a little brown bottle.' This was the case on that particular dhow.

'They all get sick,' Herrer explains. 'I didn't know at first. He was like, "Oh we're all sick," and said they needed their medicine, and then got it out and then we realised it was their methadone. So they all drink up and then they come good again.'

But by the time they boarded the dhow on its return journey north, the crew had run out of methadone.

'The master was a gibbering wreck who had been alternating between talking to me and vomiting and pleading for methadone,' Hodgkinson says. 'I said, "I don't have any methadone to give you."'

'So they'd obviously done a drop-off,' says Armfield. 'But he was not really making sense when we were talking to him.'

Even on the legitimate fishing boats there are a lot of heroin addicts on methadone.

'It's a bit of an eye opener,' says Herrer. 'These men are aged. They look like they're in their fifties and you read their paperwork and they're twenty-eight.'

Like the master of the dhow on which they had made the weapons haul, this skipper was from Baluchistan.

'Most of them aren't criminals,' Herrer says. 'They just need to make money for their families.'

On one of the dhows they found a crew member who had actually gone to college, Kelly says. 'That was really rare.'

'So they live in a rural village in Baluchistan,' says Hodgkinson, 'and then go to Chabahar on the Iranian coast looking for work, or they know someone who's a fisherman and they get told it's a pretty good way to earn. We had a few guys that had been builders and stuff like that but that work dried up and they couldn't get a job so they'd gone to Chabahar to get a job on a fishing vessel. They go and do two-month trips.'

Chabahar is a big fishing port on the Makran coast of southern Iran. The illicit drugs come out of there and several other ports around the porous border between Iran and Pakistan in Baluchistan. They then travel down either the hash highway to Yemen or the smack track to East Africa and especially Tanzania, although some do get to Kenya, Mozambique and South Africa.

As James Hodgkinson says, 'I don't know if you saw that little fishing village right on the mouth of the river as you went out [of Dar harbour] but if I was running drugs and I was picking them up off the coast of Tanzania that would be a good place to go in.'

17

Jackpot

Day five of *Darwin*'s 'Out of Africa' patrol on Saturday, 21 May 2016, dawns fine and sunny with a moderate breeze and a rising sea. All is well on board the warship and there is renewed optimism among the crew as Orko is up and running and ready to resume the hunt.

At about 10 a.m. word filters through that the French P3 maritime patrol aircraft has located a suspect dhow about eighty kilometres from the ship's position, steaming southwest towards Tanzania. This contact and the fact that several other suspect vessels are steaming south and west of the Seychelles confirms suspicions that the smack track has moved even further south as the smugglers risk longer journeys in even rougher seas to avoid detection.

The decision is taken to board the dhow. A boarding huddle for a pumped and excited 'red' team on the ship's waist at 11.10 a.m. is followed by the command brief at 11.25 a.m., before the launch of the first RHIB in choppy seas.

As they prepare to leave the comfort of the ship, the excited boarding team members, both male and female, conduct final checks of their gear. They are wearing helmets and goggles as well as life preservers over their uniforms and are armed with 9 mm pistols and batons as they line up behind Hodgkinson and John Armfield, who also carries a large sledgehammer known affectionately as 'the key'.

Darwin has emerged from the shadow of Madagascar, and the sea state is right on the outer limit for boarding operations, with strong winds and waves of three to four metres in height. However, as the ship approaches the target, the RHIB is launched from the port (left) side and the coxswain (driver) employs his considerable skills to position the inflatable boat on the starboard side of the moving frigate so that the team can safely climb down the ship's wriggling rope-and-timber ladder and into the bucking, bobbing and increasingly wet inflatable boat. There is plenty of chat about the conditions as we watch the twenty-metre dhow disappear below the growing swells and jump around the angry sea like a frog in a sock.

James Hodgkinson is first to scramble down the ladder and into the wildly pitching boat, followed by Armfield and the rest of the team. One team member realises that the conditions are outside her comfort zone, so she is immediately replaced. Finally, the inflatable is loaded with six boarding team members, but as it speeds towards the dhow it appears unlikely that they will be able to board it in such marginal conditions.

'When we approached from the stern we did a lap around looking for any obstructions or places where the crew on the dhow may have been hanging things over the side,' Hodgkinson says later. 'We also look for any identifying marks or, from the intelligence tripwires point of view, places you could see scrape marks on the side or freshly splintered wood that might indicate that that dhow has done an at-sea transfer with another dhow, one of the indicators that they've transferred drugs.'

Several minutes later as the RHIB nears the vessel, a large set of waves hits the dhow, causing it to rock violently and roll through about forty degrees.

'At that stage I pulled the RHIB off and said that we weren't going to board,' Hodgkinson says. In addition, he says their radios had become waterlogged and they could not talk to the ship.

On their way back, the radios dry out and the skipper tells them to have another crack and to instruct the master of the dhow to steer down-sea so that the waves will come from behind, making it slightly easier for them to board.

Whenever boarding teams approach a dhow they try to identify the master and use hand signals and loud voice commands to push the crew to the bow of the vessel.

'Most of the crews we've had so far have understood what that means and they all move up onto the forecastle and gather up there,' Hodgkinson says. 'It's also an indication of whether they've been boarded before. Some dhows will see the RHIB approaching or they'll see a warship approaching and the crew automatically moves up onto the forecastle and sits down to wait for you to board. Some dhows even lower ladders or ropes or are there to help you get on board because they know the procedure. It's the nature of doing business in this part of the world that they get boarded by warships.'

They soon identify the skipper. Hodgkinson instructs him to go to the wheelhouse and turn the boat so he will have a following sea.

'The waves were a bit more predictable and because we had the sets coming from behind us we could see where the bigger waves were going and we moved up alongside and commenced boarding,' he explains later.

In calm conditions the boarding party will put a portable ladder up the side of the dhow to provide access. On this occasion, with the vessel behaving like a cork in a vortex, the sea state means that one minute the RHIB is almost level with the gunwale or deck rail of the dhow and the next it is three metres below. Instead of using the ladder they simply wait for the peak of a wave before leaping from the RHIB directly onto the dhow. The dangerous seas mean that the security detail does not go aboard in advance. Instead, all the boarders scramble on in quick succession.

'Two or three of the guys were grabbing on at a time and then scrambling over and then helping up the rest of us as we came up,' says Hodgkinson. 'So it wasn't graceful, but every time we'd come up at the top of the set the boat would manoeuvre in close to the side of the dhow, we'd climb on board, grab the gunwale or one of the posts and then pull ourselves into the dhow.'

Once the first six are safely on the dhow the inflatable returns to *Darwin* to fetch Agent Lerza and the terp. Meanwhile, the rest of *Darwin*'s crew enjoy a hot lunch that includes a tasty beef stir-fry. Afterwards, some play a game of uckers while others watch the Sharks versus Sea Eagles NRL match live on TV, while James Hodgkinson and his boarding team begin the arduous task of checking the vessel's bona fides and commencing the search.

The interpreter speaks to each crew member, starting with the master, who is escorted back to the wheelhouse and asked to produce his paperwork. It is in disarray. The registration certificate is five years out of date and there are discrepancies in the crew manifest – the master has said that he has sixteen or seventeen crew members but the manifest lists just fourteen.

'They only had twelve ID cards and when we counted them there were fifteen people,' he says. 'So, those sorts of inconsistencies.'

In some cases, an extra crew member will be the drug agent who has come on board at sea and will depart with the drugs at the destination. That person has no papers and no intention of going through normal immigration channels at either end of the journey. Many of the dhows have papers that were amended by simply crossing information out with a pen.

In this case the dhow has come from Gwadar on the Makran coast in Pakistan. That is traditionally a key fishing port, and in recent years the Chinese have poured millions into its facilities. They are creating a 'friendly' deep-water port with direct access to the Arabian Sea from a new Chinese-funded road that is being built up through Pakistan to China. The port will be also be configured to handle large surface warships and could become a vital strategic outpost for Chinese ships during any future conflict. With tensions rising between the United States and China, Washington and its allies, including Australia, will be closely watching developments at Gwadar.

Hodgkinson thought the master of the dhow was a slippery customer. 'He was smoking and arrogant with this little smile the whole time and just kept talking about how, "I'm just a fisherman I don't know anything." So I asked him where he was going and he said, "Oh, it's so windy that I've decided that we're going to go drive to the Seychelles so we can get all the big fish that are near the Seychelles," and so I went along with that.'

When Hodgkinson asks him again if he is sure that he is heading to the Seychelles and what heading he is on he replies, 'West on 220 degrees.'

'I said "Oh, that's interesting, because the Seychelles is actually the other way, it's actually back towards the east,"' says Hodgkinson. 'So then we started to get a bit stronger in our responses and I said, "So where is it that you're actually going if you're not driving towards the Seychelles? Where are you going?"

'At this point he started to splinter a bit in his story and he went, "Oh actually I'm not sure where we're going, I don't know where we're going," which is odd, because if you're the master of the vessel and responsible for its navigation and the safety of all the crew on board, how do you not know where you're going?'

Finally, the master admits that there is someone else on board who is the real navigator. It is his brother – the same fellow whom Petty Officer Armfield has already identified as the probable drug agent. This man speaks a little English and is sitting back doing nothing, wearing a clean white shirt when the others are all clad in filthy fishing gear. The story does not alter, so Hodgkinson and Armfield plan the search to start with the forecastle area where the crew is being held.

As they move through, they find rats' nests and cockroach infestations both in the cramped crew quarters, which are simply a platform beneath the captain's cabin, and elsewhere throughout the typically filthy and stinking boat. The dhows and the crew members are always dirty and after fifteen days at sea this vessel is reeking. The crew tend not to wash; they eat and sleep in close proximity and go to the toilet over the side. There are hazards everywhere but especially in the engine room where wheels and belts and flywheels spin without any protective measures. Occupational health and safety is not a priority in the world of poor South Asian fishermen.

At this time, each crew member is paid about $600 for a drug smuggling run and the skipper gets around $1500 – much more than any of them can earn from a legitimate fishing trip.

'This dhow in particular had half-eaten food in amongst the sleeping space which was just being feasted on by the vermin on board,' Hodgkinson says. 'It has really given me a deep appreciation of how good we have it because these men are honestly on the edge of survival and they are trying to make money for their families so they can eat. They have no grand aims of achieving anything more than surviving and providing.'

At about 5 p.m. the boarding teams are changed out and as the 'red' team is leaving the dhow, a team member falls off the ladder and into the drink. It is a tense moment, but soon one of the screens in the ops room clearly shows the sailor being rescued, fortunately without incident. The soaked boarders are soon safely back on the ship for a shower, change of clothes and a hot feed.

About two hours into the boarding, a crew member on the dhow quietly tells the interpreter that he wants to give the team some information.

'One of the guys [crew] had gone to the bathroom and as he went through he tapped the interpreter on the shoulder and started speaking to him,' Hodgkinson says later. 'I didn't catch what he was saying. He was speaking in Baluchi and the interpreter grabbed him and just sort of brought him back aft and sat him down and he just started saying, "I need to tell you that there's drugs on board. I'm a good man, I'm a good Muslim, I've been caught up in this and this boat is carrying drugs." So that really confirmed the suspicions that I already had that we were definitely onto something.'

The informant becomes agitated and it appears to the Australians that he is coming down off a drug high of some sort.

'Once we calmed him down he said that he didn't see the drugs come on board but he'd heard the others talking about it and he'd principally heard the guy we'd identified as the drug agent,'

Hodgkinson says. 'He said, "Yeah, I heard this guy talking about it, he said that they're in the snow." The translation was initially not quite right. He said the place with "all the snow", which we interpreted to be the ice tank, but the more I talked to him about it and drilled down, we got it down to, "It's in the ice hold," was what he said. He didn't know where but, "It's somewhere in the ice hold."'

They reassure the man that they will not go straight there and uncover the stash, but will continue with their methodical search. 'We then redoubled our efforts further forward in the net hold and the engine space to check tanks and things like that and actually left the ice hold and I passed that back to command.'

At about 8 p.m. word comes from the dhow that the 'black' team has found a large quantity of what appears to be heroin deep in the ice hold. The Australians have spent hours breaking up and removing about four tonnes of ice that had melted and formed into a solid sheet.

Given the length of time since the weapons haul back in February, there is great excitement on board the ship, with everyone from Phill Henry down delighted to finally have a drugs haul under their belt. Early estimates put the find at about 380 kilograms, with fifteen large sacks containing twenty-five one-kilogram bags of the drug. That is around $100 million worth on the streets of a Western city.

'A good deposit for a new frigate,' Phill Henry says happily.

As the night wears on, the CO and several chiefs go to the galley to help prepare toasted sandwiches for the weary boarding team members. At 12.30 a.m. we watch the inflatable pull alongside the ship and the first six mail sacks containing the heroin are hoisted onto the ship and into the arms of a delighted Kelly, who carries them to the torpedo magazine on the port waist to be stored under lock and key (there are just two keys on board). A temporary table is set up inside the magazine and the racks of torpedoes provide a bizarre backdrop to the sacks of contraband. The Naval Police Coxswain, Chief Petty Officer Denis McKenna, and XO Tina Brown begin the painstaking task of weighing, cataloguing and testing the drugs, which are also photographed by the ship's photographer, Able Seaman Sarah Ebsworth.

Small samples are taken for the Australian Federal Police and they are carefully labelled and stored in the captain's safe. Agent Lerza arrives to take samples for further testing ashore by the US Drug Enforcement Agency (DEA).

Phill Henry has also come down to witness the transfer and to examine his ship's first heroin haul of the 2016 patrol. There is no official competition between RAN ships, but his broad smile indicates that he is really happy now that *Darwin* has both heroin and weapons on her score sheet. The second load arrives back on board just after 1 a.m. With all boarding team members and their bounty safely in the ship it is time for a well-earned rest.

Sunday, 22 May, begins with a late start for many who have been hard at it for more than twenty-four hours during the latest boarding operation. Over breakfast in the chief's mess, the discussion turns to the vexed question of the fate of the informant on the drugs dhow. It transpires that the man has appealed for sanctuary on board *Darwin*. He has told the Australians that the skipper of the dhow and the drug agent will kill him if he stays put. Commander Henry takes a hard line and after consulting with headquarters he has little choice but to refuse the man's request and leave him to his fate.

Given the unpleasant task that many RAN sailors have had in turning asylum seekers back at sea only to hear of them washing up on rocks in Indonesia, leaving people under duress to their fate can be a genuine moral dilemma and emotional test for those on the front line.

'It is a tough call but the right one for sure,' says Warrant Officer Tim Brading. 'The hardest part of the job sometimes is putting your personal morals to one side to do the job and accept the command decision.'

Navy sailors and other defence personnel regularly have to deal with such grey areas. Phill Henry, who ultimately must make the call and has spent his fair share of time turning back asylum seekers off northern Australia, freely admits that the decision was a tough one. Unfortunately, when the informant initially told the boarding team about the drugs he did so in front of the dhow's helmsman. While the search wore on he repeated the claims and he indicated to the Australians that he had felt threatened during the dhow's journey south. He also revealed a long history of personal conflict between himself and the master.

'It also would appear from the questioning that the NCIS agent and interpreter formed the opinion that the gentleman concerned was also a drug user and was coming off a high, which is when people are often paranoid,' Henry says.

Under the Safety of Life at Sea obligations he would have been obliged to bring the man onto *Darwin* if he judged him to be under imminent threat. After consulting with those on the dhow, as well as his bosses at Task Force 633 and Combined Maritime Forces headquarters in Bahrain, Henry took the decision to leave him on the dhow.

'It was a bloody horrible decision,' he says frankly.

To help to salve his conscience and as added insurance, the Combined Maritime Forces headquarters reported the incident to Pakistani authorities, who undertook to check on him when the dhow arrived back in its home port. To further ease his own considerable concerns and those of his shipmates, Commander Henry kept the ship's optical equipment zoomed in on the dhow as the two vessels parted company.

'We kept an eye on the vessel for over an hour to make sure that there was no sign of anything untoward going on,' he says. 'The last sight that we had of the gentleman concerned, he was actually helping to reorganise all the stuff that we'd pulled out and re-stow the boat so there was no visual indication as we departed that anything was going on.'

With a successful boarding under their belts, *Darwin*'s crew are exultant and the talk around the ship has turned to the chances of achieving the magic 'one tonne' of heroin. Grumblings about the lack of shore leave in Dar es Salaam have evaporated as the ship's company focuses on the prospect of boarding more smugglers and finding more drugs. Only one RAN ship has ever hit the 1000-kilogram figure for heroin, and that was *Darwin* during her 2014 deployment under Commander Terry Morrison.

The Marine Engineering Officer, Lieutenant Commander Trevor Henderson, rates their first heroin bust of 2016 as the biggest morale boost of the entire deployment. He concedes that after the seven-tonne weapons haul the ship had lost momentum following the two long empty-handed patrols, a maintenance period in Bahrain and a port visit to Dubai. Due to workloads and security concerns many of the crew did not get a decent break during this time, so by the time they reached Dar es Salaam at the end of the third patrol the mood on board had been tense.

'When we got the drugs you could just see the batteries suddenly recharge,' Henderson says. 'You could feel it. I can feel things in the ship. I get around all decks – that's my job, to go down below, and you can feel it. I talk to all the sailors, senior sailors, young officers and there was a lift. We had the guns, we got the drugs and we're hoping to get more because now we feel like we're actually really doing something good for everyone around the world getting these drugs, [this] insidious substance off the streets. Throw them over the side because that's where they belong, they don't belong inside your veins, mate. They belong in the garbage.'

With several other suspect vessels in the area, optimism is spreading from the ops room to all parts of the ship. Most departments have members attached to the boarding parties and the joy of a successful boarding soon spreads.

Boredom is the natural enemy of morale and after the lack of results on the two earlier patrols Chaplain Richard Quadrio was as happy as anyone that the ship had bagged her first heroin haul.

Says Quadrio later, 'I remember vividly talking to one of the sailors and he said to me, "Chaplain, this is why I joined the navy. I didn't join the navy just to stooge around doing exercises off Jervis Bay. I joined to go on operations and make a difference for my country, do something important."

'There have also been lots of days at sea where we haven't done anything and that's like any war story. In between the battles there's a lot of down time – "Hurry up and wait." But you don't get one without the other.'

The crew does not have to wait long for the next morale-boosting job.

Just a day after the first 380 kilograms of heroin have been secured in *Darwin*'s torpedo magazine, the frigate intercepts another suspect dhow, flying a Pakistani flag. Similar in size to the previous smuggler, this vessel is lying a little lower in the water. Fortunately, the seas have abated slightly, making boarding a little easier. Once on board it is soon clear to boarding officer James Hodgkinson that the vessel, also from Gwadar, is dodgy.

'When you get on the boats where they're legitimate the crew are really calm, they welcome you on board, they start hitting you up for things, "Oh, Mr Navy man, have you got a radio?" Even before the interpreter gets on board they're trying to get food and water because they know that you're there to help them,' he says.

On suspect dhows such as this one there is none of that interaction. That absence, the general intuition that experienced boarders feel and the master's dodgy paperwork often add up to smugglers. The dhow's manifest lists ten crew names but there are twelve men on board, so the team is authorised to carry out a flag verification boarding and search. In addition, the master's story about why they are in that location is so ridiculous that alarm bells are ringing loud and clear. The master tells Hodgkinson that he was fishing in company with four other dhows off Somalia when they were attacked by pirates in skiffs, who fired AK-47s at them.

'Because of his swift actions they cut the nets, turned and ran and because they had the wind behind them this little dhow was able to apparently outrun a skiff,' Hodgkinson says drily, explaining that this is hardly likely since skiffs do thirty to thirty-five knots, whereas at best a dhow might manage eight knots with a following sea and wind.

In addition, Hodgkinson has previously been told by genuine fishermen that the Somali pirates are running an extortion racket and have no interest in killing fishermen because there is no money in it for them. He goes forward to see John Armfield, share his thoughts and see what he has found.

The first thing Armfield says to him is, 'Sir, when the blokes went down to do their security search in the ice hold a few of the crew members said, "Oh you don't need to go down there, there's no need to search down there, don't bother. Nothing to see down there, don't go down there."

'That means there is something that they don't want us to see down in the ice hold,' Hodgkinson says. 'We had a bit of a chuckle to ourselves and knew we were definitely onto something here.'

On some smuggling dhows, the crew are in a hurry to get home so they just confess immediately and point out where the contraband is located. In this case they angrily insist that they are just fishermen and to prove their innocence they even provide a demonstration of how they cast their nets.

Armfield says the reaction of the crew tells the tale. 'Real fishermen are like tradesmen, they're just professional, they want to do their job. If they want to do something they'll tell you because they've got nothing to hide. If they want to go to the toilet, they'll just tell you. If they want to eat, they'll just tell you. They'll put out a fish, cut it up and you just go, "Yeah these guys know what they're doing." These guys were worried and you could tell they weren't being themselves because they held off on things and even prayers.'

Hodgkinson says that the crew's unusual behaviour at prayer time was a dead give-away because on all of the legitimate fishing boats that they have boarded, praying is not negotiable.

'We make every accommodation that we can for that because a lot of what we do here is building goodwill, particularly amongst the genuine fishermen. The only way we're going to actually try and improve the situation on the ground is through building those relationships,' he says. 'But the dodgy guys, they didn't pray the entire time that we were there. They didn't even ask for food, and we prompted them. We said, "Do you want to eat now? Go and get lunch?" and they were like, "Oh you want our food, here go and take our food," and we're like, "No, that's not what we're saying." We got the interpreter who was speaking in their language to say, "We're happy for you to eat now."'

Once clearance is given to begin an intrusive search, the team heads straight into the ice hold. They immediately notice a newly fitted section of the aft bulkhead towards the rear of the hold, but it proves to be an innocent repair. A couple of hours later some team members working in one of the smaller ice holds uncover a brand new hatch in the floor. Removing the ice is hard work and it has to be chipped into small blocks that are then removed and stored, to be replaced should the vessel be clean. Chipping ice in a filthy fish hold in a madly rocking wooden dhow is not a fun job.

Several hours into the search the team chipping away in one of the smaller bays notices a place with much less ice than the rest.

'The guys started clearing that one and when they cleared it down to the deck level they could see that the deck plating of tin was brand new and that all the bulkhead was rusty so John gave me a hoy,' Hodgkinson says. 'I was back up doing questioning and I came forward and had a quick look down into it. You could just see bright as day that it was different, so we went, "Yep, that's the next spot," and that's when I started to get pretty excited.'

They peel up the tin and underneath a layer of Styrofoam they find a fifty-centimetre wooden hatch. When they lift it up they discover that the void beneath is packed with plastic and synthetic hessian sugar bags. Some are marked 'Matiari Pakistan Refined Sugar' and others say 'model management', and all of them are full of what looks like heroin. The bags are wrapped more simply than yesterday's seizure, which was wound tightly in foil, plastic, cotton and then two more layers of plastic.

John Armfield says several new members of his team became excited when they saw the contraband. 'They've worked really hard, as you know, on all the other boardings to pretty much do eight hours of work without a win,' he says. 'We rotated them all through, brought them all down so they could actually experience that's where they're hiding it, that's how they're hiding it. Because they're able seamen, they'll probably do another ten years [in the navy] and hopefully when they're petty officers or chiefs they've got the experience.'

18

More smack on the track

By the time they find the stash, the dhow has begun to take on serious amounts of water. *Darwin*'s engineer cannot get his portable bilge pump into the bilge behind the dhow's engine, so they have to shut down power to ease the flooding. With no power the vessel just wallows like a tyre tube in a choppy surf as they repair the leak around the propeller shaft and get an extra fire-fighting pump from *Darwin* brought over to dry the bilge out.

Through all of this the master has been offering advice that contradicts what his own and the Australian engineers are saying about the emergency.

'I just got him to sit down and stay out of it while we fixed it,' Hodgkinson says.

About forty-five minutes later they are able to start the engine and move forward, which eases the wallowing of the dhow. Meanwhile, John Armfield and his team have uncovered the extent of the initial drug find and have tested the contraband to confirm it is indeed heroin. The sailors use a portable tool called a Trunarc handheld narcotics analyser that fires a laser through the bag to identify the drugs within minutes and without risking contamination. They remove the booty from the hold and onto the deck, and radio back to *Darwin* that they have found about 160 kilograms of a substance that has tested positive as heroin.

After the initial find Agent Lerza and Hodgkinson summon the master to the wheelhouse for a serious heart-to-heart chat.

'We started to get a bit sterner with him,' Hodgkinson recalls. 'We started off again saying, "All right, we've been on board. You know what we're looking for – we've already talked extensively. What do you think we're looking for?" He answered, "Oh, you're looking for drugs but we're just fishermen," and he kept sticking to his bullshit story.'

The pair decide to play good cop bad cop. Hodgkinson quietly urges him to come clean and to help them out as Agent Lerza reads him the riot act about where the drugs end up and how the drug money funds terrorists who kill innocent people. At this point the master shows signs of concern, so Agent Lerza pulls out a bag of heroin.

'This is what we've found in your ship,' he says. 'Are you the master of this boat? You're the master of this boat, you're responsible?'

'Yes, yes I'm the master, I am responsible'.

'So you're the one responsible for the transporting of these drugs to sell to make terrorists money,' Lerza says.

After thirty minutes the skipper finally comes clean and tells them the whole story.

'He changed his story completely and told us how he left Gwadar and went to another port to pick up an uncle before going to his at-sea transfer spot,' Hodgkinson says. 'He loaded the drugs from another dhow which gave him radio frequencies to call when he reached a certain position.'

The master said he had been told, 'We expect you to be there at this time and then we'll send another boat out.'

Under further questioning he spilt the whole story and even confessed how much he and the crew were being paid.

'This guy just started telling Paul everything he knew and it was apparent that he's not really that deeply involved, he's just a mule,' Hodgkinson says.

From Hodgkinson's discussions on the dhows it is clear to him that the major drug syndicates usually pay the owner of a dhow a handsome fee and outfit the vessel with fuel and stores. The owner then finds a crew and a master to make the run to Africa with the illicit drugs on board. The master and crew may not even be aware of what the illegal cargo is. They are simply told to sail from point A to point B to meet someone's cousin and return home again.

In this case they were aware of the drugs because they helped to load and hide the cargo under the supervision of the drug agent. Once the first stash is uncovered it is no-holds-barred as the search becomes a 'destructive' exercise. Hodgkinson draws a diagram of the vessel and asks the crew to point to where the drugs are hidden. They point to a hatch on the opposite side from the first hiding place, and that is where the main stash is discovered.

John Armfield sends Able Seaman Eddie Tomsana, who is celebrating his twenty-third birthday, into the drug compartment. Birthday boy comes up with seven more sacks.

'That's about 140 bricks worth millions of dollars,' Armfield says.

Tomsana is the last of *Darwin*'s newcomers to have been cycled through the boarding party team. His first boarding two days earlier ended in a slight anticlimax because after spending hours searching the dhow it was time to hand over to the 'black' team – who then made the 380-kilogram find. So for him, this huge haul is second time lucky.

'We do two patrols just to get our work experience up. So I was pretty lucky to have got on a team and then have a find. That was pretty exciting for me,' he says happily.

Tomsana is no stranger to fishing vessels. Born and raised on remote Thursday Island in the Torres Strait, he worked on the local Indigenous crayfish boats before joining the navy. While the rough life lived by the crews on the dhows plying their trade in the Indian Ocean come as a shock to some of *Darwin*'s sailors, it had a familiar ring to Tomsana.

'It's a bit similar to back up at home actually, like when we go out on crayfish boats – our vessels are that big as well,' he reflects. 'It's sort of like that dhow and, yeah, they're [a] living environment. You can actually see where they've got their little beds set up for themselves. When we do a sweep around, some of them are up forward [on the bow]; some of them are [below decks] and they're cooking. Yeah, they've got some food on there, some dishes. When we went on board they had a little rice and chicken going. It's pretty much the same – they just crash anywhere around the ship.'

What is different on the dhows is the filth and the infestations of rats and cockroaches.

'Yeah, there was a few [rats] on there,' he says laconically. 'I actually saw a few when I was down under the bilge area, underneath the lower deck. There was one crawling around there. I had one on my leg as well.'

Like many children from the Torres Strait islands, Tomsana went to school in Cairns and Townsville. He was on his way to becoming a rifleman in the army when he received a letter from the Defence Indigenous Development Program inviting him to apply for the navy's Indigenous development course.

After a five-month residential training course based in Cairns, he was one of twelve out of fifty candidates who were selected. 'And that's when it started for me in the navy. It was good, I was happy with it – get away from home for a bit.' His parents were pleased too. 'Yeah, my mum and dad were heaps happy with that. My dad was actually in the army. He was a sergeant in Charlie company in Darwin.'

Of Tomsana's four sisters and four brothers, one – his youngest sister – has also joined the navy. He was posted straight into *Darwin* as a boatswain's mate, and by May 2016 he had been with the ship for nine months, including the six-month work-up period.

The navy has put a lot of work into Indigenous recruitment, and Phill Henry was able to see for himself just how much the families appreciate it when *Darwin* passed through the Torres Strait on the way to the 2016 deployment. The frigate stopped in Prince of Wales Channel north of Thursday Island and from across the open ocean came a tiny flotilla of 'tinnies' (open metal runabouts) bringing family members from the island out to the ship.

Says Henry, 'We only had about forty-five minutes or an hour with them but it was just brilliant, because their families couldn't make it to Sydney for the departure and so we just decided to do that. When we arranged it I didn't quite realise the families were going to come quite some distance by very small tinnies but it's what they normally do.'

Some fifteen family members came aboard *Darwin*.

'It really was a magic afternoon,' Henry says. 'Just to see the faces of the families, seeing what their kids are doing – I can't really put words into it. And then [there were] the younger kids, their brothers and sisters and nieces that came on board and were able to look around the ship and see what these guys are doing, and they're telling me that there are some planning to join the navy now.'

While Tomsana is unfazed by the squalid living conditions on board the dhows, they have come as more of a shock to his shipmate Pete Irvine who was in the team that made the seven-tonne weapons haul in February during his first 'real' boarding. He had been with Tomsana in the 'red' boarding party that was on the brink of finding the initial heroin haul on 21 May when they had to hand over to the 'black' team. They were both determined not to miss finding the drugs this time.

It is also Irvine's first experience of boarding during very rough conditions.

'When we were up north it was a lot flatter,' he says – not that the sea state particularly bothers either of them.

'Well, for us two, we're pretty small and light, pretty mobile,' he explains. 'We go to the gym a fair bit so we sort of just bounce up on to [the dhow], but for the bigger boys I think it would be harder. I reckon it's more fun. In our team no one gets sea sick, so we enjoy ourselves over there. I do.'

Tomsana says that as soon they climbed into the RHIB he had a strong feeling that they were going to find some drugs on the dhow. 'But I didn't want to jinx us, so I didn't want to mention anything. I had that sort of [feeling] that, "Oh yeah we're going to find something," because I did want to get it down under my name that we actually found something, that I was part of that.'

Irvine was just as keen. 'I thought when we first got there, "Yep, there's definitely going to be something." And then we'd been over there for a few hours and we had no indication that there was anything. We weren't finding anything until one of the boys just noticed a small little thing, you know. Then we knew it's got to be there. So that was good.'

As for the crew of the dhows, Irvine says, 'Most of the dudes you can tell are like proper fishermen, they're just out there trying to earn some money so you sort of feel sorry for them a bit – to an extent. But realistically they know that they're not doing fishing – like they're coming down south. We've been on dhows before where they're legit fishermen and they're happy and they'll always offer you food and they're a different bunch of people. So you know they're not the head people but I guess they're just trying to make some money as well. They're not really the real drugs smugglers. They're not there to make the big dollars.'

But he says there are always one or two who are part of the smuggling ring. 'You can always tell them because they're a bit smarter, cleaner and their attitude – they're a bit more cranky once they know what's going on, like one of those dudes the other day was starting to get a bit shitty because he knew he was in the shit. So you don't have any time for him because realistically he's not there to help us – and they don't help. He's not there helping them very much [either] when it comes to like pulling out the nets and that. You know he's not a fisherman.'

Irvine describes the living conditions on the dhows as 'atrocious'.

'I definitely couldn't sleep there,' he says. 'Four hours on one of those is enough for me. Compared to our growing up I think it's terrible because they don't have showers, they drink water out of this drum that everyone shares and they wash their hands with, and like the toilet is just a cut out into the ocean. They obviously don't do washing and they all don't look like the healthiest most hygienic people, so their sleeping conditions, they'll sleep in the engine room, they'll sleep in the fishing nets, they'll sleep wherever they happen to have a pillow and rug. It's filthy, it stinks.

'There's been farm animals – goats, all sorts of non-hygienic things. It's totally different, all different culturally. Another thing – it's pretty amazing to see – we're pretty respectful of them when it comes to their prayer time and that. So we've been on boardings where the sun rises and so you give them their prayer time and they still take all of that, their culture seriously even though they're doing the wrong thing. So that's a big culture thing, their prayer time.'

During the boarding the pair spent hours down in the ice hold, chipping away at the ice with a crowbar.

Tomsana says, 'They used to be just blocks of ice but they [had] all just sort of melted together so it's pretty easy to start chipping away to see where all the blocks are and then you're just carving through just to get to the bottom. We started from one end and then sort of just worked our way across instead of just trying to dig a big hole in the middle. The first part we found, you could see where the cut-out was. It was just in the centre, so when I started hacking on the other side I just worked around and went straight into the middle then spread out from there and then yeah I saw that new plate that was on there, and knew straight away, "Yeah there is something under there."'

With the help of the crowbars they managed to remove the top, and that's when they saw all the bags.

'There were more than what I expected too,' Tomsana recalls. 'Pulled out five at first and it was such a small space, once you go under there you can't sit up, you have to lie down. But then once I got under there I asked for a flashlight and then I had seven more bags under there and I was like, "Oh shit, there's still more down here," and there was just rat poo everywhere – crawling around in rat poo. I could feel one just crawling up, it wasn't bugging me, it was just trying to get away from me as well so I just sort of let him find his way out of the hole and he was out of there.'

Irvine was not quite as sanguine as Tomsana when a rat crawled up his own leg.

'Brad yelled out to me, "Pete, there's a rat on your leg." I just screamed like a girl.'

But once they saw the drugs, excitement took over.

'Because it was my first drug [haul],' Irvine explains. 'We had a good idea that there was more than the previous day and it was just like, "Oh this is pretty cool, that's what we're out here for!" Because I've done heaps of boardings now where we've got nothing and it's pretty disappointing when you spend twenty-four hours on a dhow taking it apart, and then you've got to put it all back together because you haven't found anything. So finding this one was like – you just see everyone's faces of the team. It didn't matter which rank it was, everyone was the same, so excited. It's just boosted morale around the ship.'

'Everyone is happy now,' Tomsana says.

'Yeah,' says Irvine. 'It just picks up not only the boarding party teams but the whole ship, everyone just gets excited because we're out here to do a job and it's finally got done, which is good.'

Each morning they go through handover at 7.30 a.m., he says. 'The off watch people who were on the previous day, they go to PT – we maintain a PT standard for the boarding teams – and then on watch, so we'll clean our guns, make sure all our kit is ready to go for the next twenty-four-hour RAST [recover, assist, secure and traverse] period and then if we don't do anything we hand over to the next team and we'll do our PT and they'll do the exact same. They'll do their kit maintenance and when it comes to a boarding and if there is something, the online team will go for it and then we'll swap out in accordance with the fatigue management.'

Neither Tomsana nor Irvine has personally seen heroin in Australia, but both have seen plenty of people affected by drugs. 'So it's a big thing to see it get destroyed and taken away. I've seen it ruin people's lives, so it's good.'

Tomsana says that back home the drug of choice is mainly marijuana imported from Papua New Guinea – but there is not so much of it in the outer Torres Strait Islands. 'You know there are drugs going around. You see people using it and people getting affected by it, so it's good to know that you stopped drugs from getting in the hands of innocent people and hurting themselves. Also, stopping all the money from getting around the bad people, cutting that cycle.'

The boarding team members are whooping it up and having the time of their lives as they stack almost $500 million worth of heroin on the deck of the dhow.

For James Hodgkinson the total half-tonne (512-kilogram) haul is vindication of a lot of hard work by a lot of people.

'The mood is buoyant on board because it is a whole ship evolution,' he says. 'I'm obviously biased and very proud of the boarding party and the work that our guys do in very arduous conditions. There aren't many people who would be able to stay on one of those boats for ten hours at a time while it's rolling around like that.'

Armfield says the navy and the Australian Defence Force are strict about fatigue, but there was no way his 'red' team was leaving the dhow until the job was finished.

'We're in the military and you roll through, but this time there was no way our team was coming off and I'm pretty sure the comms [radios] would have been turned off at that point,' he says. 'We punched out a nine- or ten-hour day, whatever it was, and when we got off the boat and we come back on and everyone's there to greet you and congratulate you, you're exhausted but you are that stoked. I've been able to achieve a fair few milestones in my career and that will be a highlight. It was the first one we've actually been able to go right from leaving the ship to going right through to saying goodbye to the crew.'

Armfield had become quite friendly on the dhow with a man who said he was an uncle of the master and who spoke good English. 'I was the last guy to get off so I went over and shook his hand and I said, "Mate, I appreciate everything," because he was nice, he was hospitable the whole time, never once did he lose it, never once was there any rage or anger.'

Armfield is even more passionately against illicit drugs than he was before his numerous boarding operations.

'The guys that are actually putting their lives on the line to get this to their suppliers and their customers are doing the most dangerous part of the job and they are not making the money for it,' he says. 'I wish we could inflict the pain that these guys are suffering on the guys at the top. They are only the guys transiting it – there's bigger much fish out there that need to be crunched.'

Hodgkinson believes that if heroin users could see what he and his team had seen they might think twice about using the drug.

'If you'd seen the rats running over the heroin, it's been cut five times and you're about to put it into your body, you probably wouldn't be as keen to get amongst it,' he says. 'Also, if you'd met some of the people that were involved in this and you knew the thorough evil that some of the head honchos in these drug trafficking networks are, you might not be as keen to support it. And the money is going back to Al Qaeda, ISIS or Al-Shabaab.'

The third and final successful boarding of the fourteen-day patrol occurs on day nine, 25 May 2016, when *Darwin* intercepts an al-Mansour dhow flying an Iranian flag. There is great excitement as all on board feel that the ship could hit the magic tonne of heroin. With 890 kilograms already collected that means they need just another 110 kilograms. At 9 a.m. Lieutenant Kelly leads a pumped-up black boarding team over to the suspect dhow and after checking the dhow's credentials a search is soon authorised.

On *Darwin*'s bridge the officer of the watch manoeuvres the ship relative to the dhow as it turns into wind to land ('recover') the helicopter that was used to locate the suspect vessel.

'Bingo!' About sixty kilograms of heroin are found hidden in the first of the dhow's nine fuel tanks. Boarding teams change out as they prepare for an 'all-nighter' and, they hope, another fifty kilograms of smack to pass the tonne mark. Sadly, the sixty kilograms are all there is, so *Darwin* will have to be content with a huge total of about 952 kilograms of the illicit drug, worth more than $800 million. That is almost enough cash to buy a new frigate to replace the ageing *Darwin*.

Morale on board has received a boost after the skipper announced an extra day's shore leave in the tropical paradise of the Seychelles, meaning that most of the ship's company should get time off the ship and a good rest.

Hodgkinson says his time on boarding-party duty in *Darwin* has given him a deep appreciation of just how good life is in Australia. 'These men are honestly on the edge of survival and they are trying to make money for their families so they can eat. They have no grand aims of achieving anything more than surviving and providing.'

The final phase of the illicit cargo's long journey south from the valleys of Afghanistan through Pakistan and Iran and down the Indian Ocean takes place on the flight deck at the stern of the frigate. It isn't every day that you get to see, touch and walk around a half a billion dollars worth of heroin. Most people can relate to a million dollars, so with each bag containing an estimated one million dollars' worth of the drug it is not difficult for the Sydney-based crew to equate the drugs with a Ferrari or a two-bedroom apartment in the harbour city.

For Agent Paul Lerza the field of one-kilogram bags of heroin spread across the flight deck is the highlight of his latest deployment on an Australian navy ship hunting narcotics smugglers. The sheer volume of the booty from the successful boardings is staggering. Surveying the haul, he says he knows US Drug Enforcement Agency (DEA) agents who would not see such a quantity of heroin during their entire careers.

'Any DEA agent would love to see this much heroin,' he says as he poses for photographs among the bags of drugs.

As *Darwin*'s XO, Tina Brown supervises the display and disposal of the drugs. The ship's crew is allowed onto an area above the flight deck to see the fruits of their hard labour.

Numerous photos are taken to record the massive haul for posterity, with the odd personal shot, including one of Commander Phill Henry with a broad smile. Then it is time to clear the decks so that the disposal team can get to work disposing of the drugs over the stern of the ship.

The bags, which carry a variety of labels including 'new gold', 'niaz', 'Siddique' and 'see shell', are carried to a table located next to the modified plastic wheelie bin renamed the 'Goonganator' after Chief Petty Officer Andrew 'Goonga' Sims' latest modifications.

Fortunately, it is not too hot for the disposal team, who are clad from top to toe in plastic 'hazmat' suits with respirators and goggles to protect them from the illicit powder. Each bag is cut open and the contents emptied into the bin where water jets suck it down and wash it out of the bottom and into the sea below. The drugs leave a slight caramel coloured stain in the ship's wake as they mix with the seawater. The plastic bags and other wrappings are stored and disposed of later and do not go into the ocean.

It takes many hours for the team to get rid of the heroin. As each bag dissolves in the sea that means about a million dollars less for the terrorists and criminals behind the evil trade and fewer caps of smack on the streets of London or New York.

Even the most junior sailors on board *Darwin* take great pride in the fact that the months of hard slog and the sacrifices of their loved ones back at home have had a tangible impact. They also know that somewhere in the world there is a syndicate of criminals who will be deeply unhappy that such a huge chunk of ill-gotten cash is literally dissolving in their wake.

THE END GAME

19

Catch and release

While billions of dollars worth of narcotics are dissolved in the Indian Ocean, the dhows that smuggle the illicit cargo simply sail off into the sunset and the traffickers escape prosecution.

'At the moment there is a limited avenue for a legal finish for the smugglers,' Phill Henry explains. 'Effectively, we seize whatever it is, the weapons or the drugs, and the boat is left to go on its way because the ability to conduct a court case is difficult.'

This so-called 'catch and release' policy generates a deep frustration about the inability to prosecute smugglers caught in international waters. That frustration goes right to the top of the United Nations Global Office of Drugs and Crime.

The head of the office's Global Maritime Crime Division, Alan Cole, is confident what the next step needs to be. Cole spent twenty years in the Royal Navy on frigates and submarines before retraining as a barrister. His last job in the British navy was legal adviser to the Combined Maritime Forces in Bahrain, before he joined the United Nations.

I interview him in the Seychelles during the piracy conference in May 2016, and Cole is in furious agreement with other speakers and attendees when he says, 'It's a great pity that we're throwing the drugs in the sea in most cases and letting the vessel go on its way. We really want to see what we call a "legal finish", the same as we've done with piracy, where we bring the vessel in, prosecute the individuals, confiscate the vessel and put the guys in prison, because it does have a massive deterrent effect.'

He knows that would require specific international agreements and complex legal arrangements, but he believes it is possible. 'You find a country that's volunteering to do the work – and we've got three in this region that have offered to do it and are doing it, Tanzania, Seychelles and Sri Lanka. It [would] then be for the government of Australia to look at whether it's prepared to enter into an agreement with them to transfer drugs traffickers in to be prosecuted. We have a dhow here in Seychelles which was detained two weeks ago. On it was a crew of twelve Iranians. They're up in prison currently waiting for trial and I saw them yesterday. The captain of that vessel, this is the third time he's been stopped.'

Everyone at the conference is pleased about the capture of the dhow, which had been boarded in international waters twice before by *Darwin*. Both times, the drugs had been disposed of overboard and the captain set free.

'It's only the third time that it's actually ended up with him being in prison,' Cole says. 'And that's what we need to see, because clearly throwing the drugs in the sea, the guy just goes back and gets more.'

The third time, *Darwin* again located the dhow but did not board it.

'We shadowed the dhow prior to its entry into Seychelles territorial waters and provided its position to the local authorities,' Phill Henry explains later. 'The arrest and interception was all local authorities. We played no part in that. In essence, we shadowed the dhow that looked like it might be heading to Seychelles and let them know it was coming.'

The Seychelles Coast Guard was then able to board the dhow inside territorial waters and they found a hundred kilograms of heroin. This enabled the Seychelles government to reach a 'legal finish' by making arrests that would lead to the prosecution and likely conviction of an experienced and well-known drug smuggler.

Henry is very pleased about *Darwin*'s role in facilitating the possibility of a smuggling conviction in the Seychelles. 'That is the one thing that is lacking at the moment.'

Says Cole, 'It would be great if Australia could go the last short distance and see if we can get these [narcotics] cases transferred into Seychelles, Tanzania, Kenya, some other suitable location. We can ensure that they're tried, prosecuted and serve their prison sentence just as we did with some Somali pirates.'

Three other narcotics smuggling test cases are underway – two in Tanzania and one in Sri Lanka. 'But they're all domestic arrests, they haven't been arrested by the navies on the high seas.'

The smuggling crew imprisoned in the Seychelles would get up to twenty years if convicted, he says. 'For some of them, it means they won't ever leave Seychelles prison. It's a hundred kilos of heroin. You wouldn't get much less if you got convicted in Melbourne.'

As for the boat, Cole says, 'Seychelles Government can confiscate it and they'll probably use it for some purpose but it certainly won't be going back to what it was doing before.'

He is confident that seizing the vessels has been a major deterrent for piracy. 'It made a huge difference. The guys were being repeatedly arrested, having their guns thrown in the sea and allowed to go on their way. The same guy was getting picked up again and again and again and eventually we found states to prosecute them and then it stopped.'

When it comes to the narcotics trade, the crews are of little concern to the kingpin, who is living a life of luxury elsewhere in a penthouse or a palatial compound. 'I don't think the trafficker really cares. He can soon get some more crew, I suspect.'

It is the combination of losing both the vessel and the captain that would really hurt. 'The captain will have some value because he's the guy who can navigate from Iran down to wherever he needs to be, but the vessel is worth a lot of money, and you can't afford to lose a vessel every time you do a delivery.'

As for the captains, he says, 'There's a limited number of people who are going to do something if they think there might be twenty years' imprisonment ahead.'

The dhow's master being held in prison in the Seychelles has quite a history, Cole says. 'He was previously in a prison in Bosaso, arrested by the Somali authorities for illegal fishing off the same vessel, and before that he was a hostage held by Somali pirates in Somalia. Doesn't speak very good English unfortunately but it's a fascinating story. So he went to sea in his same dhow, got taken by pirates, held hostage, got released after a couple of years, went back to sea illegally fishing, got taken and put in a prison in Bosaso with the pirates who'd held him as a hostage, who had been captured by that point, got released again and now was caught with a hundred kilos of heroin.'

He says large Nigerian gangs operate in Kenya and Tanzania, handling the onward consignments of heroin and other narcotics.

'We believe quite a lot of it goes to West Africa but a lot of it also flies out of Kenya into Europe. Addis Ababa airport [in Ethiopia] is very popular as well. Addis airport has one of only two direct flights to South America from Africa, so cocaine comes one way and heroin goes the other way.' Much of it is 'body-packed' by mules, who swallow it.

'One of the ways in which it can be detected at airports in Africa is by watching men [who go] into the toilet and spend a long time in there,' says Cole. 'What they are doing is passing out the drugs that they swallowed – it's such a long flight that they've started to come out the other end – and then re-swallow them.'

At some airports, customs officers approach suspicious characters and smell their breath. If it exudes faecal matter, the officers know they have probably re-swallowed the drug and so pull them aside to be body-searched. There are regular instances both in Africa and elsewhere of packages bursting inside people on aircraft. 'They are dying horribly.'

He also says, 'If you make the trade more and more expensive you put the price of heroin up. The worrying thing is that the price of heroin in Europe is extremely low at the moment, which suggests that plenty is getting through.'

Added to that, the purity of the drug is improving. 'If you've got to smuggle something that's bulky you want it as high purity as possible, cut it later on.'

As for the captain imprisoned in the Seychelles, he says, 'This guy is now completely written off and he's never going to go back to Iran if he's convicted. And a lot of his friends will know that if we've caught him three times he must have done it many more times than that. They're suddenly going to hear he's in prison for twenty years and they're going to go to their employer and say, "This was all very good when he was telling us, I've been stopped three times by the Australian navy, every time they let me go. But now he's in prison for twenty years this was never part of the deal."' Now the message is going out in Sri Lanka, too, in Tanzania and here that they're getting nicked. That's a pretty big deterrent.'

Anyone who watches television would have heard of the American crime series *NCIS*, which stands for Naval Criminal Investigative Service. Few fans have ever met a real NCIS agent. Unlike most of the fictional agents, Agent Paul Lerza had a background not in the US military but in law enforcement, most recently as a US Customs Service criminal investigator, before he joined the NCIS nine years ago.

'I'm strictly civilian,' he tells me. 'There are elements that are in the military within NCIS but by and large we are a civilian agency.'

Head office is in Quantico, Virginia, but he works out of an office in Bahrain called the Middle East Field Office.

'Within that is the Transnational Organised Crime Unit and we see its mission as counter-narcotics and counter-terrorism,' he explains. 'So we're kind of dual-hatted. We're looking at it from a criminal violation [perspective] as we are criminal investigators but we also do see the impact and believe that there is funding of terrorism involved.'

In mid-2016 Lerza is nearing the end of his two-year posting. He has only deployed on Australian ships and his time in *Darwin* is his third at sea, with five successful boardings under his belt. From his perspective nothing is more important than ensuring the chain of evidence in narcotics operations is unbroken.

He approaches each boarding as if executing a search warrant. 'We look at "articulable facts". That gets us to "probable cause" and those are just legal standards that we're looking at, our levels of suspicion. And so very quickly we can go from "reasonable suspicion" to "probable cause" and it's looking at … the totality of circumstances when you're on the boat.'

NCIS agents work closely with a combined research and intelligence-sharing agency known as the Regional Narcotics Interagency Fusion Cell, but once on board, he says it is still hit or miss. 'We just had three seizures. Two of the dhow masters would not speak even after we found and confronted them with the drugs – just, "I don't know, I don't know."'

A vital link in the chain is a reliable interpreter, or 'terp'. After the boarding party secures the dhow and corrals the crew, a RHIB goes back to the ship and collects Lerza and his terp. On this patrol, the terp is a Baluch, living in the United States, and as well as interpreting he throws some light on the mainly Baluchi skippers and crews. He cannot be identified for security reasons.

'They are poor people, fisherman,' he confirms. 'People use them for drug [transportation], they don't come themselves or appear on the sea. Sometimes they use them one time, the second time the master doesn't want to go, they tell him, "Oh yeah, you already got some money, you need to go again."'

The payments vary. 'Each one we ask, and everybody says different. They might get like $1000 average, for each person on the boat. There is a difference on the amount of the drugs. There's a lesser [amount of] $500 they might get. I think the most they get is like $1000 if they succeed.'

This is a lot of money. 'Oh yeah, because one time we were asking some people, they were saying, "Okay, if I go to fish it's three months or two months I'm on the sea, I come back, I don't make enough money."'

The terp grew up in the region but says that does not mean he can figure out who is telling the truth. 'I cannot judge them –

there's nothing written on their forehead. I can't tell if they are lying or telling the truth. The one thing that they never tell you is, "I have drugs." The master would say, "No, I don't have drugs," until we find it. Most of the time after we find something they start cooperating. They tell their story, where they got it, how, where they are going to take it. Other than that, they don't. One load of drugs, they pass, they're good for six months. No need to come out to sea.'

The crews always say they are fishermen, even when there are tell-tale signs including that their nets have not been used. Mingling with real fishing dhows also provides cover.

'Then they do it so quickly. They don't really talk like those real fishermen [who] don't know where they got [the drugs] on board and where they're taking it, because they do this job very secretly,' says the interpreter. 'Sometimes I said, "Why you don't tell us, it's not yours, it's the owner? They can make money and then you are suffering in the sea, so why are you not telling? When we get over here, you know we're searching everything." He said, "Because we take an oath, we swear we never talk until they find it on their own." So when we find it alone that's okay.'

Baluchistan is the size of Germany and the interpreter is well versed in the politics of the troubled region. With other routes closing up, it has become a vital waypoint for smuggling.

Lerza and his terp endure the same hardships as the navy boarding party members. They risk their necks boarding RHIBs and dhows in rough seas and spend many hours on board the suspect vessel before returning to the frigate. Once back on board *Darwin* the drugs are tested and Paul Lerza sends samples to the US DEA for analysis. First up, they determine whether a sample actually is narcotics.

'The test that we do aboard the dhow is a presumptive test so we need that laboratory report to say whether it's truly narcotics or not. We need that certification because one of the things that NCIS will do is create a law enforcement report that we hope can be used [as evidence] if it can be tied to an investigation on one of the networks.'

He treats each seizure as a criminal case, following all the stringent rules of evidence. 'The young men and women who work very hard on the ships, they're war fighters, but I'm a law enforcement officer, so a lot of what I'm here to do are fundamentals of law enforcement.'

He and other NCIS agents are trained in the physical demands of getting on and off the dhows at the Federal Law Enforcement Training Center in Charleston, South Carolina. 'What we're doing this mission is very much what the coast guard does every day. The coast guard is not operating in this area of the world so that's how NCIS ... organically grew this ability, and in large part we did it going out with the Royal Australian Navy, so we've documented, photographed and captured a lot of this information. We hold onto it, we add to it and then that's where our knowledge base comes from – getting out here and doing it and then we pass that on to the next agents.'

He admits that boarding the dhows is his least favourite part. '[It's] definitely not the most fun part of the job. Anytime, interdiction operations are a lot of fun. However, whenever you add "at sea" to anything it becomes that much more dangerous and that's why the skill of the Royal Australian Navy really comes in handy. They keep me safe and sound while doing the job.'

As for the condition of the dhows, he says, 'Ah, they are a mess. They don't handle very well in the sea and rats, colonies of roaches, really filthy.'

Despite the increasing flow of drugs down the smack track, Lerza does think his work is worthwhile. 'I believe that the Royal Australian Navy hopefully with our assistance is making a difference. We're definitely disrupting and that's one of our main goals, because we know we're not going to stop the flow of heroin or hash coming out of Pakistan, but we are hoping to disrupt and dismantle organisations. And I do believe we do that. We document everything, so we're keeping track of what's going on out here, the trends, how they're smuggling [and how] they will change their techniques and tactics based on the fact that the Royal Australian Navy and the other navies are seizing this much of their product.'

Lerza attributes the terms 'hash highway' and 'smack track' to the Australian navy. 'It's credit where credit is due! The Royal Australian Navy came up with those terms.'

As for why the trade can't be stamped out, 'There's always that lure of money', he says. 'If we can get the regional partners in Africa, in Pakistan, in Iran to deal with their own corruption, we feel that promotes regional stability ... But when you have a large influx of cash in a very poor country that lure is great.'

None of the strategies aimed at stamping out the production of opium poppy crops in Afghanistan have worked.

'Afghanistan has been referred to as the graveyard of empires,' he reflects. 'So again we have to look at some way of getting regional stability there. Maybe peace and education and hopefully not needing so much money will follow. I don't believe the farmers are getting rich from this crop. I believe they're being exploited just like the dhow crews are.'

He says Australia's commitment to the vast problem is commendable. 'We may want to say that it's Afghanistan's problem, its East Africa's problem, it's a southwest Asian problem. It's not – it's a global problem. Truly a global problem.'

*

While Agent Lerza sends his samples to the DEA in the US, other samples are taken back to the Australian Federal Police's Forensic Drug Intelligence Unit. The Sydney-based unit provides intelligence support to investigations, expert policy advice to government and manages the Australian Illicit Drug Intelligence Program.

Team leader Dr Mark Tahtouh says they analyse all of the AFP's illicit drug seizures, whether imported or seized inside Australia, as well as samples from state and territory police forces and those seized by the navy. They manage and house the central Forensic Drug Intelligence Database and liaise with the government's National Measurement Institute (NMI) laboratories in Sydney, where the chemical analysis takes place.

'The chemical profiling that we do … is based on similar programs in the US,' he explains. 'We also mirror some techniques used in Europe in some of the large forensic institutes.'

Speaking at the unit's state-of-the-art laboratory complex on the outskirts of Canberra, Dr Tahtouh says there is no global narcotics database, but the agencies harmonise their methods and share information based on mutual understandings and methods of interpretation, including the margins of error. This is not as straightforward as it seems, he says. In comparing drug samples, it is always preferable to analyse them in the same laboratory on the same day at the same time.

'You're always going to have natural variations, even within the same laboratory on the same instrument, when analysing it on different days or with some time period in between,' he says.

Tahtouh's team members have experience in either forensic science, like himself, or law-enforcement intelligence.

'I always like to say we try and teach the chemists a bit of intel and we try to teach the intel analysts a bit of chemistry,' he says. 'We find that middle ground to use the technical information that we derive from the analysis of the drugs to produce forensic intelligence.'

As well as the drugs' chemical profile there is their 'physical signature' – how they are packaged and wrapped.

'It's particularly relevant for some of the seizures that the navy has made,' he says. 'There might be stamps and logos – those sorts of physical characteristics can be very useful to link different seizures together and to identify syndicates involved in their manufacture or transporting.'

They collect and collate all that information, monitor changes in manufacture practices and drug purity, link seizures and build a picture of the manufacture and trafficking networks. Each drug seizure must be treated as a crime scene and strict rules of evidence apply. Like Lerza and the navy, his unit does 'presumptive' testing before samples are sent to the NMI. 'That gives us an idea of what drug we're dealing with,' Tahtouh says.

The NMI's Australian Forensic Drug Laboratory conducts two types of analysis. First is the identification of the drug and its purity. The hand-held instruments used by the navy to identify drug samples cannot measure purity. They show only how similar the sample is to a reference spectrum of a known drug like heroin.

'The Commonwealth legislation around drugs is actually based on the pure weight of drug present,' Tahtouh explains. 'So if someone imports ten kilograms of cocaine but it's only fifty per cent pure then the [criminal] charges will be based on five kilos rather than the ten kilos. So the purity is very important for that purpose and there's a certificate of analysis that's issued around that.'

The heroin seized by the navy and analysed in Australia has been of relatively low purity, averaging less than fifty per cent.

The second set of tests conducted in the NMI lab is the chemical profiling for intelligence purposes.

'It's about working out where the drugs were made or how they've been manufactured,' Tahtouh says.

Because heroin is derived from opium poppies and is therefore plant-based, chemical profiling can help determine where it came from and the only way to do that is by comparing a sample with 'known-origin samples'.

How far it is possible to drill down into particular regions depends on the number and range of known samples. With heroin the range is quite limited. They can determine whether it comes from the Golden Triangle of southeast Asia or the Golden Crescent of southwest Asia but cannot yet identify specific cultivation spots inside Afghanistan.

However, a lot of work is being done to improve profiling techniques. The hope is that Isotope Ratio Mass Spectrometry may enable them to drill down further to the 'isotopic ratio' of drug samples, to help pin down the locations.

A big problem is gaining access to enough known-origin samples.

'We have obtained samples from all around the areas but using the techniques that we have, [the samples] may be too similar to each other,' Tahtouh says. 'Afghanistan is not exactly the most quality-controlled environment. There are natural batch-to-batch variations even within the same facility. Sometimes we would say that within one region there's more variability batch-to-batch than there is between one facility and another facility. That kind of throws everything out.'

Heroin from the Golden Crescent is mostly packed as loose powder in one-kilogram bags, such as those seized by the navy. Workers go around the poppy fields and score the unripened seed pods with a bladed tool. The opium gum oozes out, is scraped off and dried out to form opium resin, which contains a number of compounds.

The five main opiates – broadly, in order of quantity, morphine, codeine, thebaine, noscapine and papaverine – are present in various ratios that are also characteristic of where the poppy was grown, Tahtouh says. 'By looking at those ratios we can tell differences between stuff grown in southeast Asia versus southwest Asia.'

Heroin manufacture is about refining the morphine. Once it is isolated, a compound called acetic anhydride is added to convert it to diacetylmorphine, a chemical name for heroin.

'Acetic acid is vinegar; this is really like two vinegar molecules joined together,' Tahtouh says. 'We call it acetic anhydride but really, when you add it to the morphine, it's a way to add vinegar or acetic acid to turn that morphine into diacetylmorphine or heroin, and that is the reason behind the vinegar smell to heroin.'

That forms 'heroin base' and the final step is to convert that to heroin hydrochloride using hydrochloric acid.

'Heroin base is not very water soluble, therefore not very useful for injection,' he says. 'It has a lower melting temperature and therefore it's more suitable for smoking whereas the hydrochloride is water soluble and therefore easier for injection. In Australia it's almost exclusively that hydrochloric salt that we see.'

Once made, heroin can be adulterated. The analysts look out for adulterants and diluents that may be added in Afghanistan or along the supply chain, including caffeine, paracetamol, methorphan and some sugars. They also have some information about the movement of interim heroin products to different production facilities, some of which may specialise in particular stages of the process.

'And there may be some processes occurring outside of Afghanistan itself, in that we do see a lot of trafficking of raw opium or morphine base or even heroin base out of Afghanistan,' he says.

While Tahtouh is not aware of the Australian navy seizing interim products, there have been large seizures of raw opium beyond Afghanistan. 'Logistically it doesn't make a lot of sense because you have to ship a much larger amount of opium compared to if you refined it into heroin. That said, there is a market for opium itself. There are user groups, particularly in Iran, that smoke opium in its raw form.'

More recently, analysts are using profiling to link different samples. 'Recent heroin seizures by the Royal Australian Navy have been profiled to be southwest Asian heroin.'

They also compare samples to other seizures. 'Even though we can't tell it's from [a] particular production facility, we can at least say that this stuff that was seized by the navy at sea on this day has exactly the same chemical profile as this stuff that AFP seized a year ago or six months ago,' he says. 'Linking samples or seizures to each other is a very important part of the profiling, in addition to just telling you it's from southwest Asia or southeast Asia. So even stuff that we seize in the next six months or so may be from the same batch or the same production facility [as that] interdicted by the navy.'

20

Chasing the Golden Crescent

During the three years to 2015, the Combined Maritime Forces seized 8300 kilograms of Afghan heroin. By the end of 2016, the figure had grown to more than nine tonnes with an approximate street value of $15 billion.

While it is the navy that seizes the drugs at sea, an important link in the intelligence chain is provided by Australian Federal Police liaison officers stationed in key locations throughout the Middle East.

Marzio da Re is a former AFP detective whose long police career included two major stints on the front line of narcotics smuggling from the Golden Crescent. At a coffee shop in suburban Perth the retired officer tells me that he was first posted to Pakistan in 1989 for three years as one of two Australian drugs liaison officers, and he returned to the capital Islamabad in 2010 for another posting that lasted nearly five years. In between, he spent twenty years in AFP jobs that included major drug interdictions, two police royal commissions (New South Wales and Western Australia), the investigation into the 2002 Bali bombings and a posting to Jakarta from 2007 to 2010 during the big influx of people-smuggling boats to Australia.

His first stint in Pakistan was spent almost exclusively on narcotics – heroin and cannabis resin in the Golden Crescent. At that time, as well as in Afghanistan, there was still significant cultivation of opium poppies happening in Pakistan, and the authorities took him out to see the opium fields. There were also many heroin processing laboratories – 'plan labs' – in the front-line province.

The heroin trafficked from the Golden Crescent was of an inferior quality, known as 'brown sugar', smoked by consumers in Europe. But Australian addicts preferred, and still do, to inject the purer white heroin from the Golden Triangle of Burma, Laos and Thailand.

'Trafficking routes back then were pretty well known,' he says. 'And once again I don't think there was just one singular route.'

The Makran coast (known as the 'smugglers' coast') was quite a prominent route but not to the same extent as today, he says. 'The dhows were still plying their trade to mainly Dubai. You were picking up small craft [mainly with hashish] back then. The dhows have been plying their trade with whatever commodity since time immemorial but we weren't then seeing that [narcotics] trade down the east African coast.'

That trade route has now grown exponentially, as has the quality of the product. Then there are the newer manufactured drugs. 'You're now going to start seeing an ice epidemic or an ice amphetamine production problem coming out of Pakistan and

Iran. You're already seeing people being picked up and seizures being made, so we're getting that capability, which is very disconcerting.'

The porous borders and tribal areas made it easy to set up labs and facilitate the movement of acetic anhydride, the precursor for heroin production.

'It has a lot of commercial applications in the textile industry, so there is a lot of it legitimately around in India,' da Re explains. 'It also came in through Karachi. There's movement of goods both ways.'

The opium itself arrived in the laboratories as a paste, dried and packed into hessian bags that weighed a 'maund' – about thirty-eight kilograms. Da Re says that during his first posting to Pakistan the AFP did want to know about the trafficking routes, but at that time they were more interested in the transactional aspects and connections with Australia.

'The Americans were playing more of that world policeman role at the time,' da Re recalls. 'We didn't have the funds or resources other than [to say], "Okay, you've got a trafficking group in Australia, it's connected with the money flowing up there or they're selling gear in the streets." There was a particular guy in Karachi and I remember during Ramadan he was importing through statues. So he'd go across from Karachi into nearby Baluchistan and conceal it in the statues at the time. This guy ended up dying a violent death in the Philippines, but that's another story.'

Heroin trading crosses all faiths and all bounds. At that time the police officers were able to get up to places like Peshawar and run informants who would bring back samples from the laboratories that were fed back to the Heroin Signature Program in Australia, which had just started up.

'So it gave us a fantastic insight as to where these plan labs were, what their capabilities were.'

While Australia did not receive a lot of heroin from the Golden Crescent, there were a significant number of Afghan refugees arriving in Australia, mainly people from the Hazara ethnic group.

'We probably could have expected to have a bigger problem directly impacting on Australia by virtue of the sheer numbers and the desperate situation the Hazaras found themselves in,' da Re reflects. 'It hasn't borne true, which is really interesting, so the seizures that are coming out of there destined for Australia are not significant. There have been some large ones of a hundred or so kilos through Iran and Afghanistan and some others, but they haven't been to the numbers that we would expect. So that's pleasing I think. Plus, we do have some natural advantages with our systems – customs, borders and good reporting systems with finance now; there's a whole range of counter measures and tools in the toolbox with undercover policing and assumed identities. There's a whole suite of things that we can do.'

Drug liaison officers from Western countries who were posted in the region would swap information and tips, but the job carried particular dangers. Just after he left his first posting in early 1992, four agents from another country were travelling out of Karachi towards Baluchistan when they were captured. 'They were kept in a cave for three weeks because they had been out of their area and didn't have permission to go there. You had to be careful even back in those days. They were lucky to get out of it at all. Imagine nowadays!'

He used to drive around in an old Toyota Corolla, but when he returned in 2010 for his second posting in Pakistan, the situation had become much more dangerous. The agents had to be supported with armoured vehicles and obtain permission to travel anywhere outside of Islamabad.

'The security situation made it difficult because you're going to seek resources from an agency that's fighting a war. These people are trying to survive getting blown up in Peshawar and Karachi – getting shot at, killed and then they wash the streets down and half an hour later they've got another piquet [guard post] up there with another set of police ready to get taken out again. So they were in a dire situation. Four hundred police officers are killed every year in Pakistan, some people I knew very closely so … it was chalk and cheese compared to the time before.'

Narcotics production and trafficking had also evolved significantly by 2010, as had the interdictions.

'The anti-narcotics force to this day is run by, or led by senior army officers mainly from ISI [Inter Service Intelligence, Pakistan's largest intelligence service]. They're plugged in, linking with the liaison officers and also doing the work in countries, so they've got more fire power to be able to interdict.'

Few opium poppies are grown in Pakistan today, and the processing laboratories have all moved to Afghanistan, he says. 'They [Pakistanis] can actually legitimately claim they are production free – "We're a transit country, we're not a producing country." So that's a big distinction that they make and they're sensitive about.'

The drugs are transported down country from Afghanistan through various staging posts. Wherever there is money, goods of all kinds will travel, not just drugs.

'The guys that were being picked up told us about the discipline that they had in moving these goods,' he says. 'You can apply it across to the other crime types, in that these truck drivers will take it a certain way and then there'll be others picking it up and going the other way, so you have that discipline in movement that they're not knowing where it's going to – they're just truck drivers.'

As well as in trucks and containers, the heroin can also cross into Pakistan on camels or packhorses because many border crossings are unregulated.

'They'll know where they can come through, whether they're paying a lot of money or whether they come through on the informal crossings. And because there's so many people moving backwards and forwards who legitimately can be in Pakistan because they're ethnic, they're refugees, [it] just makes it so difficult.'

Some drugs are also stockpiled up country. In poor countries such as Pakistan, inevitably, money talks. Few transactions take place without cash changing hands all the way along and up the line.

He says the Pakistani military is highly disciplined. 'Of course they have to be on their toes because it's now not just a narco issue, it's a terrorism issue. They're fighting for their lives. So when you had big massacres like the December 2014 massacre in Peshawar with 150 school kids, it was pretty much a line in the sand that the military guys drew then and they said, "Right, we want to take this to its natural consequence." In other words, "Gloves are off and we are going to go in after you hard," and that's why they went into Waziristan [a lawless tribal zone between northern Pakistan and Afghanistan] and found all those bomb-making factories.'

Baluchistan, the transit area for heroin to the Makran coast, not only has its own nationalist movement but its own social system. 'Tribes and kinship, that's their first line of loyalty. If you control an area, if you're a Baluchi, you're not going to do anything that's contrary to that. So the movement of goods is going to still be relatively straightforward.'

The consequence is that a shipment of heroin can travel from the processing plant in Afghanistan to a port in Baluchistan without any proper law-enforcement exposure and, from there, down the smack track.

'They were back-trading in charcoal,' da Re recalls. 'Some smart Alec suggested we should call it "Al Kebab" because the charcoal is going back to Dubai to make the kebabs with coal.'

He expects the heroin trade to persist into the future and to continue to fund terrorism, and says that while piracy is under control for now the problem still has to be solved properly. But he warns that the situation could change. 'If these things start to make a big dent on them they will reinvent themselves somehow or another because they are clever people. They've survived for hundreds and hundreds of years against the odds. So it will continue whilst there's a demand and in places like Iran and Africa there'll be a probable growing consumption issue of their own. We have started to see already, that they'll change their product to methamphetamine because they know that's going to be the product in demand and its going through to Malaysia.

'You can track these things and you can see the developments. But you really need to have your intelligence on the ground because the locals know it better than any of us smart Alecs that come in from the West. They know. When we were giving management training to the Pakistanis for terrorism – we have designated programs – 95 per cent of the presenters were the locals from each of the areas, who all gave an account of terrorism amongst themselves. No point bringing someone from Australia to start teaching them about terrorism, they're fighting for life and death. They know the Baluchi area, they know the Peshawar area, they know all the areas. The method I adopted was "indigenise, indigenise", so if you're going to run any courses up there get the locals to run it and they can facilitate it.'

On his first posting he dealt with his own informants and paid them directly, which can be very dangerous for agents. By the time he returned in 2010 the system had changed and they had to go through the local agencies. It became a reward-based system rather than cash up front. Informants knew that if they could get information to a Western drug liaison officer through official channels they were likely to get a far greater reward.

'That was a satisfactory arrangement for us. It [also] gave us the protection in the country, because you're diplomats as well.'

One of the difficulties with human intelligence is continuity of contacts. While he was in Pakistan for nearly five years on his last posting, the Americans were more likely to be there for twelve months. 'You get a relationship in twelve months if you're lucky. We talk about "three cups of tea" or "ten cups of tea" before you're even doing business. So the poor old Americans on a twelve-month posting are getting nowhere and even on a two- or three-year posting they knew that there was another person coming. The Pakistanis are also being moved around, so your relationship with the head guy would change as well.'

As to the navy patrols, da Re says, 'It's like I guess any massive problem, whether it's in Australia or elsewhere. You've got to attack it from all angles. If there's a demand they're going to keep supplying it. So whilst there's a demand there, there's got to be enforcement. If you're on the ground you're going to understand the situation a hell of a lot more than from a distance.'

Catching the kingpins is another matter. That involves not just chasing the product but following the money with international law-enforcement cooperation through the great money-laundering centres in the world. Australia has strong restraint laws such as the proceeds of crime legislation making it is possible to freeze assets. In other countries that is not the case.

'So that's the bigger issue in terms of whether you are going to stop it. Whilst the kingpins aren't getting prosecuted, whilst there's a demand, it's going to keep flowing.'

Australian Federal Police Detective Superintendent Anthony Fox spent the first ten years of his life in the Middle East Region when his father worked in Qatar as general manager of one of the Sheikh's construction companies. In 2016 he was back there, based in Dubai as one of two AFP liaison officers. The other officer is his wife, Kate, a sergeant. He had not learnt Arabic as a child. 'But in saying that, I did some language training for this posting and picked it up pretty quickly. I think that's because subconsciously, as a child, you probably pick it up.'

Educated in Toowoomba, Fox, or 'Foxy' as he is known, did a variety of jobs, including running in partnership a security and investigation business in Brisbane, before joining the AFP at the age of twenty-six in 2000. A year later, 9/11 hit.

'And that's when it all started,' he says. For the next eight years he was deployed out of the Sydney office to jobs including the bombing of the Australian embassy in Jakarta in 2004; investigations in Asia, Europe and the Solomon Islands; and Project Wickenby (the Australian whole-of-government taskforce targeting international tax fraud and money laundering). In 2010, based in Canberra, he became the AFP's national coordinator for people smuggling, which involved a close working relationship between the AFP and the navy, Customs and Defence.

This led to his posting to Dubai in January 2014. However, in July he was suddenly sent to the Ukraine to investigate the shooting down of Malaysian Airlines MH-17 on 17 July. All 283 passengers and 15 aircrew died. He was the first AFP member to deploy to the terrible crash site.

After some weeks he returned to the Middle East to his position as senior police liaison officer, which involves quite a lot of travel.

'The main crimes of interest here at post are terrorism, which includes terrorism funding; organised crime; and money laundering. So they're the three big hitters for us in this region,' he explains.

Narcotics smuggling crosses all those categories and Dubai, being a major international transport and financial centre, is also a convenient meeting point for key organisers.

'Whether it's the CT [counter-terrorism] targets we're looking at, or organised crime or the money launderers, it's a convenient nexus point,' he says. 'Some guy jumps on a flight from Australia, guys jump on a flight from Africa, from the UK, from the US and everyone is here within a day, they have a meeting and then they organise the shipment and the money and everything else. Two days later they all fly off. Targeting organised crime and terrorism, particularly where the local jurisdiction may not have the legislation to support what you need, is a challenge.'

With terrorism funding so heavily tied up with the heroin trade there is a big focus on the smuggling of drugs from the Makran coast. Fox says his job involves liaising with the Gulf Cooperation Council countries – Saudi Arabia, Kuwait, Qatar, Bahrain, Oman and the UAE – Yemen and Iran, and the Horn of Africa and central African countries Djibouti, Eritrea, Chad, Sudan, South Sudan and Somalia. The officers stationed in Islamabad look after Pakistan and Afghanistan.

'One of the roles here is information and intelligence exchange,' Fox says. 'So that's with a range of partners, whether it's law enforcement – security agencies – or sources in the community or people [who] just have information they want to pass on.'

Other countries, including Australia's 'five eyes' partners – the US, UK, Canada and New Zealand, plus the Netherlands, Germany, France as well as foreign law enforcement agencies, pass on information relevant to Australia and vice versa. 'So that information can come from anywhere.'

Generally, intelligence about a drug load is received at the point when it is being transported towards or away from the Makran coast. The ability to track a load depends on where it is going. Some countries are more proactive than others in cooperation and targeting narcotics trafficking.

But success has mainly come from well-connected sources inside the smuggling chain. Usually it is broad information, such as a tip that a certain vessel is carrying narcotics.

Sometimes they know the name of the vessel or the captain. 'But it's never as simple as having all of the information in one hit [so] that you can go, "Right, that's the boat." It needs that analysis behind it and to start feeding in with other intelligence coming in from other sources and other areas.'

They conduct analysis and gather as much information as they can from their sources before passing it to the Australian navy people in Bahrain. 'Then they throw that into their systems and they see what information seeds they have that connect with it, and then if it's enough they will go, "Right, let's have a crack at this boat – we think it's this one, let's go and board it, let's have a go."'

Sometimes the intelligence is just not enough. The ships can't be everywhere and they are patrolling a large ocean. 'They have to go for whatever the best result looks like, and sometimes it isn't the information we pass; they have to make that decision based on other information they have.'

Of *Darwin*'s three heroin seizures in May 2016, Fox's office provided information in relation to only one. 'Once a vessel has come south past Somalia and they're on a certain bearing, there's not really any fishing grounds there. But these dhows' saying, "We're down here for fishing, that's what we're going down there for," doesn't quite stack up. So that's where they've had most of their success.'

Where dhows used to leave directly from a port along the Makran coast loaded with narcotics, they are now more likely to rendezvous with a mother ship in the waters forty or fifty kilometres off the coast.

'The smaller dhows come up and they'll offload there and then they'll all have a go,' Fox says. 'And that's really for the syndicates. Instead of having that one big load, the risk of having one big load busted, they now have five or six boats and if two get caught well, who cares – the other four get through.'

Fox isn't prepared to offer a view about the role played by corrupt officials at senior levels and at the borders in enabling narcotics cargo to reach the ports. But he observes, 'It's pretty rough terrain where it's coming from. It is the bad lands, from Afghanistan to Pakistan [and] Iran through those mountains. There's not a lot of control from the military or law enforcement up there. The effectiveness and commitment seems to vary but there is commitment at some levels. As an example, a colleague visited the Iranian counter-narcotics police college and museum and they actually have a wall of honour there with the names of the officers who've been lost in the line of duty. And I think it's over 4000 they've lost combating the narcotics trade. When they get into a gun battle [it is] pretty fierce and some of the stuff that has been seized includes heavy machine guns, automatic weapons, armoured vehicles. That sort of stuff is what the narcos have.'

The terrain also makes it especially difficult to monitor what is coming through. And Pakistan's many internal security issues take up their resources.

Some dhows drop into ports on the way down the Gulf but that is mainly to deliver and collect legitimate cargo before heading south. 'I don't think we've seen any information to suggest that there's narcotics coming directly in here [Dubai].'

The main drug that is causing problems in the Gulf region itself is the psycho-stimulant Captagon that is often taken by insurgent fighters going into battle. It comes mainly from Lebanon and also from Iran.

The difficulties of putting together counter-narcotics teams in developing countries are well known. 'Trying to get a vetted team, out of a team of twenty guys you might have nineteen who are committed and you might have one corrupt guy, and that just brings the whole show down. That's the difficulty you're always going to face, particularly with the developing countries. But the majority of law enforcement officers are committed and the support given to them by law enforcement agencies from developed countries in training them up has been phenomenal. But again, it's just trying to keep resourcing that, keep them trained, keep them committed.'

Nearly three-quarters of the successful boardings have been conducted by RAN ships, followed by the Canadian and then New Zealand, Saudi, German and French navies. Fox is not sure why the Australian ships do so well. 'I think experience has a lot to do with it but I think there's a fair bit of commitment there. Australians are always ready to have a fair crack. All the work I've ever done with the navy, whether people smuggling or over here, they'll always give their utmost, always have a crack or always let it run and see what comes out of it.'

He believes that the AFP's close relationship with the navy was forged on the people-smuggling taskforce back in Australia. 'I think all those agencies now understand that no one can do a task on their own in this environment, whether it's in Australia or whether it's offshore.'

After arriving in Dubai in 2014 he set about augmenting that relationship, building up informants and working with local law enforcement. It is now at the point where they know who to call. 'When we get information we can just pick up the phone straight away and say, "This is what we've got and we'll do more analysis on it, but just to give you a heads up," so that they can pre-plan to have vessels in the area, that type of thing. If it starts looking good, well then, it might look towards a boarding. And vice versa – they'll give us a ring and say they have information, they're looking at a boarding saying, "Hey, we're about to do this boarding," or, "We're looking at this boat, you got anything on it?"'

The intelligence provided by his office is just one element that goes into the counter-smuggling operations. 'But when we get information, it's usually pretty good, it's fairly reliable.'

As for the war on drugs, he says, 'The way I look at it is that every seizure is a win. It might be a little win but if you didn't seize it what would happen? That might be a million, two million hits on the street and really that's the way that you need to look at it. It's a hard game, really hard game over here just because of the environment. It is nothing like executing an official warrant in Australia where we can put protections in place to increase our safety when kicking in a warehouse door or a house. You can't move into Iran or in the highlands of Afghanistan or Pakistan and do the same thing! They're just places you can't get to, so you can only be effective at certain points along the chain.'

He says Iran, Pakistan and Afghanistan have formed a useful counter-narcotics unit to target drugs in the border region. 'As an example, a few years ago there was information passed to the Iranians from a law enforcement country here, and as a result of that they seized seven tonnes of heroin in a cement truck in Iran.'

Since the Syrian war closed the border to narcotics traffickers, he thinks the main changes in strategy have been in reducing the earlier, bulk loads to smaller loads of higher purity and in becoming better at devising hiding places on the dhows. 'So methodology is changing, as you would expect. We need to change with it.'

He says that sometimes only the master of the dhow knows that there are narcotics on board because it has been loaded secretly at night. 'We've had information where the crew have been moved to the end of the deck and told, "Turn around and do not look," while the gear is loaded on board. So they know there's something on board, they just don't know where it is. Other times, the crew come on board when it has already been loaded so they won't have a clue, only the captain may be aware of what's on board. And a lot of the time that's because the syndicates know that law enforcement or navy personnel will question the crew and they might give up where it is.'

One navy seizure where the AFP was involved right down the chain started with a tip-off in the region that a load was heading towards a port.

'Then essentially the vessel was identified and followed and it was boarded by the navy,' he says. 'It was late in the afternoon so the navy members went on board trying to find the narcotics. Had no luck – it was getting too dark – so they got off the vessel, reboarded it the next morning then after a couple of hours finally found the narcotics.

'And for us, that was a fairly big relationship-building exercise because the navy got on board, they drilled a lot of holes and weren't finding anything. It wasn't until we started to really push that we got a better indication of where it might be in the vessel. And then to have the navy just sit there that night, surveil it and then go back in the next day, trusting us, and actually finding it where we said it was, I think that really helped build the relationship.'

Another interesting development is that a few people who went to Australia on people-smuggling boats are involved in the drug trade direct from Iran to Australia.

'So it's something else that we are conscious of. Some of them are playing with a habit as well. People think that in the Middle East Region there's not too much of those drug habits because [of] the death penalty and other punishments, but the reality is, a lot of these countries have the social issues of drug addiction.'

The AFP's work in the region is not well known in Australia. But Fox says, 'Being able to try and identify the funding or locate and seize narcotics as close to the source as we can, which is what we're trying to do, has been pretty effective.'

21

Bringing them home

There is growing excitement on board HMAS *Darwin* as she sits gently at anchor in Jervis Bay on the afternoon of Saturday, 16 July 2016. It is the last night at sea after seven long months for the thirty-two-year-old frigate and her 228-person crew.

The birdies have safely deposited on board the special 'welcome home' guest – Commodore Luke Charles-Jones from Fleet Headquarters – and the speeches, promotions and awards presentations are out of the way.

Now the officers and sailors and a handful of visitors are tucking into the final 'steel deck' barbecue dinner of the old warship's final deployment to the Middle East. Somehow the rissoles, sausages, chicken and salads that we washed down with the obligatory cordial taste better as the lights of Huskisson and Vincentia twinkle in the distance.

Since 1990, when she joined *Adelaide* and *Success* in the first Australian Task Group for Operation Damask 1 following Iraq's invasion of Kuwait, *Darwin* has deployed to the Gulf a record-equalling seven times.

During her 2016 tour the ship has steamed more than 50,000 nautical miles or 92,500 kilometres. Her chefos have dished up more than 100,000 meals and the crew has conducted dozens of boardings that have turned up the record seven-tonne weapons haul and hundreds of millions of dollars worth of illicit drugs.

Chief of the Australian Defence Force Air Chief Marshal Mark Binskin regards the Middle East as an important training ground for the Royal Australian Navy's future leaders.

Sitting in his expansive office on the top floor of building R1 at defence headquarters in Canberra, with a beautiful view over Lake Burley Griffin and the Brindabella mountains, Binskin reflects on the thousands of naval personnel who will have served in the Gulf region during sixty-four ship deployments to mid-2017.

'If you look at each ship with about 250 people on board, that's a lot of people from navy over the years,' he says. 'On the list of the captains' names or the commanders of the operation during Damask and Slipper there are future chiefs of navy – there are a lot of two stars in there. They took those skills from there on their future careers.'

The variety of tasks has also been a great operational and training opportunity.

'We went through counter-piracy for a bit, then the drugs, trying to interdict the finances of terrorists, rebels, depending on where they might be fighting in those particular areas in the Middle East and then in the last few months weapons have started to come to the head on the dhows that have been picked up,' Binskin reflects. 'We're not sure if this is a longer term trend or will we start to see more drug interdiction again, but it just shows the variety of what we're seeing out there and what our crews have to be ready for.'

While the impact of the interdictions on terrorist finances is not huge in global terms, Binskin is confident that the RAN is making a difference. Every bit counts.

Many Australian sailors have spent a substantial chunk of their careers patrolling the waters around the Middle East Region and not just in the frigates.

'We've had FFGs, we've had Anzacs, we've had HMAS *Kanimbla* over there during the 2003 Gulf War, we've had *Westralia* and HMAS *Success*,' Binskin says. '*Success* was over there just before Anzac Day [2014] and she was actually resupplying and refuelling ships that were on station, as well as doing some missions herself. We then chopped her to NATO and she did a couple of weeks as the only NATO ship on Ocean Shield, which is a counter-piracy patrol, before she went up the Red Sea and then up for Anzac Day commemorations. So their ability to chop between the various task forces and missions shows they're pretty versatile, pretty good people and ships.'

Binskin was a navy fighter pilot before he transferred to the RAAF when all fast jets moved over to the air force. Like many of the senior navy officers he refers to, he has had personal experience with the mission. Before becoming chief of the air force he spent four months serving in the Middle East as commander of the Combined Air Operations Centre in 2004, an intense period directing all military air movements in the area of operations. He was the first RAAF officer to run it and direct its vast array of air power.

While there, he flew out one day to the American aircraft carrier USS *Enterprise*.

'We landed in the C2 greyhound quad [resupply aircraft] and as I got out I looked to the portside and there was HMAS

Melbourne tucked in close as the rescue destroyer and in close protection,' he recalls. 'Just seeing a red kangaroo on the side of the ship was really good and then being able to see how our ships could seamlessly integrate with their task force in doing that in close protection for them was terrific.'

Binskin knows just how hard navy crews work in the region.

'There's a lot of activity so I can't see them getting much sleep there when they're in the Arabian Gulf,' he says. 'That is not just for those doing the navigation and the bridge work and the operations area. There are a lot of crew members volunteering for jobs such as boarding parties, so a cook will be trained up and be roping out of a Seahawk onto vessels, or in the RHIBs and doing boarding parties. It's a pretty exciting life.'

The other important aspect is the opportunity to operate alongside warships from other nations. 'That helps to tie down the tactics, techniques and procedures and it gives our sailors the chance to see that we are a pretty slick operation when you compare us to other navies around the world. We're very professional and we're very capable.'

Binskin's military career has been moulded by the instability of the Middle East.

'I can't see it changing in the shorter term anyway and so for us, we might not be in the Middle East in ten years' time but we may well be somewhere else,' he says. 'Adaptability is the key [for] any acquisition that we make, any training that we do, any exercise constructs that we have. We're always cognisant of the fact that we've got to be interoperable with our major ally, the US, and then with those that we look like we're going to be operating with into the future. A lot of those are NATO forces, NATO navies.'

Nothing happens in the military without a strictly ordered set of official arrangements. The Chief of Navy is responsible for raising, training and sustaining the nation's maritime forces and for positioning all ships and submarines and ensuring they can do the job. But the Australian warships deploying to the region are 'force-assigned' from the navy to the ADF's Chief of Joint Operations, based in Bungendore near Canberra, who is the operational commander of all Australian forces deployed overseas.

Since the 1999 East Timor crisis, when the realities of a truly 'joint force' and the ADF's own shortcomings hit home, the joint model has been fully implemented and the handover of warships from navy to Headquarters Joint Operations Command is now virtually seamless.

'I look at where we've come to now from back then [1999] and we are well ahead, with a far better understanding that joint isn't doing everything the same,' Binskin says. 'Joint is about bringing the best of the three services and the public service together to get the best combination you can for that particular operation. We've done it so many times but what we're tending to do now is that JOC [Headquarters Joint Operations Command] will have a lot more oversight as the ship is transiting or doing other operations. It's easier now because JOC has all the command and control systems to do it.'

Operations in the maritime domain will dominate future ADF operations, he thinks. 'It's very obvious that we're a maritime power, not a naval power, and we should structure ourselves that way. That means the three services being able to operate in that maritime environment, whether it be archipelagic or a bit broader. You're going to see a lot closer integration between the three services.'

Interoperability has been a catchcry in the defence force for years and Binskin believes technology will enhance it. 'For example, having the frigates being fully interoperable with the air warfare destroyers means that the air warfare destroyers can detect, target and designate and use the weapons off the frigate to engage. So the air warfare destroyer doesn't have to be a long way down threat [close to the enemy] – you can have frigates down threat doing anti-submarine warfare and the air warfare destroyer can use its weapon systems in the anti-air battle. That's the sort of integration that you need to have in the modern battlefield.'

Navy chief Vice-Admiral Tim Barrett does not believe there will be a significant change to the single-ship Gulf deployment model for some time to come.

For a small navy to deploy a warship for seven or nine months, at least three ships need to be engaged in the rotation. One deploys as another trains up and the third returns home. Given that the RAN has just twelve surface warships or major combatants (one air warfare destroyer, three guided missile frigates and eight Anzac Class helicopter frigates), the Middle East commitment occupies twenty-five per cent of the fleet and places a heavy strain on resources.

'We have been sending single ships there for decades now and we have only a finite ability to be able to do more,' Barrett says.

From his office at Sydney's HMAS *Kuttabul* overlooking Garden Island and the old and the new of the Australian navy, the former navy helicopter pilot acknowledges that the RAN enjoys a very strong reputation within the Combined Maritime Forces and many others in foreign military and political command chains.

'We are at the sophisticated end of the navies that are in that force,' Barrett says.

His own experience in the region dates back to 1981 when as a young midshipman he served on board the guided missile destroyer HMAS *Perth* in the northwest Indian Ocean during the Russian war in Afghanistan. At the height of the Cold War between 1981 and 1986 it was the activities of Russian warships and planes rather than pirates or drug smugglers that were on the radar of Australian ships deployed to the US-led naval coalition. Barrett was back in the region in 1992 on board the guided missile frigate HMAS *Canberra*. This time the job was enforcing sanctions against Saddam Hussein following his invasion of Kuwait.

'So what started for one reason has largely developed over time,' he says. 'It's a demonstration of national resolve in having a capability to have ships there almost permanently to be able to support a variety of actions – be it Soviet presence, the invasion of Kuwait, maritime security issues in terms of piracy or a fear of state-sanctioned transport of illicit drugs and goods.'

That is not to say that Australia's commitment to the CMF is open ended or permanent. There is constant scrutiny of the mission, the reasons why the navy is there and the effect that is being achieved. To date, successive governments have judged that the cost and effort are worthwhile. As the officer responsible for ensuring that the navy can meet the national commitment, Tim Barrett is fully engaged in that review process. But with strife in Yemen and the Red Sea area on the increase he thinks there is no reason to believe that the navy will be out of the Middle East Region in the foreseeable future.

Most of the world's navies face more work than they have the capacity to do. Responses have to be carefully weighed up and are driven by risk-based intelligence fed from a variety of sources – human intelligence, surveillance by aircraft and satellite and information shared by like-minded countries.

'Rarely would we send a single ship out there to do its sole surveillance on the basis it might come across something,' Barrett says. 'It might be patrolling in an area, but its movement within it will be directed by an intelligence-led side and with that you're going a little further than what's within the ship.'

While he has witnessed huge amounts of technological change during his forty-year naval career, in many ways the job remains much as it did. Back in 1976 he was at sea in a patrol boat off Darwin looking for Vietnamese boat people. Today he sends sailors to sea still to look for boat people from Vietnam, Iraq or Afghanistan. 'It's important to understand what it is we are required to do and differentiate that from how we do it. It's the difference between the nature of war and the character of war. One's enduring, one's ever-changing.'

Continual motivation is vital to the task. 'To actually motivate and to get people to do it again and again and again, it's still important, I think, that they understand where they fit and why they're doing the things they're being asked to do. I insist and persist with all my COs that we need to tell our sailors why it is they do the job and put it in context, not just for the navy but in context of the nation and why it's significant and why it's important.'

The strategy is evidently working, with recruitment and retention levels at record highs. Recruitment is running at about ninety-six per cent for sailors, while separation rates are down to 8.2 per cent. With an entirely new fleet coming on line during the next decade the future looks bright as young people are attracted to a career at sea in comfortable, highly technical, state-of-the-art warships and submarines. That process is underway with two landing helicopter docks and three air warfare destroyers and will continue with a new fleet of offshore patrol vessels and two new tankers by the early 2020s. Then comes a new Australian-built frigate fleet and twelve new French-designed submarines. The total cost will be in the order of $200 billion, making navy the biggest Australian defence capital equipment buyer by a long way.

To Barrett, it is not just about beautiful shiny new ships but also the advanced technology they will carry.

'Where we're going now is the combat system design and the way the technology will be used and that's the bit where I think there is absolutely a greater deal of excitement around how it might look,' he says. 'To some extent it is what I think younger people today would expect to see. It almost provides the things they would expect to see if they were playing games at home. It is the ability to make rapid decisions based on fused data that is now readily apparent and not having to be done through manual intervention.

'A lot of it comes down to bandwidth, it comes down to connectivity, it comes down to the protocols that are used, but it also comes down to the ability to feed certain information at certain levels. All of those things are advancing rapidly and we're in on that. Not every navy gets to see those advances in the levels that I think we have over the last couple of years.'

HMAS *Darwin* will not see the advances that Tim Barrett refers to, but the fine old warship is a classic example of the tough, high-speed escort frigates built to protect US aircraft carriers during the Cold War.

After a final journey down Australia's east coast following a gala stop in the Top End, where the ship and crew were lauded by the citizens of her namesake city, the frigate unloaded her munitions in Twofold Bay at Eden on the New South Wales far south coast before turning north, bound for Sydney and home, starting with a quick dash up the coast to Jervis Bay.

There *Darwin* anchored off one of the navy's idyllic havens – HMAS *Creswell* near Huskisson – to drop off a few family members who had joined the ship and experienced life on board for the final leg of the voyage.

From ashore at the picture postcard base, the ship is the embodiment of a sleek fighting vessel anchored about 500-metres out in the bay.

A group of 'early leavers' from the crew, who left the ship in Muscat for a break so that they could man her when the rest of the crew took leave, board the ship again for the cruise up to Fleet Base East at Garden Island in Sydney Harbour. A TV crew from Network 10 also climbs aboard to record the ship's homecoming.

For me, the landlubber author who spent a fortnight on the ship in the Indian Ocean as it pursued and caught drug smugglers on the 'smack track', the welcome at the top of the ship's ladder is like reuniting with old friends. There are warm greetings all around and the mood on board is much more buoyant than it was in Dar es Salaam – the crew can almost smell home. First stop is the captain's cabin for a cuppa with Commander Phill Henry and a quick update before climbing down to the chiefs' mess to prepare for my final night on board.

Great news. There has been a 'promotion' for me and a move up the night-time pecking order, which means shifting down from the top rack to a more accessible middle rack for the last sleep on board.

Excitement builds, but ship life goes on as the crew undertake their duties with growing smiles. I join Marine Engineering Officer Trevor Henderson and Chief Ty 'Sparrow' Davis on the forecastle supervising an engineering team who are trying to repair a faulty capstan on the anchor. The men and women work hard as the sun dips below the Great Dividing Range above the pure white sands of Jervis Bay and the temperature begins to drop. The skipper will be reluctant to leave the shelter of the bay without a fully functioning anchor system.

Soon after dark, the warship is ready to sail. She weighs anchor and slowly steams out of Jervis Bay and past Point Perpendicular for the steady cruise up to Sydney in choppy seas. The crew spends this final leg tidying up and packing their personal gear in advance of tomorrow's homecoming. For those operating the vessel it is business as usual as preparations are made for the arrival in Sydney Harbour. For navigator Lieutenant Scott Benstead that means plotting the complex course along the busy harbour to the main wharf at Fleet Base East.

Sunday, 17 July 2016 dawns overcast and cool as *Darwin* makes her final turn for home off the New South Wales Central Coast, to arrive in Sydney right on time for the official welcome.

Even the chefos take the morning off so the routine hot breakfast is replaced by coffee and toast in the chiefs' mess. No one is thinking about food as, dressed in their formal winter uniforms called the 'W2s', they are busy shifting luggage between decks in preparation for a speedy escape at Garden Island.

As we pass Broken Bay, the skipper conducts a TV interview on the starboard bridge wing before a final pipe to remind the crew of their great achievements and to ask them to spare a thought for their deceased shipmate, Leading Seaman Cameron Acreman.

The city skyline is shrouded in fog as the warship turns into Sydney Harbour and slows for the transit to Fleet Base East. After passing the HMAS *Sydney 1* memorial mast on Bradleys Head where the traditional 'still' (call to attention by the bosun's whistle) is piped and those on the upper decks stand to attention, the crew shifts as one across to the port side for the final run into the main wharf at Garden Island.

The smiles grow wider and the banter becomes more excited as all on board strain for that first glimpse of their loved ones. The ship edges into the wharf and the large crowd breaks into cheers, waving excitedly as they spot their husband, wife, brother, sister, son or daughter lining the ship's rail.

'Welcome Home Goonga' reads one of the biggest banners as Chief Andrew 'Goonga' Sims waves to his wife and kids. Children with balloons, pet dogs and even a group of mates wearing panda bear masks add to the carnival atmosphere as *Darwin* finally ties up and everyone gets ready for that first wonderful hug.

Before the long-awaited lunge down the gangway into the loving arms of families and friends there are some formalities to be endured. Prime Minister Malcolm Turnbull, Deputy Opposition leader Tanya Plibersek and the Chief of Navy Vice-Admiral Tim Barrett wait patiently for the troublesome gangplank to fit into place.

Having marched off the ship and saluted the PM, Commander Henry can finally embrace his wife Adele, kids Samuel and Brodie and stepkids Lachlan and Kiele. The family will soon embark on a 'busman's holiday' – a two-week pleasure cruise around New Zealand with several thousand other holidaymakers. You can bet that Phill Henry will spend very little of that time alone in his cabin.

There is a surge of bodies ashore and the emotion on the wharf is palpable as a seven-month separation ends in a whirl of hugs, kisses, laughter and tears.

Six weeks later the crew is back on board as *Darwin* prepares for another month at sea – including a trans-Tasman visit – before a stint on emergency callout duty during the festive season. She is on hand to assist with disaster relief when a destructive earthquake hits near Christchurch in November. There is little rest for the reliable workhorse as she prepares for her scheduled retirement in late 2017 following another busy twelve months around Australia and beyond.

Bringing his ship back into Sydney was a bittersweet moment for Phill Henry. Before disembarking he sat alone in his cabin taking an emotional moment to reflect on the fact that he was not returning with all of his sailors. The loss of chefo Cameron Acreman in the port of Muscat hit the whole ship hard, but for the man in charge it was a life-altering experience.

The memory of the sailor's untimely death came flooding back to him as he prepared to go ashore to meet the VIPs and then his family.

'Grief can hit at unexpected times and at that moment I felt I had failed because I did not bring everyone home,' he says simply.

Through all of the ups and downs of the long deployment Henry had constantly reminded himself and those around him of his first 'pipe' as they departed from Sydney Harbour on 31 December 2015.

'Sydney put on a beautiful day,' he recalls. 'We had a fantastic send off, the Prime Minister, Chief of Navy, Fleet Commander, local Member of Parliament and a thousand friends and family were there.'

After they sailed, he had said to the ship's company, 'Remember this day, remember standing up there and looking back at all those people who are supporting you, because on your worst day away, they are there helping us do our job. If you could just capture that image and remember it, that's going to help us while we're away.'

Acknowledgements

This book would not have been written without the efforts of my wife, literary partner and editor extraordinaire Verona Burgess. My daughter Lucy and stepkids Dan and Jenna have been as supportive as ever.

Pup Elliott from the office of the Chief of Navy was a tireless advocate and went above and beyond on numerous occasions. Commander Geoff Fiedler, formerly of CN's office, was also helpful and responsive.

A special thanks to the Chief of Navy, Vice-Admiral Tim Barrett, who has been right behind the project from the start as was his predecessor, Vice-Admiral Ray Griggs, who got the ball rolling.

Once again, the Chief of the Australian Defence Force, Air Chief Marshal Mark Binskin, was generous with his time and support.

I am greatly indebted to the commanding officer of HMAS *Darwin*, Commander Phill Henry, and the entire crew of the wonderful old warship for their hospitality and friendship during my stint on board on the 'smack track'. Special thanks go to the Ship's Warrant Officer Tim Brading, Chief Petty Officer 'Swaino' Denis McKenna and the other chiefs who welcomed me into their mess and transformed me into something of a shipmate.

The Maritime Logistics Officer, Lieutenant Commander Neil Krauklis, got me to the ship in Dar es Salaam on time and in one piece.

I am very grateful to everyone who was interviewed for the book for their time and generosity and I hope you enjoy the telling of your stories. A special thank you to Captain Terry Morrison, Captain Brian Schlegel and Commander Catherine Hayes.

Former navy officer James Lawless provided numerous contacts and crucial guidance, and ex-Admirals Chris Ritchie and Rob Walls were also very helpful.

Captain Mike McArthur and John Perryman at the RAN Sea Power Centre opened their doors and their files with great generosity.

Former AFP Commissioner Mick Keelty was helpful, as was the AFP national media team and Dr Mark Tahtouh from the Forensic Drug Intelligence Unit.

A sincere thank you to our wonderful transcriber Sharon Horwell for her outstanding work.

Finally, to our publisher at Harper Collins, Catherine Milne, editor Nicola Robinson and the team, thank you for getting book number six off the ground and for your ongoing support of Australian authors.

Appendix

RAN Middle East deployments 1990-2017

Operation Damask 1 (warlike)
August to December 1990: Her Majesty's Australian Ships *Adelaide*, *Darwin* and *Success*

Operation Damask 2
November 1990 to April 1991: HMA Ships *Brisbane* and *Sydney*

Operation Damask 3
April 1991 to October 1991: HMAS *Darwin*

Operation Damask 4
September 1991 to February 1992: HMAS *Sydney*

Operation Damask 5
February 1992 to August 1992: HMAS *Darwin*

Operation Damask 6
September 1992 to April 1993: HMAS *Canberra*

Operation Damask 7
June 1993 to December 1993: HMAS *Sydney*

Operation Damask 8
April 1996 to September 1996: HMAS *Melbourne*

Operation Damask 9
April 1999 to September 1999: HMAS *Melbourne*

Operation Damask 10
June 2001 to November 2001: HMAS *Anzac*

Operation Slipper 1 (warlike)
October 2001 to March 2002: HMA Ships *Sydney*, *Kanimbla* and *Adelaide*

Operation Slipper 2
March 2002 to June 2002: HMA Ships *Newcastle*, *Manoora* and *Canberra*

Operation Slipper 3
May 2002 to November 2002: HMA Ships *Melbourne* and *Arunta*

Operation Slipper 4
October 2003 to May 2003: HMA Ships *Anzac* and *Darwin*

Operation Bastille
December 2002 to April 2003: HMAS *Kanimbla*

Australian Clearance Diving Team 3
January 2003 to May 2003

Operation Slipper 5
April 2003 to August 2003: HMAS *Sydney* (fifth MEAO deployment)
May 2003 to November 2003: HMAS *Manoora*

Operation Slipper 6
July 2003 to December 2003: HMAS *Newcastle*

Operation Slipper 7
October 2003 to April 2004: HMAS *Melbourne*

Operation Slipper 8
March 2004 to September 2004: HMAS *Stuart*

Operation Slipper 9
July 2004 to January 2005: HMAS *Adelaide*

Operation Slipper 10
December 2004 to June 2005: HMAS *Darwin*

Al Muthanna Task Group
April 2005 to June 2005 and December 2006 to January 2007: HMAS *Tobruk*

Operation Slipper 11
May 2005 to November 2005: HMAS *Newcastle*

Operation Slipper 12
October 2005 to April 2006: HMAS *Parramatta*

Operation Slipper 13
March 2006 to August 2006: HMAS *Ballarat*

Operation Slipper 14
July 2006 to January 2007: HMAS *Warramunga*

Operation Slipper 15
January 2007 to July 2007: HMAS *Toowoomba*

Operation Slipper 16
June 2007 to December 2007: HMAS *Anzac*

Operation Slipper 17
November 2007 to May 2008: HMAS *Arunta*

Operation Slipper 18
March 2008 to September 2008: HMAS *Stuart*

Operation Slipper 19
August 2008 to February 2009: HMAS *Parramatta*

Operation Slipper 20
January 2009 to July 2009: HMAS *Warramunga*

Operation Slipper 21
June 2009 to December 2009: HMAS *Toowoomba*

Operation Slipper 22
October 2009 to April 2010: HMAS *Stuart*

Operation Slipper 23
March 2010 to September 2010: HMAS *Parramatta* (fourth MEAO deployment)

Operation Slipper 24
August 2010 to February 2011: HMAS *Melbourne*

Operation Slipper 25
December 2010 to June 2011: HMAS *Stuart* (fourth MEAO deployment)

Operation Slipper 26
May 2011 to November 2011: HMAS *Toowoomba*

Operation Slipper 27
September 2011 to March 2012: HMAS *Parramatta* (fourth MEAO deployment)

Operation Slipper 28
February 2012 to August 2012: HMAS *Melbourne*

Operation Slipper 29
July 2012 to January 2013: HMAS *Anzac* (fourth MEAO deployment)

Operation Slipper 30
December 2012 to June 2013: HMAS *Toowoomba*

Operation Slipper 31
April 2013 to October 2013: HMAS *Newcastle*

Operation Slipper 32
August 2013 to March 2014: HMAS *Melbourne*

Operation Slipper 33
January 2014 to August 2014: HMAS *Darwin*

Operation Manitou 1 (non-warlike)
August 2014 to December 2014: HMAS *Toowoomba* (fifth MEAO deployment)

Operation Manitou 2
November 2014 to June 2015: HMAS Success

Operation Manitou 3
April 2015 to September 2015: HMAS *Newcastle*

Operation Manitou 4
August 2015 to February 2016: HMAS *Melbourne* (seventh MEAO deployment).

Operation Manitou 5
December 2015 to July 2016: HMAS *Darwin* (seventh MEAO deployment)

Operation Manitou 6
June 2016 to November 2016: HMAS *Perth*

Operation Manitou 7
December 2016 to August 2017: HMAS *Arunta*

Operation Manitou 8
September 2017 to May 2018: HMAS *Newcastle* (sixth deployment)

www.ingramcontent.com/pod-product-compliance
Lightning Source LLC
Chambersburg PA
CBHW071149070526
44584CB00019B/2724